Praise for

PROPHETIC CITY

"Klineberg's meticulous research makes a strong case that Houston, with its growing inequalities, demographic shift to a nonwhite majority, and rising social and environmental consciousness, is at the forefront of America's future. This eye-opening and accessible study deserves a wide readership."

—*Publishers Weekly*

"It's a relief to read a book where Houston isn't just the backdrop—it's the story.... Critical reading for anyone interested in the Bayou City."

—*Texas Monthly*

"Houston epitomizes the America that has emerged over the last half century—immense fortunes coupled with widespread privation; world-class cultural institutions nestled alongside impoverished slums; ethnically diverse and ambivalent about it; divided between the religiously devout and the religiously disconnected; a sprawling metropolis with colossal commutes; environmentally challenged; culturally individualistic. This book summarizes four decades of the longest, most systematic, and yet perhaps least known research project in American sociology. Its lively prose is must reading not just for Houstonians, but for any Americans interested in where we are headed."

—Robert D. Putnam,
research professor at Harvard University and
author of *Bowling Alone*, *Our Kids*, and *The Upswing*

"Stephen L. Klineberg's *Prophetic City* is a masterfully researched and eloquently written investigation into what makes America's fourth largest city tick. All stereotypes about Houston are shattered. There is a staggering amount of fresh historical observations, environmental concerns, and urban lore in his epic book. Highly recommended!"

—Douglas Brinkley,
Katherine Tsanoff Brown Chair in Humanities and
professor of history at Rice University and author of
American Moonshot: John F. Kennedy and the Great Space Race

"Houston is one of America's largest and most vibrant cities. Stephen Klineberg does a great service illuminating the key factors that have driven this city's remarkable wave of growth and change, while detailing its pressing challenges with inequality, gentrification, and climate change. Based on four decades of detailed research, Klineberg's insights provide an alternative story, and model, of urban development that adds much to what we know from existing models based on cities like New York, Boston, Philadelphia, Chicago, and San Francisco. A must-read for all those concerned with the future of cities and urban development."

—Richard Florida, author of
The New Urban Crisis

PROPHETIC CITY

HOUSTON *on the* CUSP
of a CHANGING AMERICA

Stephen L. Klineberg

with Amy Hertz

AVID READER PRESS
New York   London   Toronto   Sydney   New Delhi

AVID READER PRESS
An Imprint of Simon & Schuster, Inc.
1230 Avenue of the Americas
New York, NY 10020

First Avid Reader Press trade paperback edition June 2021

AVID READER PRESS and colophon are
trademarks of Simon & Schuster, Inc.

For information about special discounts for bulk purchases,
please contact Simon & Schuster Special Sales at 1-866-506-1949
or business@simonandschuster.com.

The Simon & Schuster Speakers Bureau can bring authors to
your live event. For more information or to book an event,
contact the Simon & Schuster Speakers Bureau at 1-866-248-3049
or visit our website at www.simonspeakers.com.

Interior design by Kyle Kabel

Manufactured in the United States of America

1   3   5   7   9   10   8   6   4   2

Library of Congress Cataloging-in-Publication Data has been applied for.

ISBN 978-1-5011-7791-0
ISBN 978-1-5011-7793-4 (pbk)
ISBN 978-1-5011-7792-7 (ebook)

For

Peggy, of course

and for

Geoffrey and Ursula, Kathy and Rick

and for

Julia, Maggie, Anna, Coles, and Emily

Contents

COMING TO GRIPS WITH
THE NEW REALITIES

Author's Note

Houston, America's fourth largest city, has been largely ignored as a subject of thorough study for the better part of the last thirty years. The two most recent comprehensive analyses of the city were published in 1988 and 1991 (Feagin, *Free Enterprise City*; Thomas and Murray, *Progrowth Politics*), and both have long been out of print. This book renews Houston's claim to serious national attention.

In the spirit of nearly forty years of collecting—through systematic survey research—the thoughts, feelings, and attitudes of Houston-area residents, we have allowed the voices of Houston to drive the writing of this book. We have interviewed dozens of people whose perspectives have greatly enriched the narrative, and we sincerely apologize to those many other worthy voices whose perspectives we were unable to include. When requested, we have changed names and identifying details.

The experiences we have recorded here exemplify both the remarkable changes that are underway across America and the ongoing efforts to address effectively today's most critical challenges. It is not yet clear how the general public, either in Houston or in the nation as a whole, will ultimately respond to the new realities that are refashioning the political and social landscape across the nation. What is clear is that those cumulative responses will determine the future of this city, state, and country as the twenty-first century unfolds.

PUBLIC PERCEPTIONS IN A RAPIDLY CHANGING WORLD

CHAPTER 1

Getting to Houston

Men resemble their times more than they do their fathers.

—Arab proverb

I am not a native Houstonian, nor did I ever travel to Texas until I went there to teach as a college professor. I grew up near New York City, the youngest of three children, and I was raised as a Quaker, a religious tradition that has continued to be an important influence in my life. I spent parts of my childhood in São Paulo, Geneva, and Paris. I majored in psychology at Haverford College, and received a master's degree in clinical psychology (*"psychopathologie"*) from the University of Paris and a PhD in social psychology from Harvard. I taught for a time at Princeton.

My path seemed set: Life would be lived along the Northeast corridor, somewhere between Philadelphia and Boston, with occasional stints abroad—a traditional Yankee destiny. But in 1972, I landed as an associate professor at a university I had known by reputation only. It was in a city I had never thought much about and where I surely would never have chosen to live. Yet it would turn out to be a perfect setting for the research trajectory I was on, an intriguing window into the changes that were occurring across America.

From the beginnings of my life in academic research, I have been intrigued by questions about the psychological impact of social change, the shifts that take place in people's attitudes and self-perceptions as they respond to (or resist) the new realities. During the thirty years of broad-based prosperity in the United States after World War II (1945–1975), the experience of profound social change seemed to be happening somewhere else. Most American social scientists thought Western societies had basically arrived at a new plateau, and all the rest of the world was trying to become as much as possible like the world's developed countries.

The nations of the First World were showing to the Third World, Karl Marx had claimed, the face of their own futures. So if you wanted to study social change during those halcyon postwar years in America, you needed to go to countries where older civilizations were colliding daily with the new realities of the twentieth century and trying desperately to reinvent themselves in order to succeed in the modern world.

In 1969, a yearlong fellowship from Princeton gave me the opportunity to explore these questions in Tunisia, on the North African Mediterranean coast. Led by the enlightened dictatorship of Habib Bourguiba, the traditional Arab culture was being challenged daily by the widespread determination to build a modern country. Working closely with Tunisian colleagues and graduate students at the University of Tunis, we conducted a systematic survey of families with teenage children living in the inner city, asking both the adolescents and their parents in face-to-face interviews about their assessments of the present and their perspectives on the future.[1]

There is a well-known Arab proverb that I heard many times during that year in Tunisia: "Men resemble their times more than they do their fathers." I watched this prophecy come to life in the perspectives of the younger generation of Tunisians: They were coming of age in a profoundly different world from that of their parents, far more comfortable with new ideas and new people, and feeling at home in the wider world beyond the closely guarded one in which they had grown up. Meanwhile, their parents, grandparents, aunts, and uncles were having much more difficulty accepting the new social order and its challenge to traditional assumptions. One generation wanted to turn back the clock, while the other was eager to embrace the future.[2]

Returning home in the summer of 1970, I saw America undergoing its own dramatic transformation. The country was being torn apart by Vietnam War protests, radical changes in sexual mores, and growing concerns about the environmental and social costs of rapid economic growth. You could already see the early signs that the well-paying, low-skilled, blue-collar jobs and the broad-based economic prosperity they had generated during the years after World War II were beginning to disappear, portending the Rust Belt decline of the 1980s.

Moreover, after four decades of America's doors being closed to all but northern Europeans, immigration was back on the agenda, bringing intimations of a demographic transformation, with America just beginning the epic transition that would make it progressively less European and more Hispanic, African, Caribbean, South Indian, and East Asian. It no longer seemed necessary to go abroad if you wanted to gain a deeper appreciation of the human dimensions of social change.

★

The American nation, as it grew from a few settlers in the northeastern colonies, had absorbed cultures from many older (predominantly European) worlds as it spread across the continent, becoming vast and complex both culturally and politically. Using the arbitrary state lines to try to make sense of the way the country's various economic and cultural characteristics are distributed across the continent would turn out to be an exercise in frustration. In 1981, while putting together a series of articles on American values, *Washington Post* editor Joel Garreau ran into exactly this problem.

As the reporters identified the demographic and attitudinal patterns that were sweeping across broad swaths of North America, it became clear that some of the patterns engulfed several states; others bifurcated them. To clarify what he was learning, Garreau drew new lines that divided the continent into nine distinct sectors.[3] His descriptions of the "nine nations of North America" advanced our understanding of the American patterns of culture, politics, and economic development—at least as they existed in the 1970s.

If you're from the Northeast, you'll recognize right away the depictions of the nations along the two coasts: New England stretches from Connecticut to the Atlantic Provinces of Canada; its capital is Boston, and its values center on education and the promulgation of liberal social policies. Ecotopia, which stretches along the West Coast, has its capital in San Francisco; its values center on innovation and the preservation of the planet.

The Islands begin in South Florida; their capital is Miami, and their language derives from Caribbean and Latino cultures, their values swinging wildly from one end of the political spectrum to the other. The Foundry, now called the Rust Belt, stretches from New York to Milwaukee and south to northern Virginia; its capital is Detroit, and its values are centered on blue-collar industrialism. The Empty Quarter begins in the extreme northwest and contains Alaska, Alberta, and much of Northern Canada. Cascading down to Arizona and New Mexico, its capital is Denver; its values are focused on civil liberties and rugged individualism. And Quebec is, well, Quebec; independent at all costs, even if it means recurrent outbreaks of secessionist fever.

Houston is the designated capital of none of the nine nations; yet it is the only city considered to be an integral part of *three* distinct nations, which converge in its region. Dixie stretches from central Virginia and Kentucky to Houston, with its capital in Atlanta; its values have to do with holding on to tradition while coming to grips with rapid change. Mexamerica crosses the country from California's

Central Valley in the west to Houston in the east; its values spring from the promise of a better life. The Breadbasket, which covers most of the Great Plains into the Canadian provinces of Saskatchewan and Manitoba, also spreads to Houston; its values are a celebration of hardworking, pioneer, Christian America.

Dixie, Breadbasket, and Mexamerica—the three nations cover much of what people in New England and Ecotopia call the flyover states. Houston is only missing a direct connection with the Empty Quarter to make it the ultimate flyover city; although since they say that Aspen is to Houston as the Hamptons are to New York, perhaps it can claim honorary geographical membership in that part of the continent as well.

The three converging nations have given Houston its Southern warmth and charm, its abundant fresh and organic produce, and its haute Mexican cuisine. As a part of Dixie, Houstonians will offer you politeness over directness; as a member of the Breadbasket, a business community absolutely convinced that if something is good for business it has to be good for everyone; and as Mexamerica, a Latino population that by the third generation is completely American even while it retains strong ties to its Latin traditions.

This combination also generated centuries of deep-seated racism, an unremitting effort to block any government programs designed to redistribute income to benefit the poor, and a diversity that belies its own Anglo bootstrap mythology. It meant an unintellectual pragmatism: Either the oil lies under the ground or it doesn't. And it meant a prejudice against books and theoretical learning so profound that it took eighty years after English-speaking Texans began to settle in the state in the 1820s before they had built a single public library. In contrast, the Puritans in Boston founded Harvard University only sixteen years after they landed at Plymouth Rock in 1620.[4]

No other city in America seemed to embody as much of the basic American experience as Houston. So when an invitation to consider teaching in that city came along, I felt we at least had to investigate. I had no inkling at the time that I would end up spending the rest of my professional life studying this quintessentially American city, and how within its particular stew of individual attitudes and societal trends we could see the future of the nation taking shape before our eyes.

CHAPTER 2

The Quintessential American City: Houston, 1836–1982

When Satan came to Houston
He beat a quick retreat;
He loved its wicked people
But he couldn't stand the heat.

—George Fuermann,
Houston Post, 1969[5]

It was a leap year, 1836, the year Houston was founded. It was a time when the Mexican government happily accepted as the newest citizens of the Mexican Empire the American, British, Irish, and German settlers who were beginning to trickle into the vast, flat, barely habitable land of the Texas frontier. The land's only value, the Mexicans thought, was to serve as a buffer between their empire and the brutal Comanche raiders.

The Comanche were feared for their brutality not only by the new settlers but by other Native American tribes as well. They had mastered the art of rapidly firing arrows atop a galloping horse, enabling them to take out ten Anglos before a second bullet could be loaded into a single-shot rifle. It was the year the Texas Rangers saved Samuel Colt's company from bankruptcy by being the first major consumers of his new invention. The revolver was the only effective weapon the Texians—yes, that's what the Mexican residents of Texas were called—had to use against the natives.

Eighteen thirty-six was also the year of the Alamo in San Antonio, where Davy Crockett died and Sam Houston, a ne'er-do-well nicknamed "Big Yellow Drunk" by the native tribes, led his men to victory against the Mexican government and then allowed General Santa Anna to go free in exchange for Texian independence. It was the year of the birth of the Republic of Texas. And the Allen brothers, fresh off the wagon trail from western New York State, had already made plans for the location of its capital.

★

Augustus Chapman Allen and John Kirby Allen had abandoned their solid middle-class lives as college professors in the lush, hilly, densely forested country just west of the Finger Lakes in upstate New York. The lure of easy riches from land speculation out in the frontier territories, powered by the inheritance of Augustus's wife, Charlotte, had drawn them south and west three years earlier, in 1833. They came by primitive and incomplete railway lines, by wagon and barge, finding safety in numbers by gathering in large flotillas to guard against the river pirates along the Mississippi, and finally arriving, most likely via New Orleans, in the hot, sticky island of Galveston. They were among the many Anglos, as the Mexican government called them, who were willing to give up their American citizenship to become Mexicans in order to make a grab at the abundant land.

At least a two-month journey from home, Galveston was a newly developing port, positioned to give New Orleans—already by 1833 on its way to becoming the wealthiest city in America—a run for its money. The Allens' plan was to purchase as much land as they could in order to control the massive trade in cotton and timber production that was coming out of the South and Southwest and shipped to the big country to the north, the recently formed United States of America. To their chagrin, however, by the time they got to Galveston, the Allens discovered that the island had all the dance partners it could accommodate. Undeterred, they headed farther inland.[6]

The rivers in East Texas are nothing like the wide, deep, capacious bodies of water in the American Midwest or even the Northeast. They are shallow and narrow, clogged with undergrowth, dotted with sandbars, and susceptible to drastic changes in character depending on the rainfall. In just a few days, they can transform from nearly dry to wild, raging, twenty-foot-deep waterways. They aren't really rivers at all: They are bayous or creeks, part of a swamp's drainage system designed by nature to allow water to recede from floodplains into the Gulf of Mexico. And, like Bangladesh, much of East Texas is one gigantic floodplain.

The Allens continued, heading north and west along Buffalo Bayou—one of the area's muddy, shallow, overgrown creeks—navigating around sandbars and sunken boats as they searched for a strategic position where goods could be offloaded or moved onto barges. The last point where the bayou was wide enough to accommodate boats traveling inland from Galveston was near the town of Harrisburg. But title to the land in question was ensnared in litigation: Years after the widow to whom it had been left had died, the extended family was still fighting over it.

So the brothers and their entourage traveled inland for another nine miles along Buffalo Bayou as it snaked and narrowed, until they found what they were looking for, sort of: Six thousand acres at the intersection of Buffalo and White Oak Bayous that were available for purchase for the princely sum of five thousand dollars. The surrounding land was relentlessly flat and swampy, choked with flora and fauna, infested with mosquitoes, and prone—they soon discovered—to frequent yellow fever outbreaks. The muddy roads, often washed away by recurring floods, swallowed wagon wheels, stranding oxcarts and shutting down the settlement's nascent commerce. And May to

September brought five months of some of the most brutal heat and humidity any of them had ever experienced.

The town's inhabitants were their own special breed—several earlier waves of settlers had been run off by the violence of war and raids and by the general cruelty of life on a ferocious frontier. The cohort who stuck it out was made of sterner stuff, and they liked their entertainment harsh. Public floggings and hangings drew crowds of hundreds. Shootings in broad daylight were common and were only considered to be a crime if the injured party was white. Drunken raids on hotels and gambling establishments were the norm. In the late 1830s, a visitor described the town as "the greatest sink of dissipation and vice that modern times have known."[7]

The Allens had staked their entire fortune on this unpromising venture. It was either going to become a successful point for the shipment of goods to and from the port of Galveston, or they were all going to die trying to make it work. And so the marketing campaign began.

"We will name our new city after you," said Charlotte Allen over dinner one night at her home, with Sam Houston as their guest of honor, "the hero of our new republic." Or so the story goes. If the town of Houston were to be chosen as the capital of the republic, its future would be assured. It would grow into an international city, a cosmopolitan center with embassies and global trade routes, a new North American power center to rival New Orleans as the inland gateway to and from the great port of Galveston.

In order to move in that direction, the new town needed more inhabitants. Friends, relatives, and any other suckers the Allen brothers could contact were papered with the brochures they printed, pen-and-ink renderings of a hilly, bucolic, and verdant village dotted with charming chalets (Figure 2.1). The drawing resembled a Swiss village, but the recipients were so far away from anyone who could give a firsthand account that no one knew the extent to which the picture didn't look anything like an East Texas town.

FIGURE 2.1: *From the Allen brothers' brochure—*
Houston: A Place of Legend and Myth[8]

Francis Lubbock, a visitor in 1837, gave a more accurate depiction when describing his efforts to find the town by steamboat. When their vessel got stuck, the group continued on in a smaller boat. "So little evidence could we see of a landing," wrote Lubbock, "that we passed by the site and ran into White Oak Bayou, realizing we must have passed the city when we struck in the brush. We then backed down the bayou, and by close observation discovered a road or street leading off from the water's edge. Upon landing we found stakes and footprints, indicating that we were in the town tract." As Lubbock's party followed the tracks, they discovered all there was of the town: a few tents, one of which was the saloon, and some small houses in the process of being built.[9]

When in 1839 a yellow fever epidemic killed two thousand people—12 percent of the population—the Texas Republic's legislators beat a hasty retreat north to the city of Waterloo, later named after the "Father of Texas," Stephen F. Austin. Though land in the Texas Hill Country is rocky and tough, and just about as hot as Houston in the summer, at least there were actual hills and lakes. It was to that city the embassies of Belgium, France, and the Netherlands would come. Galveston, the portal for trade with the industrial cities of Europe, was bustling with money and culture. Houston, now just another unpromising East Texas town, was left to find its way or die in the floodplain, where the waters of the Breadbasket drain into the Gulf of Mexico.

One thing about the Allens' brochure was true: The land was cheap and abundant in this interior settlement. More people began to arrive, and, like the Allens, once there they did whatever they had to do to survive. Few of the settlers had the resources to return to their distant origins. Thus the DNA of the community was injected with a combination of both boosterism and a determination to exploit every available opportunity. Houston began life with no particular ideological motivation beyond pretending it was something it wasn't and doing everything possible to ensure its success.

★

This relentlessly flat, swampy prairie land did have some advantages. While many farmers abandoned the surrounding Beaumont clay for what they were sure would be more fertile land to the west, the farmers who stuck it out discovered remarkable fecundity in the mineral-rich soil. The clay may have looked like a bad bet, but it managed to make everything grow: corn, all varieties of potato, wheat, barley, rice, every imaginable tree or grain. Sugar plantations sprang up to the south, near a town that came to be known as Sugar Land. King Cotton would fill the coffers of many. The nearby East Texas timber fields stretched far beyond what the eye could see.

For white men and their families, opportunity abounded. William Marsh Rice, who left his fortune in a trust that would establish Rice University upon his death, arrived broke from New York, after his ship, full of the merchandise he had been planning to sell, sank in the mud of Buffalo Bayou; he went on to become one of the richest entrepreneurs in America. Englishman Thomas House moved to Texas in 1836 to join the revolution against Mexico. He parlayed his ownership of a bakery and ice cream shop into the city's premier commodity brokerage house. The belief that hard work will be rewarded was woven into the psyches of Anglo Houstonians across the social classes.

The nascent economy blossomed, but the fate of Texas in that time of perpetual warfare was still uncertain. Santa Anna may have agreed to exchange his freedom for Texian independence, but the Mexican government was not about to accept that outcome without a fight. The emperor's forces headed north again in an effort to reclaim the lost territory. In looking for allies, the new republic spurned Britain's overtures: Joining forces with the UK would have required giving up slavery, and Texas, its economy now firmly rooted in cotton, was intent on keeping its slaves. In 1845, Texas became the twenty-eighth state; it fought the victorious war with Mexico from 1846 to 1848, and in 1861 joined the Confederacy in the Civil War.

Agriculture and commerce continued to expand. Texas was pouring money into the Confederacy, and Houston's resources were deployed to the east where the major battles were being fought. The rail lines that were being laid down in earnest before the war were now abandoned; some of them were ripped up and moved to bolster Confederate supply lines, especially after New Orleans so easily fell to the Union forces.

Galveston at the war's end was the third largest port in America. It had succeeded in surpassing New Orleans as both a cultural center and a point of entry and exit for commerce. While its arts and culture flourished, its economy remained narrowly focused and repetitive: load, unload, ship in, ship out; load, unload, barge in, barge out, train in, train out. Tick, tock, crates moving, humming along.

Meanwhile, the residents of Houston weren't just growing food, cutting trees, raising cattle, or planting fields of sugarcane and cotton. Grains and sugar were being refined and made ready for sale in city factories. Timber was processed and engineered to be turned into building and flooring, into wooden boxes and custom-made crates. Cotton brokers built warehouses for storage and processing, and by the 1870s, two-thirds of all the cotton grown in North America was coming through Houston. Financial institutions were formed by the cotton magnates to grease the wheels of commodity trading, incubate the birth of new industries, and spur the planting of more crops. The proliferation of production and services was becoming integral to all of Houston's commercial enterprises.

Then on September 8, 1900, an unnamed category 4 storm destroyed Galveston and ruined its dream to be the great port on the Gulf Coast. It is an operatic and ruthless tale: An unprecedented wall of water, a storm surge of more than twenty feet, swept across the island, claiming in one night at least six thousand lives, countless ships, and an entire city. Those are indeed the facts, and the Great Storm still ranks as the single most lethal natural disaster in American history. But the cutthroat outcome, in which Houston mercilessly stepped on the chests of Galveston's dead to steal its place as the biggest port in the South, didn't happen quite the way many still spin the tale.[10]

By the time the storm hit, Houston was already well on its way to beating out Galveston for Gulf Coast dominance. There had been enough hurricanes, enough wrecked ships, and enough property washed out to the Gulf of Mexico to convince developers and ship owners that Galveston was too vulnerable to be a long-term option as a major port. But more than vulnerability to the elements, it was Galveston's single-minded identity as a seaport that would ultimately undermine its prominence on the world stage.

Rail lines and railroad companies had figured in Houston's plans from the beginning. The Allen brothers themselves were part of a railroad scheme that collected more than fifty thousand dollars but did nothing. Three other companies tried to build rail lines and were sued

by soon-to-be governor Jim Hogg for pocketing the money without
so much as laying a single ton of ballast to support the rails. In 1853,
Harrisburg, to the east of Houston, in partnership with Galveston,
incorporated the first railroad in Texas.[11] There were still no rail lines
in Houston other than the narrow-gauge rails going out to the timber
fields; and Thomas House, William Marsh Rice, James A. Baker, and
other early entrepreneurs saw an opportunity to stop both Harrisburg
to the east and Galveston to the south from becoming rival centers
of commerce.

First, they managed to convince the state government that allow-
ing Galveston to build a rail bridge to the mainland would be unfair
to Houston, since it would steal the city's traffic, and so construction
was brought to a halt. Then, in 1856, they built a short, seven-mile
line heading south to tap into the east–west Buffalo Bayou, Brazos
and Colorado Railway that was beginning to connect to the rest of
the country. They built their seven mile line at a fraction of the cost
of a full-blown rail line, and in one fell swoop they managed both to
steal the traffic from Galveston and to stop Harrisburg from becoming
an inland port.

The final blow came when Galveston's leaders journeyed to Austin with a proposal to build a fan of lines emanating from their port,
only to discover that Houston had beaten them to the punch with a
better plan: Since Houston was already connected to an east–west line
thanks to that seven-mile tap, the infrastructure to link up with many
more lines was in place. And the rails would be less vulnerable there
than if lines converged on a single, exposed, and vulnerable island.
Houston had solved its overland transportation problem: With the
new railway lines, real ships started to worm their way up the bayou
to the city; and local business leaders began their long campaign of
lobbying Congress for the funds to dredge the Houston Ship Channel.

After that first railroad line took hold, many others followed, more
than in any other city at the time, including New York and Chicago.

By the 1890s, Houston had become known as the "iron-ribbed city," the "Manchester of America," the commercial junction "Where Seventeen Railroads Meet the Sea." This remote city had all the services to be found in older, larger metropolitan areas, but without the harsh winters to complicate commerce. And Houston, rather than Galveston, was now positioned to provide the quickest access to the ocean for the products of America's Breadbasket.

FIGURE 2.2: *A fitting symbol of the mercantile era: Houston's city seal (1840)* [12]

The city's official seal (Figure 2.2) depicts a plow and a locomotive, appropriate emblems for an economy firmly based on agricultural products being brought by rail into this commercial city. Though travel over land had seemingly obviated the need for a shipping channel into Houston, business leaders and politicians were unwilling to let it go. They lobbied Congress relentlessly until they secured, in 1896, the funding needed to dredge the bayou into a twenty-five-foot-deep channel, and finally, in 1914, to open the Houston Ship Channel to oceangoing vessels.

★

Houston's bayous, when the water was high enough, were swimmable; the water was drinkable, and in fact most of the residents had gotten their water from Buffalo Bayou and from rainwater cisterns while the city was still small enough for everyone's needs to be met. But as the population grew, and few paid any attention to the environmental costs of the growth, the bayous were polluted by dead animals, along with human and animal feces and runoff from a smallpox cemetery and an oil mill. Houstonians were getting sick, and doctors were advising people not to drink the tap water.

By 1887, some private citizens were digging for water on the eastern edge of downtown and to the north in Second Ward. Sure enough, they found the pure stuff gushing up two feet into the air from what would turn out to be the third largest underground aquifer in the country. In a stroke of extraordinary good fortune, Houstonians discovered that there was plenty of underground water for everyone to have all the clean drinking water they wanted, at least as long as it was developed in a sustainable manner.

"This city had nearly if not quite a hundred excellent churches, but had very few sewers, less than one-half the necessary water service . . . and only a small percentage of scattering sidewalks . . ." said Frank Putnam, writing about Houston at the turn of the century. "I gained the impression that while the people of Houston were admirably equipped for living in Heaven, they were rather poorly equipped for living in Houston."[13]

By 1900, responding to the lure of opportunity, people were coming from rural areas in burgeoning numbers, and Houston became the fastest-growing city in America. Its strong mercantile, blue-collar economy would propel it past all the older cities of the South. Then, in 1901, a new discovery would transform the business landscape of Houston along with that of the entire world.

Legend has it that oil was first discovered in Texas by a Mexican cattle rancher in 1854 in Duval County between Corpus Christi and

Laredo. He was digging for water when he found a smelly, black viscous liquid bubbling up, which he used to lubricate his wagon wheels. He had heard that the Native Americans used the substance to help their digestion, as an eye salve, and for treatment of rheumatism. For him, it was mostly of no value, so he sealed that hole and kept searching for water. Four years later, the industrializing parts of America along the East Coast and in the Midwest would become addicted to the cheaper, cleaner-burning kerosene that replaced whale oil as a source of fuel. The race was on to find new sources of oil in the Northeast.

The first oil boom occurred in 1865 in Titusville, Pennsylvania, when a team of drillers added a steam engine to the drill bit, breaking through rock and reaching unheard-of depths. Oil gushed, and it was drilled until dry. Pithole, Oil City, one oil boom after another was tapped and went dry, leaving companies without the resources to move west into Ohio and Indiana, the belt around the Great Lakes, where industry giants were sure most of North America's oil was to be found. Meanwhile, John D. Rockefeller had cornered the market on refining and transportation, and soon began buying up oil fields all over the Northeast. His Standard Oil, and the subsidiary companies he'd formed as trusts, was now a monopoly, producing 25 percent of America's oil and refining 95 percent of it.

Rockefeller had become one of the world's richest human beings, but East Texas was nowhere on his radar. So when a one-armed Beaumont Sunday-school teacher started raving about the bubbling gas and smell of sulfur from the nearby salt flats, local residents laughed. Rockefeller slammed the door when Pattillo Higgins's partner came looking for financing. There would never be anything substantial, Rockefeller was convinced, in any part of the area known as East Texas.

But everyone who was living in Beaumont knew there was oil under the salt fields, even if they all made fun of Pattillo Higgins. And the fact that nobody knew how to get the oil out made Rockefeller decide to pass on the opportunity. Drillers in the Northeast pumped their holes full of water to keep dirt and rock from collapsing in on the drilling equipment. In the salt fields, however, the sand was so fine it absorbed the water. Nobody had gotten much below three or four hundred feet.

FIGURE 2.3: *The Spindletop Gusher (1901)*[14]

The Hamill brothers were hired by Anthony Lucas, who had pushed Pattillo Higgins aside when the Mellon family in Pittsburgh offered financing; they filled the hole with mud instead of water and continued drilling for two years. On January 10, 1901, they surpassed one thousand feet, then eleven hundred feet. The limit of the equipment was twelve hundred feet. They were running out of pipe and money when suddenly Spindletop shook and then exploded, erupting two hundred feet into the air and raining oil on the fields below (Figure 2.3).

It took two days to cap. A mile-long lake of oil had formed before they could get it under control. They thought their estimate of fifty barrels a day was too optimistic; Spindletop produced eighty thousand barrels of oil per day. U.S. oil production increased to the point of making America the source of one-fifth of the world's oil supply.

Beaumont was a boomtown. During those heady days, half the whiskey consumed in Texas, they said, was drunk in Beaumont. The pervasive gambling and fighting resulted in two or three murders every day. One night, sixteen bodies were dragged from the river, all with their throats slit.

More than five hundred new companies were born because of Spindletop. Andrew Mellon tried to sell his gusher to Standard Oil; when Rockefeller rejected the offer, Mellon started Gulf Oil, with a refinery in Port Arthur and his own pipeline. It was also the birth of the Texas Fuel Oil Company, Texaco, and hundreds of wildcatter start-ups. By the time Standard Oil got around to wanting to drill along with the others, the company had been broken up in the 1911 Supreme Court antitrust decision. Standard itself was barred from drilling in Texas.

As a memorial near Spindletop proudly proclaims: "On this spot, on the tenth day of the twentieth century, a new era in civilization began."[15] Spindletop was the largest strike in history. Already endowed with access to a vast freshwater aquifer and with the modern railroad and banking facilities of an agricultural and commercial center, the town of Houston was well-positioned to make the most of the possibilities that were suddenly unleashed. The country, and the world, would soon become addicted to the viscous black liquid that Houston was prepared to extract, refine, and ship to all corners of the earth. Houston had the lumber for the oil barrels, the banks with the money, the railroads and the infrastructure. Beaumont was co-opted and Galveston, just a few months after the Great Storm, was left in Houston's muddy, oil-soaked wake.

Throughout the first third of the twentieth century, more and ever larger oil and gas reserves were being developed under the lands surrounding the city. In the early 1930s came the discovery and development of the vast East Texas oil fields, one of the most abundant deposits of oil and gas on the planet. By the mid-1930s, half of the entire world's oil production was located within six hundred miles of Houston. That this city was so ready to embrace the shift from commerce in cotton and agriculture to oil and manufacturing was part of its scrappy character, always ready to reinvent itself whenever necessary in order to exploit new opportunities for additional wealth.

That Houston was also able to develop the infrastructure needed to accommodate so many new oil companies with such open arms was due in part to the efforts of one man in particular. He had arrived from Tennessee at the age of twenty-four, and he would become one of the most powerful men in America. He was the one who lured the Gulf Oil headquarters to Houston, snatching the biggest development in oil production from the arms of Beaumont. The man's name was Jesse Jones.

★

It was a cool spring day, buds just beginning to emerge from the lush landscaping of the Rice University campus, when the amiable and impeccably dressed writer Steven Fenberg came to my office to talk about one of his favorite figures, Jesse Jones.[16] A tale that begins with a young man sent from Tennessee to Texas with only an eighth-grade education primes the listener for a rags-to-riches story. But not so, says Fenberg, lighting up at the chance to talk about the subject of his definitive biography: "He wasn't poor. His father was a tobacco farmer and international merchant who did quite well."

In 1898, twenty-four-year-old Jesse moved to Houston to work in his uncle's lumber business. A natural leader with a remarkable gift for business, he learned quickly and his fortune grew. He and his uncle bought up thousands of acres of timberland spreading over East Texas and into Louisiana. From there, he began a flurry of building activities, constructing the city's first skyscrapers, eventually becoming responsible for dozens of modern buildings, mostly concentrated in downtown Houston. Jones was the embodiment of what became the city's unspoken motto: If it's good for the community, it's good for my business. And its corollary: If it's good for my business, it's good for the community.

Jones helped to forge the agreement reached with the federal government in 1909 to secure the funds needed to complete the dredging of the Houston Ship Channel, with the city paying half the cost. As the owner of the National Bank of Commerce, he helped sell the bonds to pay for Houston's share of the port improvements. He was elected the first chairman of the Houston Harbor Board and oversaw the dredging of the bayou—a project one mile longer than the Panama Canal, which was undertaken at the same time.

When the channel officially opened in 1914, with President Woodrow Wilson pushing a button on his desk in Washington to fire the celebratory cannons, it turned the city almost overnight into a major international port, capable of accommodating large cargo-laden ships from all over the world. Though Galveston was up and running not long after the Great Storm, Houston had already sucked the air out of the older city's sails, as it became a safer international port and the undisputed center on the western Gulf Coast for both manufacturing and commerce.

Jones traveled the nation and the world as his success grew, and he saw that every great city had put the arts and culture front and center. He set about gathering people and resources in an effort to push Houston into becoming a city that would attract the wealthy, sophisticated, and successful to what was still perceived by most as a bit of the Wild West. So in the early years of the twentieth century he built Houston's first major convention hall, which doubled as a performing arts theater. He backed Houston's preeminent impresario Edna Saunders, who not only brought the Ballet Russe and Enrico Caruso to the city, but she also managed to convince New York's Metropolitan Opera to break its "Dallas only" tradition when touring the country and coming to Texas.

Jones first stepped onto the national political stage in 1912 when prominent banker and Democratic Party operative T. W. House Jr., son of Houston's first and biggest cotton, sugar, and banking magnate, introduced him as a potential cabinet member to the newly nominated Woodrow Wilson. Wilson was drawn to Jones because of his business acumen and because he was one of the few prominent Southerners who did not view the government as the enemy, going back to the days of the Civil War. Though Jones would develop a close friendship with the new president, he turned down three back-to-back offers from Wilson in order to stay in Houston and keep building his businesses and his city. By then he'd added the *Houston Chronicle* to his collection of banks, luxury hotels, movie palaces, and office towers.

It was America's entry into World War I that would push Jones into national public service and compel his first move to Washington. He served on the newly formed American Red Cross War Council, raising money and coordinating medical aid both at home and in the European theater. It was also Jones who pushed the president to make the speech at a packed Metropolitan Opera House in New York City that would galvanize the world, establish Wilson as one of the great orators in American history, and lay the groundwork for a burst of national generosity. American Red Cross fundraising broke all records that year as printed versions of the speech spread across the country in the nation's newspapers.

Political conventions have been mixed bags for host cities, sometimes bringing chaos and violence, as was the case for the Democratic conventions of 1924 in Madison Square Garden and 1968 in Chicago. But they also bring national attention and plenty of new business. By 1928, Jones had become well-known as a fundraising and executive powerhouse for the Democratic Party. He wanted the convention to be in Houston, in June, and this was before the advent of air-conditioning. The competition was San Francisco, Detroit, Atlanta, and Memphis. Jones outbid them all by offering the party a blank check and, in the great tradition of the Allen brothers, perhaps exaggerating Houston's advantages just a tad. Twenty-five thousand people would descend upon the city. It was the biggest event Houston had ever hosted, the first national political convention to be held in a Southern city since the Civil War, and one of the first to be broadcast nationally over the radio.

In 1931, as the country entered the economic free fall of the Great Depression, two Houston banks were about to fail. They were holding precarious notes from agrarian areas across Texas and Louisiana, and if the two banks collapsed, others across the region would fall like dominoes, taking the whole economy with them. Jones summoned the city's major bankers, business leaders, and politicians, reportedly locked them in a room and cut off the telephone lines. He insisted that everyone stay put until all had agreed to contribute to the pool he had started with $120,000 of his own money, to enable them collectively to make the loans that might well be needed to rescue any troubled banks. As a result of this effort, not a single regional bank failed during the economic collapse, and Houston came to be known as "the city the Depression missed." That success did not go unnoticed in Washington.

President Hoover had reluctantly agreed to open the Reconstruction Finance Corporation (RFC) in 1932 to save the country's banks, railroads, and insurance companies, and to restore confidence in the overall economy. Hoover thought trying to legislate the recovery from an economic crisis would be no more effective than passing a law to stop a hurricane. But he liked what Jones had accomplished in Houston and so invited him to come to Washington to serve on the board of the new government corporation. After FDR's election the following year, Jones was appointed chairman of the RFC and then the U.S. secretary of commerce. He played pivotal roles in saving the national economy and in militarizing industry for World War II. In its May 1940 feature story, *Fortune* magazine referred to Jones as "the fourth branch of government."

When he finally came home in 1946, he had put Houston squarely on the national map. After his return from Washington, he began transferring much of his wealth to Houston Endowment Inc., a phil-anthropic organization he and his wife, Mary Gibbs Jones, formed in 1937, dedicated to the support of the arts, education, health, human services, and community development. As of this writing, Houston Endowment Inc. has assets of approximately $1.7 billion.

★

Jones's vision of how to turn around the economy did not depend on government spending. "Instead," says Fenberg, "Jones relied on judicious lending." As head of the RFC and then of the Commerce Department, he oversaw the installation of the electrical infrastruc-ture across rural America and financed the sale of modern appliances in local stores. Every dime the government spent on the appliance program was repaid at a profit by tiny increments on the residents' monthly electricity bills. The Reconstruction Finance Corporation, under Jones's leadership, not only helped people; it actually made money for the U.S. Treasury.

Back in Houston, a new generation of local business leaders was growing ever more convinced that if government programs were not explicitly designed to help business, they would be counterproductive and should simply stay out of the way. In the 1930s, the "Suite 8F Crowd"[17] emerged as a powerful and cohesive clique of very wealthy and politically active businessmen. A coterie of lawyers, politicians, founders of insurance companies, bankers, one oil magnate, one woman, and wealthy contractors seeking New Deal projects would meet regularly until the mid-1960s in George Brown's suite at the

Lamar Hotel, one of Jones's many buildings, where he lived in the penthouse until his death in 1956.

The group raised the money designed to ensure the election of politicians who supported their conservative business and political views; they were also major figures in the city's philanthropic endeavors. They basically determined the outcomes of mayoral races, and their influence continued to grow in Washington as they brought House Speaker Sam Rayburn into the fold along with Lyndon B. Johnson. They built hotels, served on the boards of Rice University and the Texas Medical Center (TMC), and funded theaters and the arts, believing that world-class cultural institutions would lure talent to the city. The Suite 8F Crowd embodied the Houston philosophy that "the business of government is business,"[18] that the only legitimate role for public policy is to facilitate and support private-sector development, all in the firm belief that this was the surest way to promote the common good.

★

As the oil patch was taking center stage early in the century, Houston's business elite lobbied the government relentlessly until it enacted the tariff and regulatory practices, the generous "oil depletion allowances," that would help ensure the profitability of the city's fledgling petroleum industries. Government subsidies allowed the oil companies to write off losses and receive more income each year than the asset was actually worth. The intertwining of Big Oil and Big Government continues to this day in a taken-for-granted dynamic of mutual assistance—all in keeping with the Houston ideology that the job of government is to help business succeed, and the confident belief that everyone will benefit from that success.

A further partnership with the federal government during World War II would bring the city yet another major new source of wealth.

With the supply routes to Asian rubber cut off, the war was generating urgent demands for synthetic rubber, aviation fuels, shipbuilding, and plastics of all sorts. Government investments poured into Houston to fuel the growth of the petrochemical industry, which was to become Houston's most dynamic sector once the war was over.[19]

Through most of the twentieth century, the flowering of Industrial America brought a seemingly insatiable demand for the products of Houston's oil and gas industries. In the 1950s, the country entered the postwar years of widely shared blue-collar prosperity, increasingly enraptured by the promise of automobility and suburbia, subsidized by mortgage deductions and forty-one thousand miles of the interstate highway system. During those halcyon years, Houston was perfectly positioned for yet another round of economic growth, one that would dwarf anything this fortunate city had yet experienced.

With no natural barriers like mountains, rivers, or forests to limit its expansion, this flat, zoning-free, car-dependent boomtown just kept spreading, engulfing incorporated towns like Pasadena, Deer Park, and Bellaire. The Houston metropolitan region was being seen as the epitome of America's newest urban form, the MCMR,[20] the multi-centered metropolitan region, with the City of Houston itself spreading across six hundred square miles—roughly the size of Chicago, Philadelphia, Baltimore, and Detroit combined—and sporting across the ten-thousand-square-mile metropolitan region some eight to ten activity centers, each growing to be almost as large as downtown San Diego.

One of those urban areas, the Texas Medical Center, again with the help of the federal government, would become the eighth largest business district in America, covering fifty million fully developed square feet. It too started as a project of Houston's philanthropy, when George Hermann donated a swath of swampland to the city in 1914 adjacent to Rice University and to Houston's oldest park. In addition, Monroe Dunaway Anderson, one of the country's most powerful cotton magnates, came to Houston in the late 1800s and left most of his enormous wealth to his foundation, with instructions that the funds were to be used to do the most good for the most people. It was with this money, along with Hermann's donation, that the Texas Medical Center was born. The continual investment over the years, from both a multitude of federal research grants and additional philanthropic gifts, would build the TMC into the largest conglomeration of major hospitals and health-related institutions in the world.

And then in 1962, Lyndon Johnson's decision to locate NASA's Manned Spacecraft Center in nearby Clear Lake City would inform the "Space City" image of modern Houston as a high-technology center. Indeed, if you think about it, virtually all of the most critical financial investments that have been responsible for the remarkable economic success of this famously anti-government, free-enterprise city were as much the products of government programs and public spending as they were of private initiatives.[21]

Despite Houston's extraordinary success during the first eight decades of the twentieth century, the city continued to fly under the national radar. When you cross the country from New York to California, you run into Dallas, but you won't get to Houston unless you make a sharp left-hand turn and head down south on I-45 for another 240 miles. Even with its focus on high technology in the 1960s and '70s, it seemed to be Houston's fate that the glamorous facets of space exploration were located elsewhere—the breathtaking liftoffs in Florida; the dramatic splashdowns in the ocean; the nail-biter landings of the space shuttle in California. Houston had its moment during Apollo 13; but there are only so many ways to make computer terminals and headsets exciting for consumers of the news.

*

Despite its investments during the 1970s in medicine and high tech, Houston's economy remained almost entirely dependent on the business of refining hydrocarbons into gasoline and petrochemicals and servicing the world's oil and gas industries. By the early 1970s, the city had become the undisputed resource and energy capital of the world, the "Golden Buckle of the Sun Belt," the favored showplace of the world's most famous architects, the triumphant expression of free-enterprise America.

By 1980, more than 80 percent of Houston's primary-sector jobs were said to be associated directly or indirectly with the price of oil. No other region in the country matched Houston's concentration of refining, petrochemical production, oil and gas transportation, and oceangoing tankers. The city became synonymous with oil, much as Pittsburgh was with steel or Detroit with automobiles, or as Silicon Valley would become with microprocessing.[22]

When my family and I arrived in Houston in 1972, this was a countercyclical city, booming even as the manufacturing belt across America was beginning to collapse. Houston had evolved into America's quintessentially anti-government, anti-tax businessman's haven, to be built purely by developer decisions unfettered by zoning codes or government regulations.

Houston was often cited in those days as the best example of the anti-bureaucratic revolt that was sweeping through the emerging sectors of the American economy and culture during the 1970s and early 1980s. Much of the country was converging on the "laissez-faire lifestyles" and "privatized services" of this new "anticity," journalist Richard Louv[23] asserted. "Houston, in other words, is catching."

This is "THE city of the second half of the twentieth century," declared Ada Louise Huxtable, the distinguished architectural critic for the *New York Times*. Houston, she announced, was the quintessential American metropolis, "where private enterprise is equated with public spirit and public action."[24]

CHAPTER 3

Launching the Systematic Study of a City in Transition

A place like Houston shows us something elemental about the American soul, leaving us at once appalled and inspired.

—James Fallows[25]

Almost from its beginnings, Houston and its surrounding Harris County had been doubling in population every fifteen years or so. The city grew from 12,000 three years after it was founded, to 45,000 in 1900, just before oil was discovered in neighboring Beaumont, to 385,000 in 1940, to 938,000 in 1960, to 1.6 million in 1980, and to 2.3 million in 2019. Between 1970 and 1982, the price of oil increased tenfold, and Houston was America's quintessential boomtown. Harris County's population doubled during those twelve years, while most of the rest of the nation was mired in the "stagflating seventies," with high rates of unemployment, decreasing populations, and long lines for gas.

This mosquito-infested, oil-lined, smoggy, and polluted swampland near the ugliest part of the silt-filled Gulf of Mexico was expanding at a rate that defied reason. "This is not a city," one reporter wrote in 1978. "It's a phenomenon—an explosive, churning, roaring urban juggernaut that's shattering tradition as it expands outward and upward with an energy that stuns even its residents."[26] Rapid growth bringing rapid transformation—it was a perfect laboratory for a sociologist interested in social change. I wanted to learn more about how this improbable, swampy, flatland city managed to grow into the fourth largest metro in the nation while claiming to show the world what Americans can achieve when left unconstrained by zoning codes, effective regulations, and even moderate levels of taxation.

★

When you look at a map showing the locations of the twenty most prestigious institutions of higher education in America, you'll find that they generally cluster along the coasts and in a few big cities in the Midwest. All alone in the southwestern sector of the country is Rice University. As a data person, I was naturally attracted to outliers.

The minute I set foot on the Rice campus, I was impressed by how much its architecture and public spaces seemed to encourage academic discourse and aesthetic appreciation. It was (and is) a remarkably beautiful campus, canopied by the live oak trees that line every walkway and the surrounding enclaves of its residential colleges. The grounds, lushly landscaped, are laid out in a coherent architectural statement celebrating the life of the mind by encouraging intellectual contemplation, with delicate columns, arches, breezeways, and courtyards; elegant brick resting on pillars, neo-Byzantine influences everywhere.

I was also impressed by the quality of the students—every bit as smart as those at Harvard and Princeton, perhaps somewhat less sophisticated, but even more eager to learn from the resources of a great university. Rice's tuition was half the cost of the Ivy League schools, yet it had twice the percentage of students on scholarship aid, a fact that appealed to the Quaker-lefty in me: The university could make a better claim than most comparable institutions that it really was accessible to the best and brightest young people in America, almost regardless of their family's ability to pay. Moreover, the faculty in this world-class research university was deeply engaged with undergraduates, and not that much more focused on graduate students; this was rarely the case in most major research institutions.

Houston lived up to its reputation as a welcoming Southern city. "Houspitality,"[27] some have called it. We settled into our Southgate neighborhood, just four blocks from the Rice campus. My wife, Peggy, was able to make a smooth transition into her second year of law school at the University of Houston. Our two children were accepted into a multiethnic magnet school, immodestly called "the elementary school for the gifted," with almost equal thirds of black, Hispanic, and Anglo[28] students. We made friends easily both at Rice and in the wider Houston community, and we even tried to master the local language—it has a bit of a twang and includes vocabulary that I thought had been left behind with the antebellum days: Yankee, Dixie, Anglos, Tex-Mex, y'all, feeder roads, and mums everywhere.

Houston itself was located on a flat, swampy floodplain, blanketed by treeless pastureland, but whatever you plant in its gumbo soil grows amazingly quickly. Founded in 1912 as an institute for the arts, science, and literature by William Marsh Rice, the university gave expression in its architecture to the aspirations early city leaders had for transforming this unpromising swampland into a beautiful urban space. "We can make up for the flatness of our terrain by the richness of our vegetation," said Ralph Cram, the Boston architect who designed the university's first buildings.[29]

The Rice campus, as its aesthetic spilled into the tree-lined, elegant boulevards and surrounding neighborhoods, anchored the experience of being canopied by nature against the harshness of the summer heat. The stands of live oaks, which line Main Street, South Boulevard, and the Rice Village, envelop Hermann Park to the east and reflect the early vision of a coherent civic landscape that got lost in the architectural cacophony of the Texas Medical Center. The TMC is a seemingly random assembly of physical structures with little thought given to building the public spaces that might have fashioned a more centered, more gracious, and more community-friendly campus.

Traveling north, the intimate, elegant civic aesthetic ends abruptly at Alabama Street, less than two miles away. This is where the battle to guide the city's growth by a shared vision of coherent urban spaces got lost in the single-minded dedication to short-term material gain. Business dominance was particularly evident during the 1950s and 1960s, when profit-making and free-enterprise individualism won out over a broader vision of civic responsibility. The new growth during the booming years after World War II, with some notable exceptions, was generally cheap, shoddy, unattractive, and seemingly random. You were free, if you thought you could make money doing it, to build an office tower in the middle of a residential neighborhood; and many developers did just that, deaf to protests from the local residents.

The benefit of being at the convergence of three of the nine nations of North America is that Houston offered a pretty good indication of what was going on in the rest of the country. It was also hard to pin down exactly what made Houston distinctive. It lacked the Hollywood dreams of Los Angeles or the international connections of New York. It had nothing like the rolling hills and lush forests of Pennsylvania. But Philadelphia had stopped growing, and Pittsburgh's steel-based economy was shrinking rapidly. Denver, the mile-high city at the foot of the majestic Rockies, wasn't yet the urban magnet it would become in the 1990s. Houston had been a singular economic juggernaut since well before the Civil War, even if all it had to offer was lots of opportunities to make money fast with the least possible interference from government.

The city was comfortably tucked into its cozy petroleum bed. The prevailing attitude of the business community seemed to be, "So what if it's ugly? Who cares if it smells? It's the smell of money!" It was so easy to find well-paid work and high profits in those days that people used to say you could dress a gorilla in a business suit, send him downtown, and he'd become a millionaire in a week! But despite its economic prosperity, Houston seemed at the time to be a genuinely unattractive businessman's town with few redeeming virtues other than the ease of making money if you had the right education and ethnic background.

New friends took us on an eye-opening canoe trip down Buffalo Bayou into the center of downtown Houston. Known as "the reeking regatta," the trip brought us into a smelly cesspool, with beer cans floating on endless oil slicks. Only after passage of the Clean Water Act of 1972 was the city eventually compelled to do something about the untreated sewage and unregulated garbage that was discharged daily, for decades, into its bayous.

There was urban planning in Houston, but as Roscoe Jones, the city planner during the 1970s and '80s, used to say, "We plan for Houston's future like weathermen for the next weekend."[30] The job of city government was to take note of where the growth was going and rush in to provide the needed infrastructure. That was the extent of the government's responsibility. Growth should be driven solely by private developers seeking to maximize their profits; the role of the city was to facilitate the process and get out of the way.

There were few government programs designed to benefit any sector other than the business class. In the 1960s, the Houston Independent School District (HISD) even refused to accept federal money to provide subsidized lunches to underprivileged students.[31] "It will suck the initiative out of them if they get fed by government handouts." When I asked about this prevailing attitude in a meeting with a Chamber of Commerce committee in the early 1970s and had the temerity to suggest that Houston may well be one of the worst places in America in which to be poor, I was firmly corrected by every member present: Houston offers opportunity, not handouts.

The city leaders proudly proclaimed that Houston's success was a dazzling tribute to the power of free enterprise, in sharp contrast with the rest of the country, suffering as it was from excessive taxation, stifling regulations, rising fuel costs, rampant unemployment, and crippling inflation. Houston had long felt looked down upon by Americans from the two coasts, and it was relishing its season of revenge. DRIVE FAST. FREEZE A YANKEE, read a popular bumper sticker in the 1970s: "Let the socialists shiver in the dark."

★

The city's African American communities, the largest in the South, received almost none of the benefits: They still had unpaved roads and open sewers in 1980 and they were largely unprotected from the toxic waste and pervasive pollution that unfettered growth was bringing to this booming metropolis. Fifth Ward, one of the last intact African American neighborhoods whose middle- and upper-class families had not yet fled to the wealthy, mostly white neighborhoods into which they had finally gained access, was bisected by the development of I-10 and US 59, two massive freeways that were pushed by the business community and that effectively cut off Fifth Ward's access to downtown and drove financial and social capital out of the area. The growing poverty, pollution, and continuing racism, along with the neglect of public spaces and the sheer unattractiveness of this sprawling metro, were all largely ignored, because addressing them would detract from the single-minded emphasis on short-term business profits.

The realities of environmental racism in America were first documented in Houston. In the early 1980s, Robert Bullard, a young sociologist at the predominantly African American Texas Southern University, was able to show that virtually all of Houston's municipal incinerators had been placed in predominantly black or Latino neighborhoods.[32] In 1977, under the approving eye of an openly racist police force, twenty-three-year-old Vietnam War veteran José Campos Torres was brutally beaten by police officers and thrown into Buffalo Bayou to drown. The officers were convicted of negligent homicide and sentenced to one-year probation and a one-dollar fine.

The city was generally unattractive, smelly, and transient. At the same time, you could see all around you that the private fortunes made from the region's abundant resources of cotton, cattle, timber, sugar, and oil were contributing significantly to the development of world-class arts institutions and other public amenities. Houston's opera, symphony, ballet, and repertory theater were among the best in the world.

The Museum of Fine Arts (MFA), within walking distance of my office on a cool winter's day, was already a premier institution; it carries the names of the descendants of the great entrepreneurs in Houston's past, including former Governor Hogg and the legendary Jesse "Mr. Houston" Jones, along with many other generous donors. As Gary Tinterow, director of MFA-Houston, recently asserted, "Houston is a cultural capital, and that it is is largely thanks to the discovery of oil."[33] The city's elite had funded these remarkable institutions with a clear eye for quality and a clear sense of their importance in creating a successful city.

John and Dominique De Menil poured much of their Schlumberger fortune into preserving and enhancing the best parts of Houston. Engaging Philip Johnson as their architect, they designed and built the campus of St. Thomas University to match the aesthetic of the nearby Montrose area rather than continuing the Houston tradition of tearing down what came before. They commissioned one of the two Rothko Chapels in existence. They founded their extraordinary cutting-edge museum, the Menil Collection, by creating an art cartel, which was joined by other wealthy Houstonians and then bequeathed to the city.

Architecturally, downtown Houston in the 1970s was a paradox of bland, expedient functionality, but it also boasted some of the most iconic skyscrapers in the world, designed by such renowned architects and firms as I. M. Pei, Louis Skidmore, and Philip Johnson, brought in by local developers like Gerald Hines. The Pennzoil building and One Shell Plaza were innovations in the use of public space, and they went up right next to exquisite art deco mid-rises, along with the few surviving late-nineteenth-century Beaux-Arts office buildings. Through it all, however, there was little appreciation for the community-building function of public spaces; each new private structure was basically isolated from its surroundings, each a "monument unto itself," as my Rice architecture colleague and friend Stephen Fox likes to point out.

Coming from the Northeast and having grown up in a culture in which government is understood to be an essential positive force in addressing issues of social and economic injustice, I was skeptical. Houstonians seemed to believe that the sheer act of amassing private fortunes would naturally trickle down to expand opportunities for all and alleviate the suffering of the poor, and that private philanthropy was always preferable to government intervention, which will only make things worse, in their view, when it tries to address these kinds of social problems.

At the same time, there was evidence that Houstonians tend to volunteer more than the residents of most other cities in America, and that Houston was awash in nonprofit and nongovernmental organizations seeking to make a difference in the lives of others. Its low taxes and minimal government services seemed to be compensated, at least to some degree, by its generous philanthropic activities and innumerable fundraising galas. As celebrated as these initiatives were, however, it seemed clear to me that the generosity of private organizations was unlikely to provide anything approaching equality of opportunity for area residents, even if they were living in one of the fastest-growing and most affluent cities in America.

★

As the 1970s came to a close, public opinion polling and letters in the local newspapers made it clear that growing numbers of Houstonians were beginning to seriously question the city's single-minded pursuit of short-term profits. Excoriating articles in the national press, such as *Newsweek*,[34] the *Chicago Tribune*,[35] and the *New York Times*,[36] were drawing attention to Houston's neglect of its most urgent problems.

They were highlighting the city's seemingly easy acceptance of the large numbers of local residents who were mired in poverty and homelessness, its worsening traffic congestion, skyrocketing crime rates, levels of air and water pollution that were seriously compromising people's health, and the increasing subsidence as businesses and residents drained the aquifer without a thought to the consequences, turning Houston into the sinkhole and pothole capital of America. They reminded their readers further that the city was home to some of the most overcrowded schools and some of the least adequate city services in the country.

In the fall of 1981, I was preparing to teach a course that spring semester on research methods in sociology, and I had originally thought of getting the class involved in developing and conducting a systematic survey that would compare Rice freshmen and seniors in their assessments of the university and their perspectives on the future. Then, quite unexpectedly, a new and more intriguing possibility opened up. Dick Jaffe from Chicago's National Opinion Research Center (NORC) and Rosie Zamora Cope from Houston had just launched a new professional research firm in Houston, called Telesurveys of Texas, and they were looking for additional projects to get better known in the community.

With the help of a firm like this, we would have an opportunity to study Houston itself, to explore the way area residents were balancing the exhilaration of the city's spectacular growth with mounting concerns about the social costs the growth was generating. Rosie, Dick, and I agreed to work together in that spring semester, to train the students in conducting a systematic survey to measure how residents were assessing life in the Houston area, and to get a sense, through objective sociological research, of the kind of city its inhabitants were hoping to build with all the oil-based affluence. The research on student attitudes at Rice would have to wait.

All survey researchers shamelessly steal from each other's work. We wanted to replicate questions that had been asked in national surveys, so we could compare Houstonians' views with those of the country as a whole. The class drew from the contemporary Gallup, Roper, and Harris polls, as well as from the more sophisticated General Social Survey conducted annually by NORC at the University of Chicago. We captured their best items and added some of our own to put together a questionnaire that would provide reliable measures of Harris County residents' perspectives on the local and national economies, on poverty programs, black/white relationships, and the public schools; it would ask for their assessments of traffic, crime, and environmental issues, and it would measure their religious and political orientations, family structures, and socioeconomic well-being, along with their age, gender, and ethnicity.

Our plan was to interview at least five hundred respondents, following word for word our new questionnaire, and to select the participants so that those five hundred would faithfully reflect the views of the 2.9 million adults who were living in Harris County at the time. Sampling theory teaches that, if you want to draw reliable inferences, within known margins of error, from the small number of actual survey respondents to all area residents, every adult in the overall population must have an equal chance of being included in your sample of respondents—the requirement known as the "equal probability of selection method," or EPSEM.[37]

Random selection is the key, and the most widely accepted technique for achieving that goal is random-digit dialing. In order to ensure that every household with a working telephone would have an equal chance to be included in our sample, we used a computer program to generate random four-digit numbers and connected them randomly with the 227 prefixes that identified Harris County telephones.

I worked side by side with eleven intrepid Rice undergraduates that spring semester as we took up positions in the new Telesurveys offices, in phone-bank cubicles with brand-new rotary telephones. The representative sample of respondents was generated in two stages. First, we dialed the random telephone numbers, discarding those that turned out to be either not in service or connected to business phones. When someone in a household answered the telephone, we asked how many adults (aged eighteen or older) were living at that residence and used a table of random numbers to select the specific adult we needed to interview.

We had developed the scripts to be read verbatim. Jaffe had trained the students in the techniques of survey interviewing. Zamora had taught them how to code and track responses by whether they had a completed survey, a break-off, or an outright refusal. They learned when a return call might be most effective—if someone was cooking, or a child was crying, or if the designated respondent was just leaving the house or was not available, let them go with thanks and schedule a callback for another time.

We had to stop the interviewing process after the first three weeks of March in order to give the students time to analyze the data and complete their research reports before the end of the semester. We had interviewed a total of 412 randomly selected Houston-area residents. A larger sample would have been preferable, but this would give us enough data to provide a useful glimpse into the Houston psyche in the midst of a booming economy, and to show the students how to conduct a scientific survey, analyze the results, and complete a research report.

We converted the responses into the tiny holes punched on IBM cards and stuck them into the card sorter at the Rice Computer Center. Out popped results that would divide and count the distribution of responses by gender, age, ethnicity, income, education, political party, religion, and whatever other relationships we wanted to explore. The hopes and fears of area residents were given numerical expression in the tabulations we recorded, and we watched the mind of the city emerge from our analyses of the data.

In many obvious respects, Houston in early 1982 was a different place from the rest of America. It was an arrogant, spread-out, automobile-dependent boomtown while most of the rest of the country was in recession. It was dominated more decisively than almost anywhere else in America by the commitment to continual press-on-regardless growth, in a single-minded embrace of an extreme version of the quintessentially American free-enterprise, business-oriented ideology of governance.

At the same time, Houston's booming economy had been drawing massive numbers of people from everywhere else in the country. I could make the case that Houston was distinctively different from the rest of America, or that it was rapidly becoming a microcosm of the country as a whole. The data comparing our findings with the national surveys could tell us which argument prevailed and where the similarities and differences were to be found.

It turned out that the second assumption was more firmly supported by the data. Houstonians were not nearly as different from other Americans as we had expected—a reflection, in part perhaps, of the earlier convergence in Houston of those three North American nations. Drawing on the rapid in-migration from all other parts of the country, this thriving city wasn't just Southern or Southwestern or Texan anymore; highly educated doctors and engineers, along with construction, factory, and service workers from across America, had been flocking to Houston during the booming decades of the 1960s and 1970s.

Although the city was thriving while the rest of the country languished under record levels of unemployment and inflation, the attitudes and beliefs of Houstonians as a whole were surprisingly similar to the views held by other Americans across the country: When we replicated the questions from nationwide surveys on issues such as abortion rights, gun control, assessments of the Soviet Union, or support for the death penalty, the responses from the participants in the Houston survey came within one or two percentage points of the national figures.

There were, to be sure, some interesting differences between city and nation. Confirming their mounting worries about the social costs of growth, the survey found that local residents were more concerned than Americans in general about traffic congestion and crime rates. Perhaps most unexpected in light of the city's dominant business-oriented, laissez-faire ideology was the extent to which the survey participants were also insistent, at least in the midst of a booming economy, on the need to protect the local environment.

When asked about various aspects of life in the Houston area, the respondents gave their lowest ratings (with 66 percent saying only *fair* or *poor*) to the control of air and water pollution; and 60 percent rejected the assertion that the requirements for pollution control cost more than they are worth. Fully 63 percent agreed that protecting the environment is so important that continuing improvements must be made regardless of cost. And 46 percent asserted that we have been spending too little on national programs to improve and protect the environment; just 6 percent thought we were spending too much in that effort.

We were surprised to see this degree of environmental concern in such a decidedly business-dominated city. Environmental controls, after all, entail the extension of government regulations. The views of the general public seemed clearly at odds with the actual policies Houston's leaders were endorsing.

At the same time, 76 percent of the survey participants in 1982 gave their highest ratings (*excellent* or *good*) to job opportunities in the Houston area. They expressed a remarkably strong belief in the American can-do ethic of personal achievement: 81 percent agreed with the statement "If you work hard in this city, eventually you will succeed." A January 1982 Harris poll found that just 58 percent of all Americans concurred with the assertion that "If you work hard, eventually you will get ahead." Houston's distinction in this regard would delight the city's Chamber of Commerce when I gave local business leaders a report on our findings later that year.

The perception of Houston (and America) as a land of abundant opportunity reinforces an ideology of personal responsibility and undergirds the belief that we live in a just world, where people generally receive what they deserve on the basis of their efforts and skills. When the survey participants were presented with four different explanations for why, on average, black Americans have worse jobs, income, and housing than white Americans, only 36 percent thought the inequalities might be due to continuing discrimination; just 48 percent cited unequal access to education; and only 18 percent thought the differences were because blacks have less inborn ability to learn. Fully 57 percent said the main reason for black inequality is because most blacks just don't have the motivation or willpower to pull themselves up out of poverty.

Houston was clearly a city that defied easy categorization. Area residents seemed to be at least as progressive as other Americans in their views of the social agenda, with a majority of the survey respondents in support of strengthening gay rights, while also calling for only modest restrictions on access to abortion. At the same time, they continued to believe, to an extent well beyond that of most Americans, in the ethic of success through individual effort. On August 22, 1982, the *Houston Post* ran an extensive front-page story on the survey findings and captured that ambiguity in its headline, "Traditional Labels Don't Apply; Survey Reveals Conservative, Liberal Mix Here."[38]

I finished analyzing the data, published a summary report for Rice's Institute for Policy Analysis,[39] and gave several talks in the wider Houston community presenting the central findings: Houstonians were clearly concerned about the social costs of the city's spectacular growth, I concluded, yet they were more optimistic than the rest of the country with regard to their personal economic prospects, and more committed to the can-do work ethic. I submitted final grades to the students in the class, put the IBM cards in a drawer, and started thinking about the next research venture.

Then the world changed.

In May 1982, two months after that one-time class project was completed, Houston's oil boom collapsed. A growing worldwide recession had suppressed the demand for petroleum products just as new supplies were coming onto the world markets, and the price of a barrel of oil fell from thirty-five dollars to twenty-eight dollars almost overnight. That might not seem like much, but Houston's business community had been building and borrowing in the confident expectation of fifty-dollar barrels. By the end of 1983, this booming region recorded a net loss of more than one hundred thousand jobs.

It was clear that it would be a good idea to conduct the survey again with a new class the following spring to measure the public's reactions to the sudden turn of events. We were especially interested in seeing whether the call for more stringent environmental protections would continue at the same high level, even after the dramatic economic downturn, and what would happen to the belief in the work ethic as unemployment rates skyrocketed. I taught the class again in the spring of 1983. Then as the changes accelerated further into the 1980s, I kept offering the class and conducting the survey in all the years after that; year after year, now thirty-eight and counting.

★

Rosie and Dick had worked as unpaid consultants on that first project, and Rice's Committee on Undergraduate Teaching had awarded us a one-year grant of eighteen hundred dollars to help pay for the rental of the telephones and for the costs of printing, keypunching, and verifying the survey data. The *Houston Post*, one of the city's two major newspapers at the time, after giving extensive coverage to the 1982 survey, offered to fund the next year's research with a grant of three thousand dollars, in exchange for "worldwide first publication rights to the survey findings."

One of the several presentations I was asked to make during 1982 was to the initial class of American Leadership Forum, a national organization that had just been founded in Houston by Joe Jaworski, with the intent of connecting and training a new generation of diverse leaders, and encouraging them to broaden their goals from the single-minded pursuit of personal success to encompass a deeper commitment to serve the wider community. With funding from the Russo Companies, ALF made an additional three-year grant of three thousand dollars per year to support the surveys.[40]

It was fascinating to track Houston attitudes during those early years of deepening recession. The proportion of survey respondents who rated job opportunities as *excellent* or *good* plummeted from 76 percent in 1982 to just 40 percent in 1983, yet faith in the work ethic remained: 78 percent in 1983 still endorsed the belief that, if you work hard in this city, eventually you will succeed. At the same time, by 60 to 37 percent, the respondents in 1983 now decisively *agreed* that people who work hard and live by the rules are not getting a fair break these days; eleven months earlier, only 46 percent concurred with that statement, and 51 percent had disagreed.[41]

It was also interesting to note the remarkable stability in area residents' commitments to improving and protecting the environment despite the deepening economic recession. The respondents in 1983 continued to give their lowest ratings to the control of air and water pollution in the Houston area; they were just as adamant as in 1982 (by 59 and 60 percent) in rejecting the argument that today's requirements for pollution control cost more than they are worth, and they believed even more strongly (71 percent, compared with 63 percent the year before) that protecting the environment is so important that continuing improvements must be made, regardless of cost. The findings suggested that environmental concerns are less affected than is usually assumed by short-term changes in economic outlooks; they seemed to be reflecting instead a more broad-based and more enduring shift of consciousness.[42]

Most Houstonians expected the price of oil to bounce back quickly, as humbler bumper stickers appeared—STAY ALIVE 'TIL '85 and PLEASE, GOD, GIVE ME ONE MORE OIL BOOM; I PROMISE I WON'T SCREW THIS ONE UP. By early 1987, the price of oil had dropped to ten dollars a barrel, and one out of every seven jobs that had existed in Houston in 1982 had disappeared.

It turned out to be the worst regional recession of any part of the country at any time since World War II. The city had been massively overbuilding in the expectation of continued hikes in the price of oil. By late 1986, Houston had more prime, downtown, vacant ("see-through") office space than either San Francisco or Philadelphia had total office space, and the city had become one of the best bargains in all of urban America.

★

In each of the annual surveys, we generally repeat verbatim about 40 percent of the questions in order to track ongoing changes. Another one-fourth of the questions are reserved for the obligatory background information (socioeconomic status, religion, political ideology, ethnicity, age, and gender). In the space remaining, we add the new questions for that year, seeking to probe more deeply into emerging themes or to explore new areas of interest.[43]

The questions we have been tracking measure the respondents' economic outlooks: What would you say is the biggest problem facing people in the Houston area today? How have you been doing financially over the past few years? How do you think you'll be doing three or four years down the road? Is the country headed for better times or more difficult times? In today's economy, is it necessary to get an education beyond high school or are there many ways to succeed with no more than a high school diploma? Do the public schools have enough money, or will they need significantly more in order to provide a quality education? Should the government take action to reduce the income differences between rich and poor in America?

The survey items also measure comfort with diversity and support for immigration: Will Houston's increasing ethnic diversity eventually become a source of great strength for the city or a growing problem? Do immigrants generally take more from the American economy than they contribute, or do they contribute more than they take? Do the immigrants mostly strengthen or mostly threaten American culture? How would you rate the relations that generally exist among ethnic and racial groups in the Houston area today?

The questions ask about social issues and urban amenities: Is abortion morally wrong or is it morally acceptable? Should it be legal for a woman to obtain an abortion if she wants to have one for any reason? Is homosexuality something people choose or something they cannot change? Should marriages between homosexuals be given the same legal status as heterosexual marriages? If you could live in any kind of housing in the Houston area, what would you prefer—a single-family home with a big yard, where you would need to drive almost everywhere you want to go, or a smaller home in a more urbanized area within walking distance of shops and workplaces?

Other questions come into the surveys and then disappear, as their relevance changes over the years.[44] Through it all, a variety of central themes have emerged, pointing to compelling changes in area residents' attitudes and beliefs as they have come to grips over the years with the ongoing economic and demographic transformations.

For thirty-eight years, the Kinder Houston Area Survey has been measuring the continuities and changes in the attitudes, beliefs, and experiences of successive representative samples of Harris County residents. Through the answers to these many questions, in systematic interviews lasting on average twenty-five to thirty minutes each, with a total over the years of more than forty-six thousand Houston-area residents, we have been watching the world change.[45]

No city in America has been followed in this way over such a long period of time. Few exemplify more clearly than Houston the trends that are refashioning the social and political landscape across the nation. Houston experienced more suddenly than most the rapid decline of the resource economy and the rise of today's restructured, increasingly unequal knowledge-based economy. Its Anglo population stopped expanding after the oil bust of 1982 and then declined slightly. All the growth of this rapidly growing city during the ensuing three and a half decades has been due to the influx of African Americans, Asians, and Hispanics.

In the 1980 census, Harris County was 63 percent Anglo, 20 percent African American, 16 percent Hispanic, and 2 percent Asian. Thirty years later, in 2010, it was 41 percent Hispanic, 33 percent Anglo, 18 percent African American, and 8 percent Asian. Ethnicity and age are intertwined in dramatic ways. According to the most recent census estimates, more than half of all the residents in Harris County who are under the age of twenty are Hispanics, another one-fifth are African Americans, and just over a fifth are non-Hispanic whites.

The demographic transformation is a done deal. You can close the border, seal off America, build an impenetrable wall, and deport all ten million people who are here without the proper papers; none of those efforts will make much of a difference. No conceivable force will stop Houston or Texas or America from becoming more Asian, more African American, more Hispanic, and less Anglo as the twenty-first century unfolds.

According to census projections for the American population as a whole, soon after 2040, less than half the country will be composed of non-Hispanic whites, and the nation's overall demographics will look very much like Harris County today. Houston is America on demographic fast-forward. This city is where, for better or worse, the future of our nation is going to be worked out.

CONFRONTING THE
NEW ECONOMY

CHAPTER 4

When All the Good Fortune Suddenly Ended

After years of drawing aces, Houston's economic luck had turned sour.

—Robert Thomas and Richard Murray[46]

The postwar era (1945–1979) was a period of remarkable broad-based prosperity across the entire nation, at least for white Americans. The country had emerged from the war in 1945 as the sole economic power on the planet; all its major economic competitors were decimated by the war experience. It was a time of Big Government and big undertakings. The Marshall Plan helped to rebuild Europe and Japan, enabling those nations to return to prosperity, so that poverty and despair would not become the spark renewing violence. By 1956, the GI Bill had sent more than eight million veterans to college or vocational training. The Federal-Aid Highway Act of 1956 provided the funds to cover 90 percent of the cost of building forty-one thousand miles of the new interstate highway system.

It was a time when Big Business, led by the likes of General Motors and General Electric, opened major factories and created around them new communities and thriving commerce. It was a time of Big Labor, when 38 percent of all the private-sector jobs in America were unionized, and the unions could negotiate with the corporations to ensure that workers shared in the prosperity of the companies. There were middle-class wages for most American workers whatever their levels of education, and there were pensions that would guarantee a comfortable retirement. It was a time when the rising tide lifted most boats at almost equal rates, creating a deep-seated sense of shared destiny and widespread confidence in an ever-improving future.

This was the golden era of American industrialism, when the average white American male, whatever his education, in whatever job he had, found himself making more money every year, literally doubling his income between 1949 and 1979. Those were also the years when we celebrated the stay-at-home housewife-mother in suburbia. Between 1946 and 1964, the average American woman gave birth to 3.6 children, and the baby boom, totaling seventy-six million overwhelmingly non-Hispanic whites, was launched upon the land.

The successors of Jesse Jones and of the Suite 8F Crowd continued to control Houston politics through most of the second half of the twentieth century. They championed the interests of developers and oil barons, and they threw their power and money behind candidates who would perpetuate the status quo, people like Jim McConn, the former developer and incumbent mayor, who was preparing to run for reelection.

McConn should have been able to waltz through the 1981 election, riding on the support of the city's 67 percent Anglo majority. He'd been president of the Greater Houston Home Builders' Association. He'd been elected four years earlier to a city council seat against an avowed racist, Frank Briscoe, and won most of the black and Latino vote. He was a steadfast friend to oil and gas, as well as to the developers of homes and offices, the two businesses that dominated Houston's economy.

Houston's mayoral elections work much like California's jungle primaries. All the candidates from every party run in the November election, and citizens can vote for any candidate regardless of party. If nobody gets more than 50 percent, a runoff is held between the top two candidates. When the dust settled, McConn was out of the race. He would be the last Republican, at least as of this writing, to hold the office. Two Democrats were left standing: sixty-three-

year-old Sheriff Jack Heard and thirty-five-year-old City Controller
Kathy Whitmire.

Kathryn J. Whitmire was born in Houston in 1946. At the age of
thirty-one, she was appointed city controller by Mayor Fred Hofheinz
to fill out a vacated term, becoming the first woman ever to hold such
an important public office in Houston's history. As a fiscal conservative
determined to rein in the excess and waste in city spending, she won the
next race for controller in a landslide. It soon became clear, however,
that she was prepared to challenge the old boys' game. She objected to
the many sweetheart deals that had been put into place by McConn,
and she enforced open-bidding policies rather than rubber-stamping
renewals for city contracts with local businesses. She was increasingly
vocal in calling attention to the rights of women, minorities, and gays.
She was a threat to the old order on every front, and she faced fierce
opposition when she ran, in 1981, for her first term as mayor.

Jack Heard had been a lifelong public servant. He held various
leadership positions since he was thirty-six years old, including chief
of police. For his mayoral campaign, Heard had nearly unlimited cash,
thanks to contributions from Houston's oil barons and city developers.
Whitmire unexpectedly pulled ahead in the polls, and she won, 62 to
37 percent. As Steven Williams observed in a November 1981 *New York
Times* article about that election, "The developers and bankers and oil
millionaires who used to handpick candidates can no longer be said
to dominate the political scene. Houston is home today to too many
different kinds of people, with too many different sets of values and
interests, for any one group to control elections so easily."

Whitmire was prepared to lead a city with one of the strongest
economies in America and to help move it in a more egalitarian and
inclusive direction. The coalition of women and minorities that elected
her was eager to moderate Houston's anti-government ideology and
to address at long last this booming city's social inequities and environmental threats. In early 1982 as she took office, there seemed to

be plenty of money, plenty of jobs, and positive change was in the air. It was a historic moment full of the promise of new beginnings.

Then the bottom dropped out.

The basic metric used to measure the health of the oil patch was the Baker Hughes rig count. Any operating oil rig anywhere on the planet meant an average of forty-five good, blue-collar manufacturing jobs in Houston. The rig count plunged from a peak of 4,530 rigs drilling for oil on U.S. territory in February 1982 to less than three thousand by the end of the year, taking with it a total of some sixty-eight thousand jobs. The overvalued dollar made American products more expensive abroad, causing a rapid decline in exports out of the Port of Houston, by then the third busiest in the U.S. Within eighteen months, a region that for more than a century had known only growing prosperity recorded a net loss of nearly 150,000 jobs.

The oil patch was in a free fall: shedding rapidly its once-generous benefits, pensions, and jobs. For people who lost their jobs during this time, support would evaporate. The door to opportunity would close, taking another person, another family, out of the economy. Houston entered the worst and most prolonged regional recession since 1945, in a city that had known only economic boom from its beginnings. Too many Houstonians had borrowed far more than they should have and were now overexposed. Developers had massively overbuilt for what was to come.

By 1984, every day on average three businesses and fourteen people declared bankruptcy. Retail and real estate hemorrhaged. Whole neighborhoods emptied out as homeowners who could no longer afford their mortgages walked away from houses large and small, luxurious and modest. Residents would pack up and drop their keys off at the mortgage broker's office on their way out of town.

New commercial and residential developments everywhere were going broke, just as they were coming onto the market. Private jets were grounded. Laid-off workers from Midland Oil Company were living in tents and refrigerator boxes. By 1987, more than 170 oil producers and oil field service companies had declared bankruptcy. Even the mega-rich and powerful were going bust, especially those whose greed got the best of them, clouding their judgment, their sense of timing, and their ability to calculate risks.

John Connally, former governor of Texas, the same man who took three bullets while riding in the car in front of President Kennedy on that fateful day in Dallas, endured one of the most spectacular flameouts of the Houston oil bust. The son of a tenant farmer tried to turn millions of dollars into tens of millions after leaving public office. He grabbed up oil wells and real-estate developments at exactly the wrong moment.

Connally had a history of bad timing. He had switched from Democrat to Republican in May 1973 just as Watergate was unfolding. As another Texas senator, Ralph Yarborough, was fond of saying, Connally was "the only case on record of a man swimming toward a sinking ship."[47] When the oil bust hit bottom, Connally had racked up forty-eight million dollars in debt. TV audiences were enthralled when auction houses came to the properties owned by him and his wife, Nellie, to buy up their belongings, as the couple sought to raise the money they needed to pay off their most insistent creditors.

Texas historian T. R. Fehrenbach, in his seminal book *Seven Keys to Texas*, quotes a favorite saying from the frontier: "Root, hog, or die."[48] Early settlers would send out pigs, and eventually cattle, to find food for themselves. If they didn't find anything, they died; nobody was going to feed them. For Houston in the oil bust, there was not much help coming from either the state or the federal government. While Washington responded to the demands of the manufacturing belt for bailouts, no such help was coming to Houston. The message was clear: Find a way to feed yourself, Houston, or you can die trying.

Local government was ill-equipped to handle the crisis. While Whitmire has been hailed as one of the city's best administrators, her response was widely seen as inadequate. The mayor's focus was on cutting costs and raising whatever small amounts of additional revenue she could, by levying fines for such transgressions as weeds that were not being cleared, and by increasing the charges for business permits—promulgating the kinds of small, aggravating regulations that would not ultimately make much of a difference. If things were ever going to turn around, the business community would have to jump in with both feet.

Developers Kenneth Schnitzer and Gerald Hines had reconfigured the commercial centers of Houston. During the 1980s, they continued throughout the recession to create sprawling office spaces, residential buildings, a new arena—the Compaq Center for the Houston Rockets—a famous upscale shopping district (the Galleria); a whole new urban neighborhood with easy access to some of the city's most valuable residential districts. Facing the same vacancy rates as the rest of the city, with no upswing in sight, Schnitzer recognized that Houston needed to be much more proactive in its economic development efforts. With money chipped in from local businesses, he guided the effort to establish the Houston Economic Development Council, and led the business community in its first-ever deliberate effort to diversify the economy and to sell the virtues of the city to the rest of America.

A small team of five businesspeople set to work gathering the statistics to document Houston as the nation's second or third busiest port; to celebrate the groundbreaking research and the cardiac surgical skills and medical inventions of Drs. Cooley and DeBakey at the Texas Medical Center; the data showing the diversification of the economy; the images of a green, lush landscape in various parts of the city; and its internationally renowned theater, symphony, ballet, and opera companies. "We went to New York and DC," said a campaign insider, "to talk to the media about all the good things going on in Houston. But no one really wanted to hear what we had to say. The Eastern

Establishment had already written the story in their minds; they had decided that Houston sucks, and good riddance."

With the national media showing little interest, the Houston Economic Development Council turned its efforts to the city's residents themselves. They worked with real-estate agents to educate homeowners on how to refinance their mortgages instead of walking away. They sent videos to cabdrivers so they would have their pitch ready for the customers they'd pick up at the airports, to tell them all about the performing arts and the museums. They created sampler packages with free tickets to an opera, symphony, or other theater event. There were Adopt-a-Park initiatives, neighborhood-revitalization projects, and targeted-research reports designed to attract industries to suburban areas closer to their sources of labor.

The volunteer force would grow into the thousands. Agencies created ads pro bono, and the media provided them with free space. "No matter whom we called or what we asked for," one staffer told me, "the answer was always yes." It was the business community, once again, that would act to save the city, or at least the parts of it in which they lived and worked. None of the efforts addressed Houston's failing school system or the increasing population of children who qualified for free school lunches. Among all the initiatives to save the economy, not one recognized the need for new skills or technical training.

★

When we conducted the first survey in March 1982, almost 50 percent of all the oil refining in America was occurring in the petrochemical plants along the Houston Ship Channel, including the plastic products, technical equipment, and industrial chemicals that were at the heart of the industry. Meanwhile, the Texas Medical Center and the Port of Houston were in the midst of their own spectacular growth.

Figure 4.1 depicts the official unemployment rates in Harris County during February in each of the thirty-eight years, along with the percent of survey participants who were giving negative ratings to local job opportunities. The objective data recorded each year by the U.S. Bureau of Labor Statistics swing right along with the impressions of area residents.

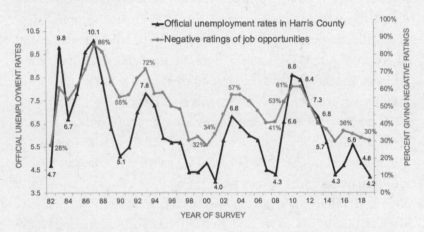

FIGURE 4.1: *The official unemployment rates and negative ratings of job opportunities (1982–2019)*
Source: Kinder Houston Area Survey (1982–2019) and the U.S. Department of Labor, Bureau of Labor Statistics

In the 1982 survey, more than three-fourths (76 percent) rated job opportunities in the Houston area as excellent or good; 47 percent said their financial situations were getting better (just 16 percent said worse), and 63 percent thought they would be even better off three or four years down the road. Two months later, the oil boom collapsed.

The recession spread from the energy sector to the entire economy, and unemployment grew to more than 10 percent. By the time of the 1987 survey, one out of every seven jobs that had been in Houston in 1982 had disappeared; 86 percent of the survey participants that year gave negative ratings to job opportunities, and 72 percent spontaneously cited the economy (poverty, unemployment, and homelessness) when asked to name the biggest problem facing people in the Houston region.

The economic forces that made Houston (and all of America) soar during the postwar years were undergoing one of the most profound shifts in U.S. history. Ahead of most of the country, Houston was hit smack in the face with the central economic and demographic transformations of our time. This city was about to emerge at the forefront of the national trends, as a bellwether of change, on many more fronts than anyone would have imagined.

★

Robert Clayton Lanier was born in Baytown, Texas, in 1925. The son of a pipe fitter's assistant, he was the first in his family to attend college and became a star at the University of Texas Law School. He went into corporate finance law, and then started buying banks, fixing them, selling them, and using the money to invest in real-estate development, much in the same way that Jesse Jones had built his fortune. Not long after Kathy Whitmire took office, and after having served as commissioner of the Texas Department of Transportation (TxDOT), Lanier reluctantly accepted her invitation to be chairman of Houston Metro.

He never believed in the light-rail Whitmire was advocating. He felt strongly that while the city might get a bump in federal funding for transit developments, Houston was too spread out to be able to persuade more than a small minority of its residents to give up the versatility of the car for a seat on such an expensive and antiquated technology. He could see Dallas heading for its own disaster as a result of overbuilding its transit system. And nothing motivates Houston more powerfully than averting a crash into a wall it thought Dallas was running into.

Whitmire's firm belief that Houston should commit to building a new transit system was not only about moving people through space. Effective public transportation, she thought, was a key to the urban experience, and it was the only way to encourage the density real urbanism requires. A great city promotes walkability—from home to work, to cafés and bars, museums and shops. Whitmire and Lanier would both turn out for different reasons to be right about the place of transit in the continuing development of the Houston region. But Whitmire was the mayor, and because of his resistance, she sacked Lanier as head of Metro.

The day he was fired was also the day of the yearly Christmas party Lanier hosted at his sprawling River Oaks mansion. It was the politico and power-player event of the season, and of course the mayor was on the guest list. As soon as Whitmire arrived at the party, she was surrounded by the press and began answering questions about the personnel changes at Metro, right there in the living room of Lanier's home. He promptly ejected her from the party, along with all the reporters, ordering them to hold their conference on the curb. Ten years later, in 1991, Lanier ran a vigorous campaign for mayor and went on to trounce Whitmire every bit as badly as she had trounced McConn and Heard in 1981. It was a rich white guy in cowboy boots with a strong Texas drawl who would guide Houston into the recovery of the 1990s.

*

Houston is known as "an elastic city," and it got that moniker as part of its strategy to feed city-government coffers. A generous policy of strip annexations enabled the city, without asking permission, to expand and absorb any unincorporated area within five miles of its borders. Houston engaged in this practice aggressively in order to keep from being ringed by incorporated townships with people who worked in Houston but lived in bedroom communities and paid taxes to a municipality other than Houston. A number of areas, such as West University, Bellaire, and La Porte, managed to incorporate as separate towns with their own local government and police, fending off annexation by Houston before the city could stop them. The City of Houston grew right around these small regions that dot the map of the Massachusetts-sized metro area.

Many of the areas Houston was able to annex were never fully integrated under the city government. Doing so would have meant having to provide full services to these outlying regions, laying down miles of water and sewage pipes, expanding and maintaining the roads, building electricity lines, providing police and fire department protection, and many other services as well. The expense was not likely to be recouped by property taxes levied in the poorer neighborhoods with lower home values.

So while the city controlled the destiny of the annexed areas, most were left in governmental limbo. Served by loosely organized MUDs (municipal utility districts), residents have no official political voice or vote in determining city policy. While their property taxes go to the City of Houston, the residents receive little by way of city services. "This has made Houston more of a 'pathetic city,' rather than what you're describing as a prophetic city," former Harris County Judge Ed Emmett told me, his voice tinged with resentment.

In his sixties now, the animated and energetic Texas native and lifelong public-office holder shows clear frustration. "It was the right thing to do at the time, in order to keep an income base for city government," continues Emmett. "A lot of Houston's annexation activity was a wealth grab, like Clear Lake City [where NASA is located] and Kingwood, which I represented in the state legislature. The residents had come to Kingwood from outside the area as a whole, and they didn't like the idea of being annexed by Houston. So I fought against that." But the city ultimately won, after a long and ugly court battle.

Houston finalized the annexations of Clear Lake and Kingwood in 1997, and all new annexations ceased after that. These two powerful, predominantly Republican and Anglo communities now receive the full array of city services along with a disproportionate influence on city policies.

Aldine is another story, illustrating the kind of blemish that keeps pushing Houston off the lists of the best places to live in America. One of the poorest areas in Harris County, Aldine's population of nearly fifteen thousand has a poverty rate of 37 percent. Its average household income is a little less than thirty-five thousand dollars. Seventy-nine percent of the population is Spanish-speaking; 41 percent are foreign-born. Its crime rate is among the highest in Harris County; there are still dirt roads, and its schools, save for the presence of a YES Prep charter, are among the worst in Harris County. When it came time for Aldine to be incorporated in the 1980s, Houston took a hard pass. Times were bad, and Aldine's shrinking tax base simply could not justify providing that additional infrastructure. Never incorporated or formed into a municipality, residents use septic tanks for sewage and dig wells for their water, since they are served by neither Houston's sewage treatment plants nor by its water systems.[49]

"Aldine is doing somewhat better recently because BakerRipley [a remarkable nonprofit] is providing many of the needed services," says Emmett. That includes early childhood education, tax services, senior services, English as a second language, and job training. But because of the old strip annexation laws, these MUDs "are left without important services," says Emmett. "They can't form as their own towns, they can't incorporate, and Houston won't finalize the annexation. They are in limbo, far from town, from jobs, and from opportunity."

According to Emmett, many of these unincorporated areas are setting the stage for even more suburban poverty. The jobs that residents can get are generally not in their MUD districts. Public transportation is inadequate, making it difficult for people to get to work.

What residents may save in their cost of housing in the unincorporated suburbs is eaten up by the cost of transportation. "There is no other urban region in America that has to deal with this kind of situation," Emmett exclaims. "No other city was given the power to do strip annexation like this."

About thirty miles west of downtown Houston, along the famed "Energy Corridor," where international and local oil and gas headquarters line I-10, is the town of Katy, Texas, which did manage to resist Houston's annexation efforts and to incorporate on its own. The area around Katy is full of master-planned communities and walkable shopping malls, and the town has its own independent school district that is much better than Houston's. Young families tend to flock there from the big city once their kids reach school age.

But travel just to the north and west of Katy and you will find, once again, pockets of concentrated poverty, with dirt roads, open sewers, and few services; and more MUDs. "The city has fully incorporated some of these areas, through Limited Purpose Annexation, grabbing recently built strip malls but bypassing the residential communities. The city is taking money without providing services; it is starving areas in deep need of additional resources," concludes Emmett.

I left the conversation with a familiar feeling of disappointment with Houston city policies that leave so many people in such difficult circumstances. And I wondered why the former Harris County judge and his county commissioners had not been able, in all the twelve years he was in office, to do anything significant to address the very obvious inequities. During his tenure, the needle hadn't moved much on improving the conditions of Harris County's two million MUD residents.

Lanier deserves some of the blame for the current situation. By almost single-handedly putting the brakes on public transportation, setting the transit efforts back at least twenty years, he deepened the plight of Houston's poor, contributing to the city's growing inequality by cutting off efficient transportation options that might have reached the more affordable but distant MUD districts.

I visited with my friend Gene Vaughan, successful financier and founder of the Center for Houston's Future, about this and much else, in the sun-filled, elegant, and comfortable salon in his River Oaks home. At eighty-six years old, this diminutive, warm, and friendly gray-haired, blue-eyed Tennessee native has a deceptively quiet demeanor. Vaughan came to Houston after receiving his MBA from Harvard and established a lucrative career in finance. He becomes animated and a bit angry when I ask him about the role that Bob Lanier, lauded by so many, had actually played in Houston's history. "Lanier loved concrete," Vaughan asserted. "And he was a disaster. The Realtors dominated everything when he was mayor. They bought up all the land ahead of the highways they knew were coming. It was a can't-lose game for them."

After his chairmanship of TxDOT, Lanier's relationship with that state agency made it easier to bring the new highways through Houston. Dallas fought for more walkable urbanism, while Houston continued to sprawl. Lanier's actions to thwart public transportation also helped to diminish economic opportunity in Houston's less affluent communities.

Algenita Scott Davis uses the example of workers who have to drive forty to sixty minutes from home every day because housing is more affordable in far-flung districts. The workers often can't afford the parking fees at their jobs; others may have lost their cars during the most recent floods. If someone gets off work at 2:00 a.m., the only public transportation option to get home will be an Uber or a cab, because Houston's Metro stops all rail and bus transit at midnight and doesn't resume until 4:00 a.m. While not as extreme as the situation in San Francisco or San Jose, where workers often sleep in their parked cars at night to avoid having to drive for three hours to get back home, Houston could well be headed in the same direction.

What you might save in rent or purchase price in your housing, you would quickly lose to property taxes and long commutes. "Houston is not an especially affordable city," says Kinder Institute director Bill Fulton, who came to Houston as a city planner from Los Angeles and Washington, DC. "The affordability that was here after the oil bust when prices were genuinely low is now a myth."

The big sort,[50] the segregation of communities by economic class and political ideology, has hit Houston hard. The city is one of the most segregated in America, not by ethnicity so much as by income. Social services and schools have generally been seen as public utilities for which the bare minimum should be spent. In dealing with crime, for example, wealthy communities can and do pay for additional constables, while the rest of the city is left with inadequate police protection.

★

Economic mobility slowed gradually during the quarter century after World War II. A World Bank study in 2016 found a significant drop in "absolute mobility," as measured by comparing children's household incomes at age thirty with their parents' household incomes at age thirty.[51] Among the adult children born in the 1940s (and who were young adults in the 1960s and '70s), more than 90 percent found themselves earning more than their parents; but among those who came of age after 1980, that was true of just 50 percent. Prime-age workers in the bottom 60 percent of American families have had almost no real income growth at all since 1980.

A child born into poverty in the U.S. today has less chance of making it into the middle class than a comparable child in Canada or Europe. The correlation between how much money you make at age forty and how much your parents made at the same age is stronger in America than in most European countries. If we are to redress the growing inequalities in America, it must come from major new investments in the education and support of the less fortunate 60 percent and in helping them develop their technical skills.

The stark contrasts in the life circumstances of the richest 20 per-cent of Americans and the everyday realities experienced by all other Americans is to an important degree attributable to differences in edu-cational attainment and in political influence. The "fortunate fifth," equipped as they are with high levels of human and social capital, are well-positioned to flourish in the knowledge-based global economy and to benefit greatly from the free trade, technological advances, and immigration flows that characterize the new economy.

After 1980, as indicated by the lighter columns in Figure 4.2, the broadly shared affluence of the postwar years gave way to growing inequalities, in a restructured economy marked by intensifying world-wide competition, declining unionization, advances in computers and robotics, and the increasing concentration of political and economic power in the hands of the wealthiest Americans.

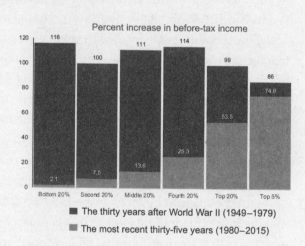

The thirty years after World War II were a period of broad-based prosperity.

The past thirty-five years have seen increasing inequalities in income and wealth.

Percent increase in before-tax income

■ The thirty years after World War II (1949–1979)
■ The most recent thirty-five years (1980–2015)

FIGURE 4.2: *Two contrasting economic eras (1949 to 1979; and 1980 to 2015)*
Source: *U.S. Census, Current Population Survey, Annual Social and Economic Supplements*

The old, once-booming factories in companies like Cameron Iron Works and Hughes Tool Company were bleeding jobs. The new organizations had less incentive to care about the success of Houston's residents. For them, the logic of capitalism in the new economy dictates that if you are doing a job that I can train a Third World worker to do, and I pay that Third World worker fifteen dollars a day to do the job, I'm not going to pay you fifteen an hour. And if you are doing work that I can program a computer to do, I will soon be replacing your job with an intelligent machine.

As a result of these forces, almost all the benefits of economic growth in the last thirty-five years have gone to the richest 20 percent of Americans. At the same time, 60 percent of the nation's families have found their incomes stagnating or declining. Like the rest of the country, Houston is struggling with the growing income disparities in today's high-tech economy, disparities that are predicated above all on access to good schools and colleges.

When I was a graduate student at Harvard in the 1960s, the average CEO of a major American company was being paid about eighteen times as much as the average worker. We sociology students were appalled by the size of that gap, since CEOs were earning just five times as much as ordinary workers in Japan and nine times as much in Germany. By 2018, the average American CEO was being paid 295 times as much as the average employee. A typical American wage earner today has to work for almost an entire year in order to earn what a CEO will make in a single day.

In 1976, when Houston was bragging about its economy and lording it over the rest of the country, the richest 1 percent in the U.S. earned about 8.5 percent of all the income earned by all Americans. Today that small group takes home more than 20 percent of the entire national income and owns 37 percent of the nation's wealth; more than the total assets held by the entire bottom 90 percent of all Americans.

Houston was not unfamiliar with these kinds of disparities. The superrich oil barons did nothing to hide their good fortune. But in

2001, the combination of oil and sophisticated financial structures came to threaten an entire sector of the American economy.

★

Reaction to the name "Ken Lay" is like a Rorschach test, indicating where in the country you're from. If you lived through California's rolling blackouts in the 1990s and the recall vote on Governor Gray Davis, you might have a hard time containing your anger at the man many residents blame for artificially jacking up the price of energy, callously swamping those in poverty with unbearable costs, leaving so many, especially the poor and elderly, without power during the horrible heat waves of that decade. If you are from the Midwest, the name may evoke indignation over the extent of corruption and greed in America. In the Northeast, if you were not working in the financial industry, you might be remembering the confident feeling, now that the main actors were jailed, that never again would the markets see this kind of excess, corruption, and greed. If you work in the financial industry, you know that it did happen again, that no one was jailed when a much bigger breach of trust occurred, and that, as long as we leave moneymaking so loosely regulated, it will happen again.

If you ask Houston's leaders about the role played by the impoverished son of a Baptist preacher from Missouri, you will hear a different story. Houstonians know the Ken Lay who for many years was the city's philanthropic hero and who led the Greater Houston Partnership (GHP)—the entity that formed out of the preexisting Chamber of Commerce and the Houston Economic Development Council. Ken Lay had also funded endowed chairs both at the University of Houston and at Rice. He had given hundreds of thousands, by some accounts millions, to MD Anderson Cancer Center, whose president at the time, John Mendelsohn, sat on the Enron board's audit committee and is an extraordinary leader who is often credited with putting MD Anderson on the world map.

Ken Lay was renowned for his generosity with Enron's money. In Houston you can make as much money as the market will allow, but if you don't give much of it away, no one will talk to you. And if you give enough of it away, people will look the other way when suspicions arise, as long as the money keeps flowing.

As Houston's economy came into line with the rest of America during the recovery of the late 1980s, and as globalization took hold, the culture of Houston was visibly changing. Longtime Houston resident Mimi Swartz remembers watching the changes unfold. "Houston had been isolated before the first oil boom," says the *Texas Monthly* executive editor and coauthor of *Power Failure*, written with Enron whistleblower Sherron Watkins. "It used to be that people who grew up here went to UT [University of Texas at Austin]. They didn't leave the state. Rich people had houses in Aspen. They were flamboyant and weird and outrageous, and it was fun. But something changed in the 1980s.

"Even as the overall Houston economy collapsed," she continues, "the kids of wealthy families were going to Harvard and meeting people from other parts of America. Houston's richest were buying summer homes in the Hamptons, Cape Cod, and Nantucket. They were starting to look more like everyone else on the East Coast." They were entering a different world from that of East Texas, different from Houston's famous openness to new people and new ideas, from its lack of class hierarchy and its handshake business ethic.

Executives Andy Fastow and Jeff Skilling, both jailed for their Enron activities, came to Houston from financial institutions just when the housing derivatives that would threaten the entire economy in 2008 were taking off. And both came to Enron from banks that would fail for similar reasons not long after they left. In fact, the bank in Chicago where Fastow practiced some of his creative moving around of assets would be America's largest bank failure until the events of 2008. Skilling left First City Bancorporation of Texas in Houston just before that entity failed as well.

"What they did in Houston could never have happened anywhere else," says an Enron insider. "Andy Fastow and Jeff Skilling came to a city that readily accepted them because they were smart and hardworking. Unethical people were coming into a handshake culture, where it was assumed that you would do things ethically."

A great many insightful books have been written about Enron, partly in response to the imperative to expose every last detail of the fiasco in an attempt at prevention. But for those who don't remember, or who've come to Houston more recently, the essence of it was this: Enron, by manipulating energy markets, made consumer costs artificially skyrocket. The managers moved assets around on the balance sheet to make it look like they had billions in reserve. Nobody checked what they were up to, and nobody asked the tough questions that would prove the data they presented was bogus.

In 2000, when Enron was at its height, Houstonians were making money hand over fist once again; positive ratings of job opportunities in the Houston surveys had risen to 68 percent, the highest numbers since the crash. "We all watched on the sidelines, wondering why Enron was doing so much better than we were," said Diana, a native Houstonian, former financial analyst, and wealthy River Oaks resident. "We were living well, but everyone at Enron was becoming superrich, like the Wall Street hedge fund traders of the mid-2000s."

"It was the excesses of energy capital colliding with the abundance of financial capital," says Mimi Swartz, "and Texans of course have the bigger balls for taking bigger risks."

The oil and gas companies with hard assets knew the train wreck was coming. Jim Hackett, who was the CEO of the oil exploration giant Anadarko at the time, was blunt: "It was a Ponzi scheme. It was all fake. There was no moral core; they never wrestled deeply with issues of morality. In Houston there is a tremendous admiration for people who succeed, but the question is, did they get there the right way? Houston tends to assume they had the merit behind them."

The Enron experience drove Hackett to explore his own sense of morality in business. At the height of his career, he left Anadarko for Harvard Divinity School. "If a room full of Midwestern Christians could go this wrong, I had to look at how it could happen and why it might keep happening." He is now teaching business ethics at the University of Texas at Austin, while also serving as CEO of Alta Mesa, a local oil and gas company.

"I knew all of them well. Jeff was in my business school class at Harvard. On the surface, Enron did all the right things. Their message was 'Respect, Integrity, Communication, and Excellence.' They published a mission statement about making the environment better. They had an amazing board. There was a Stanford professor on their audit committee. So if they were making all the right moves and claimed to hold all the right religious values, what went wrong? Three years later at a Harvard Business School reunion, I started asking classmates about their faith, and if it had any real impact on how they functioned at work.

"They told me they weren't religious," he continued, "but they quoted Bible passages every day. This was especially true of Ken Lay. These guys had intellectual values that encouraged them to do what was expedient, but they didn't have the spiritual values that meant you would do the right thing. They thought about the company's growth and about self-preservation, not about the tens of thousands of people whose wealth and savings were being destroyed." When Enron collapsed, it eliminated twenty-nine thousand jobs and all the pensions along with them.

Rich Kinder, who had been in line to take over as CEO of Enron, left to start his own pipeline and trading company. He became one of the richest men in America and, along with his wife and partner, Nancy, grew the Kinder Foundation into a major strategic philanthropic force in Houston. "What was the Enron story really about?" I asked him one day in his office with a panoramic view of the sea of green that is River Oaks. It was overlooking the newly developed Buffalo Bayou Park, a project that the Kinder Foundation had made possible. "It was greed getting out of control, wasn't it?"

"I don't think so," he replied. "It was hubris. It was about believing that they were the smartest people in the world, and so could do no wrong. It was an excess of pride, plain and simple."

Sherron Watkins, the Enron VP who blew the whistle that took down the companies Enron and Arthur Andersen, insisted that Enron was not an aberration. Andersen, the bankers, everyone was in on it, she contends in her book. There was plenty of evidence, as shown during the congressional hearings, that the blame was widely shared. Watkins claimed that everyone was complicit, including the banks, and warned that this sort of collapse would happen again. And of course, it did. Houston, in 2000, was indeed a prophetic city. And like most prophecies, such warnings are rarely heeded.

The inequalities are larger in America than in any other industrialized nation, and they are larger now than at any time in American history, with the sole exception of 1928, just after the Roaring Twenties, and before the total collapse of the American economy in the Great Depression. Inequalities this large will inevitably distort the political process. As Supreme Court Justice Louis Brandeis warned in the late 1920s: "We can have democracy in this country, or we can have great wealth concentrated in the hands of a few, but we can't have both." It was the one issue Jesse Jones feared would cause the destruction of capitalism.

The 2019 survey asked the representative sample of Harris County residents what they would do if they suddenly had to come up with four hundred dollars to deal with an unexpected emergency. Almost four out of ten (39 percent) said they either would have to borrow the money or they would simply not be able to come up with that kind of money right now. Just 60 percent of Harris County residents said they had enough in savings to meet a four-hundred-dollar emergency expense.

Similarly, the Texas Medical Center may be the greatest conglomeration of medical institutions in the world, but Houston is also among the major cities that have the highest percentage of children without health insurance. Fully one-fourth of all the participants in the 2019 survey said they and their families did not have any health insurance. Almost one-third reported total household incomes of less than $37,500. In the 2018 survey, 35 percent said they had difficulty paying for housing, and 33 percent in 2017 said they had a serious problem buying the groceries they needed to feed their families during the past year.

Houston, like much of America, has hit an economic brick wall. For far too many, upward mobility has basically ended.

CHAPTER 5

The Growing Opportunity Gap

*Gone forever are the days when a high school graduate could go to work
on an assembly line and expect to earn a middle-class standard of living.
Students who leave high school today without skills and unprepared for
further learning are unlikely to ever earn enough to raise a family—let
alone buy a house. They are being sentenced to a lifetime of poverty. A
generation's future is at stake.*

—Tony Wagner[52]

During the postwar years of the 1950s and '60s, the United States
had the best public schools in the industrial world, and through
much of the nineteenth and twentieth centuries, the nation's vigorous blue-collar economy provided the rungs that enabled the classic
formula for success. It generally took three generations for families to
climb the proverbial ladder in the expected progression from peddler
to plumber to professional.[53]

Through most of the twentieth century, you really didn't need
much education to strike it rich in this city, state, or nation. The big
money in Texas came from buying and selling land, and harvesting
raw materials and turning them into finished goods. The great Texas
fortunes were built on cotton, timber, cattle, sugar, and oil. Technical advances have long since displaced the low-skilled jobs that the
exploitation of natural resources used to provide. The undereducated
wildcatter's path into the middle class is not coming back.

Given its historical reliance on the resources of the land, it is perhaps not surprising that the state of Texas has generally shortchanged education. In 2016–2017, Texas ranked 38th of the 50 states in the amount of money it was spending per student in its public schools. It was 49th in the proportion of residents aged twenty-five and older who had high school diplomas, and 30th in the percentage with college degrees.

Such lackluster performance may not have been so important back in 1973, when 32 percent of all the ninety-one million jobs in America were available to high school dropouts and another 40 percent required no more than a high school diploma. Almost three-fourths of all the jobs that existed in America in 1973 required a high school diploma or less. By 2020, however, as indicated in Figure 5.1, the Center on Education and the Workforce at Georgetown University predicts that fully 65 percent of all the 164 million jobs will require some kind of credential beyond a high school diploma.

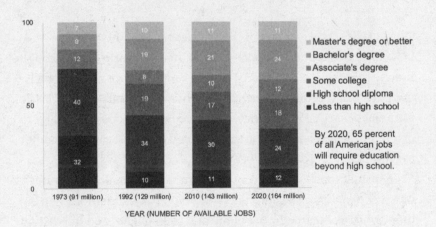

FIGURE 5.1: *The educational requirements for jobs across America (1970–2020)*
Source: Georgetown University Center on Education and the Workforce, 2014

When all the 74,398 eighth graders who were attending Houston-area schools in 2006 were followed for the next eleven years,

Figure 5.2 indicates that only 75 percent actually graduated from high school. Fully one-fourth of all the young people in the greater Houston area have dropped out of high school and are unlikely to find a job that can support a family in the new high-tech, knowledge-based economy. More than half (55 percent) began some kind of program after high school, but eleven years after starting eighth grade, just 22 percent had obtained any kind of postsecondary certificate or degree. Yet two-thirds of all the jobs in America in 2020 will require a certificate attesting to the technical skills such work will demand.

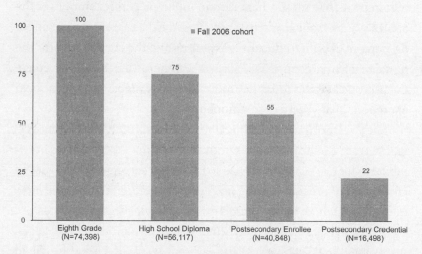

FIGURE 5.2: *The fates of all eighth graders in the Houston region through eleven years (2006–2017) Source: TEA Division of Performance Reporting for Region 4*

The Houston Independent School District (HISD), with its over-crowded, underfunded, inner-city schools, is actually more segregated today than it was before the landmark *Brown v. Board of Education* decision mandated the integration of the public schools in 1954. HISD serves more than 214,000 students, fewer than 8 percent of whom are non-Hispanic white and more than 75 percent qualify for reduced-cost or free lunch programs. We know that success in school requires strong and consistent social-support networks, like the ones that middle-class parents automatically provide for their children, but which are sorely missing in so many HISD schools.

This nation generally does an excellent job in educating the top 15 to 20 percent of America's children, nurturing their talents in some of the best public and private schools and universities in the world. In contrast, we do an abysmal job by world standards in educating the bottom 60 percent of our young people, who are falling ever further behind in comparison with their counterparts in other industrialized countries.

Houston, like most other cities in America, gets its money for the school system from property taxes. It used to be that the state paid for 60 percent of public education expenses and the county paid for the remaining 40 percent. "Now," says Ed Emmett, "that ratio is reversed. Local property taxes today pay more than sixty percent of educational expenses. That's just not sustainable."

The Greater Houston Partnership has several education initiatives, and I served on the executive committee of their Early Matters pre-K initiative for five years. "Why has so little been accomplished?" I asked current GHP president Bob Harvey in a meeting at the brand-new ultramodern, luxe Partnership Tower. "The needed money has not been raised, not an additional dime has been spent. After five years, not a single child has obtained any early education that he or she would not otherwise have received." The response from him and other business leaders, like Bracewell's Pat Oxford, is that Houston has hit the limits on both its sales taxes and property taxes, and philanthropists are unwilling to pour any more money into the deeply troubled HISD.

Because of inadequate government social services in Houston and in Texas, the city's traditional entrepreneurial spirit has been key to helping its nonprofit sector become one of the most robust in America. KIPP Academy and YES Prep both started in Houston and are now among the most successful public charter schools in the country. KIPP, founded in 1984 in Houston and the Bronx by Mike Feinberg and Dave

Levin, has more than two hundred schools in America, and several more in other countries. Students are admitted by lottery, and their parents have to sign contracts in which they commit to supporting their child's homework, attending weekly school meetings, and promising not to send them to school with junk food.

These are exceptional schools, but there are not and never will be enough charter schools to close the education gap, and many are mediocre at best. Above all, we need to rebuild the social safety net and the support systems that children need to succeed in school. Linda Lorelle, former NBC-TV news anchor and founder of Linda Lorelle Media, sees the need for more social supports. The African American daughter of a pediatrician from the South Side of Chicago, she came to Houston with an undergraduate degree from Stanford and a master's in journalism from Missouri. She and her husband, a former educator, saw that there were programs to address the needs of those at the very top and at the very bottom, but too little was available to catch that C student who, with a little more attention and social support, could become a B or A student.

Lorelle used her platform to create the Lorelle Scholarship Fund, targeted to those students; but important as it is, raising money for scholarships is only a small part of what her organization does. Students who win the scholarships are required to attend eight seminars focused on different aspects of what it will take to get through high school and succeed in college. These include learning from prior scholarship winners about how to overcome feelings of inadequacy when they encounter the challenges of college, including the experience of racial bias; learning how to prepare for interviews; instruction in how to secure additional grants; finding ways to overcome transportation issues; and etiquette lessons from Linda herself, which is usually sponsored by one of Houston's finest restaurants. "We have five former scholars on our board now. And all of them tell us that it was the life classes that helped them even more than the money."

"Yes," agrees Stephanie, a former Lorelle scholar who is now a teacher and a board member. "Especially the etiquette class. It was the first time I felt like I could belong in a world like that."

"This is all wonderful and amazing, but how do you scale it?" I asked Linda.

"That's the problem. That's what we are trying to overcome by seeing if the kids who went through the program, one of whom is high up at Shell in Louisiana, can take over and grow this whole thing," she says.

Dedicated individuals continue to chip away at the problems. "Houston was the last place I wanted to come to when I signed up for Teach for America," says twenty-seven-year-old Adeeb Barqawi. Born in Virginia, Barqawi grew up in Kuwait, where his father owned a construction company. He returned to the States for college and entered graduate school in biophysics at Johns Hopkins. We sat outside at a noisy café along Memorial Boulevard. "I didn't want to work in research for the rest of my life," the animated and casually dressed young man told me in his accented, rapid-fire English, as we struggled to be heard over the sounds of the street, "but I didn't know what I wanted to do with my life.

"So I signed up for Teach for America. When I filled out the forms, Houston was literally at the bottom of the list of the places where I wanted to teach. So of course they sent me here, to Kashmere Gardens High School. The predominantly African American school had spent more time in the Improvement Required (IR) category than any other school in the district." Barqawi was assigned to teach ninth-grade physics. "I asked my students if they could tell me what percentage of the U.S. population was African American. The average of all their answers was 75 percent. Most of them had never been outside the area," he adds, his voice rising with passionate disbelief.

"One morning, I noticed that a student, a young woman who

was normally very attentive, kept falling asleep. When I got the class started on an assignment, I kneeled down next to her desk. 'What's wrong?' I asked her. 'My mom was murdered last night,' she told me. I asked her why she came to school. 'I didn't know where else to go,' she replied. She had no one else at home. I told her to go back to sleep. And I started asking the other students about their lives at home. My kids were hungry, abused, stuck in the middle of gang violence, or their families were falling apart; many were on the verge of homelessness or in desperate need of health care. Most of them were coming to school with PTSD. And inside of me, a voice is screaming: *What do I do? What do I do?* I didn't know how to help them, let alone teach them anything about physics."

Adeeb is one of probably thousands of teachers who have felt the same kind of panic in a Houston-area classroom facing these kinds of challenges. Day care and pre-K teachers report children as young as two coming to school on a Monday and asking for additional helpings of cereal. "Because I didn't eat much since Friday," they answer to questions about why they're so hungry.

In addition, one quarter of all public-school students in Texas have experienced traumatic violence. It is from these conditions that we are expecting our future workforce to emerge, to somehow miraculously overcome life-threatening obstacles, and to grow into calm, kind, clearheaded, and well-educated young adults. I don't see how this can happen without much more support from the rest of us, without providing the array of tools these students will need for learning and for coping. This isn't just Houston's problem, of course. It's America's problem. And we have to find effective ways to solve it soon.

Trying to figure out what to do to solve these intractable problems in Kashmere Gardens has been the driving force in Adeeb Barqawi's life, after he failed many times in his attempts to help. "I got three hundred kids into college from my physics classes, and I ruined 285 lives," he asserts. "I didn't understand the challenges they would have just trying to stay in school. I didn't think about them not being able to find transportation, or keep their scholarships, or what it would do to them if they couldn't find a way to stay in college. In the world my kids were coming from, you don't bounce back from a hit like this. And I didn't think about how sending all the smart kids somewhere else was contributing to the decline of the neighborhoods."

Using the Salesforce.com software, Barqawi found a way to change the cycle of failure among his Kashmere Gardens High School students. Eighteen months after implementing the ProUnitas program, the school came within two students of being lifted out of the Improvement Required category, for the first time in years.

The secret was in using sophisticated data management tools to build a form of social capital into the schools. Adeeb created a system that could record and monitor fluctuations in attendance, behavior, and coursework for every high school student. Once a week, he would look at the data on each of the students and if any of the numbers had gone off the rails, he'd be alerted to the needs of that particular child. "We weren't looking to punish kids when they missed class or didn't turn in an assignment. We wanted to ask about the problems they might be facing that were interrupting their schoolwork and pro-social behavior.

"So we asked them what was preventing them from getting to school or from being able to concentrate. Was it hunger? Violence in the neighborhood? Abuse at home? A need for medical or dental intervention? An incarcerated or absent parent? Lack of heat in the winter? We would sit down with the kids who were having trouble and find out what they needed." Additionally, students and teachers could enter an alert into the system at any time, calling attention to a need for help, indicating that someone hadn't eaten or was facing a terrible situation at home; and this would send a notification that immediate intervention was needed.

Barqawi also vetted a network of service agencies and set up a tracking system to make sure the agencies were fulfilling their commitments. ProUnitas receives grants from donors and disburses the money to the appropriate agency on condition that the child will not have to leave the neighborhood in order to access the needed services; the agency would have to come to Kashmere High School itself. "I didn't have any problem finding appropriate agencies," he said when I asked him if the services were really so readily available.

"We are a program-rich city. There is a lot of money out there and many nonprofits. The problem is that we are systems-poor. We are asset-rich and systems-poor. What was missing was a way to connect all these sources of help with those who most needed the help. I'm trying to fix that." Barqawi now has the records of nine thousand students in the ProUnitas system, including those from all the Kashmere Gardens elementary and middle schools. His next goal is to tackle all the schools in Harris County, and eventually in the state of Texas and the rest of America.

★

According to the latest U.S. Census, more than 70 percent of everyone in Harris County today who is under the age of twenty is black or Hispanic. More than half are graduating from high school unprepared for college and unqualified for jobs that will pay a living wage and enable them to find a place in the new economy.

If today's African Americans and Hispanics are not succeeding in the public schools, it is because these two communities are by far the most likely to be living in concentrated poverty and to be attending underfunded schools that offer too few of the critical resources that enable young people of all ethnicities to graduate from high school and go on to obtain the needed postsecondary credentials. The Houston Independent School District reports each year on the percent of graduating high school seniors who were able to meet the criterion of "college readiness" on the SAT or ACT tests. The figures for the class of 2016 were 6.5 percent for the African American students and 7.5 percent for Hispanics, compared to 50.4 percent of the Anglo graduating seniors and 58.1 percent of the Asians.

Among all of Houston's Latinos and African Americans who manage to go on to enroll in community college courses after high school—in the hope of acquiring the credentials needed to qualify for the better-paid jobs, such as welders or health technicians—more than half find themselves in remedial courses that repeat material they should have learned in high school and for which they receive no college credit. It is not surprising that so many become discouraged and drop out of school before they have received any certificate or degree that will enable them to advance in their careers.

By 2040, the rest of the country will look a lot like Houston today, and the country is generally not much more successful than Houston in providing the needed education. The trends point inexorably to a future in which the majority of young Americans will not be spending much in our stores and will have to rely increasingly on government services.

If we are unwilling or unable to make significant improvements in the education we are providing in these underserved communities, who will you be able to hire to work for your company? Who will buy its products? Who will have enough earning power to purchase the home you are planning to sell in order to feed your retirement nest egg? Who will fill the leadership roles as the years unfold? It will ultimately mean the difference between a First and a Third World nation.

The Texas legislature is well aware of today's education requirements and lawmakers have officially endorsed the goal of "60x30," which stipulates that by 2030, at least 60 percent of all Texans aged twenty-five to thirty-four will have a postsecondary certificate or a college degree. The difficulty Texas will have in meeting this goal is obvious.

At the same time that we are growing an underemployed, undereducated population in Houston, we are also facing an increasingly serious skilled-labor shortage. Yet the solutions are out there and, according to early-education experts, so too are the studies showing conclusively that many of the most serious problems in high school can be prevented by starting education much earlier than ages five or six. The impact of high-quality universal preschool on a child's future, and on the ability of the future workforce to participate in the economy, is real and measurable.[54]

At Houston's Urban League, President Judson Robinson remarks that for decades he's been doing the same kind of collaborative work that Adeeb Barqawi is doing through ProUnitas. "We have been providing a vast array of services from preschool all the way to senior citizens. We have professional organizations for young people and guilds for graduates. And we do it where black people live. But Adeeb gets funded, and we don't. That is the essence of the racial issue. No one says maybe the Urban League can solve the problems of the black community since they have the infrastructure and numbers to prove that what they have done works. Nobody.

"Our role is to help people move into the middle class and to prosper beyond that, to create generational wealth. That's the real discrepancy between whites and blacks in America. The income gap is big, but the wealth gap is bigger. At the current rate, it will take another two hundred years to close that gap. There is a growing black middle class, but there is a growing underclass at the same time. The needle hasn't moved on equality of opportunity across the ethnic groups in America. So we are doing whatever we can to leapfrog progress, to engage in a revolution of thought about education, family, and mobility.

"If you build a road and you know it's going to take a hundred years before it's paid for, we can accept that because we know that the commerce coming in from a new highway system makes it worth it," Robinson continues. "We should see education the same way. We think we've already spent money on the schools. We see they haven't gotten any better, so now we are cutting taxes. But how do we get people who can participate in the economy if we don't educate them and if we don't pay teachers enough to live on? And how do we help teachers become more effective in helping families that are falling apart?"

If we are able to make impactful improvements in education, investing in children from birth to college, from cradle to career, raising teacher pay and providing far more social supports for less-affluent children, we would help to ensure the future of America. Indeed, you could make the argument that achieving substantial improvements in early education will be as important in building the conditions for this city's and nation's prosperity in the twenty-first century as was the dredging of the Houston Ship Channel (1910–1920) or the completion of the Interstate Highway System (1956–1991) in contributing to the thriving economy of the twentieth century.

But it's a long game that too few seem willing to play. Houstonians, like many Americans, have voted for decades against providing significantly more money for the public schools. "That means you want to raise my taxes," says a wealthy Houstonian friend, whose kids all attended private school at St. John's, "and I don't want to see that happen." It's a pervasive attitude, echoed until recently in the surveys, and particularly among older Anglos: *These are not my children. Why should I have to pay any more to educate them? We already provide a free public education. Let them take care of their own.*

Houston native Carol Shattuck spent twenty years at the Collaborative for Children, working to raise awareness and open minds to the cost-effectiveness of high-quality early childhood education. Founded and supported by many of Houston's major foundations, the organization works to strengthen families that have young children and to improve the quality of childcare. "There are so many studies," she says, "so much evidence, that the younger the children are when they begin to get some real education, the better off they'll be. If there is an adult who has been singing to them and talking to them and reading to them from birth, their brains actually become better wired for further learning. If those interactions aren't happening, the deficit grows and it's often irreversible. Other Texas cities like San Antonio and Dallas, and other states like Oklahoma, Pennsylvania, and North Carolina, have succeeded in making early education much more widely available than it is in Houston.

"Texas was actually a national leader in providing Pre-K," she continues. "Starting back in the fall of 1985, the state has been offering a half-day program for at-risk four-year-olds, but it has been falling behind the national norms by failing to specify maximum class sizes and teacher-to-child ratios. In 2019 as part of a major school-reform effort, the state approved a significant increase in funding to enable more districts to offer full-day Pre-K. The research is there, and so is the data," says Shattuck.

The Collaborative for Children concentrates its efforts on improving childcare in Houston's low income communities. The United Way and ExxonMobil teamed up with the Collaborative to create United Way Bright Beginnings, which is working to improve the quality of childcare in approximately forty centers and homes in the Houston region. "So much more needs to be done, through improved state standards and financial support, to make sure teachers and classrooms are prepared to deliver high-quality early education to the growing number of children in their care," Shattuck says.

"What does it say about Houston that the city lags so far behind other urban areas in providing universal pre-K? How do we get business and government leaders to improve the coordination and funding of the city's early-education programs? Early Matters, a local coalition of business, education, and nonprofit organizations, worked for several years with only minimal success to develop a coordinated effort to improve access to quality early education. It's become clear that it will require elected officials, from the U.S. president to county and city officeholders, to prioritize investments in education, from early childhood through K-12 and college, as the foundation for our community's success."

The surveys have tracked over the years the way Harris County residents have evolved in their understanding of the new realities. Are members of the general public coming to recognize more clearly the importance of education in today's economy and are they more willing to pay for the investments that will be needed to turn around the generally dismal levels of educational achievement in Houston and America?

The 2019 survey asked the respondents about this statement: "In order to get a job that pays more than $35,000 a year, you need to have at least one or two years of education beyond high school." As indicated in Figure 5.3, 67 percent of all the survey participants agreed with that assertion; fewer than a third disagreed. The findings also reveal that the U.S.-born Anglos, by 55 to 45 percent, were much *less* inclined than African Americans or Hispanics to agree with the assertion that a decently paying job today requires education beyond high school.

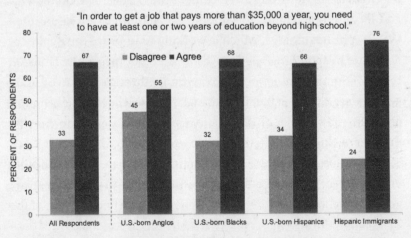

FIGURE 5.3: *The need for education beyond high school to qualify for a well-paid job (2019)*

I often fight a losing battle with many of the wealthy and powerful in Houston who assert that if only Hispanics and African Americans valued education and understood its importance the way Anglos and Asians do, we would have no problem: Everyone would get the education they need to succeed in the new economy. So it is important to acknowledge, as Figure 5.3 makes clear, that U.S.-born African Americans and Hispanics (at 68 percent and 66 percent) are much more likely than Anglos to affirm the importance of postsecondary education. Hispanic immigrants (at 76 percent) are by far the most insistent of all on this score.

Stephanie's story illustrates the way this ambition sometimes works out in practice. "My parents came here from a small village in Mexico when I was three," says the quiet twenty-four-year-old kindergarten teacher. "They had a second-grade education; they can barely read or write. I'm the youngest in my family and the first to go to college. My parents and siblings invested everything to make sure I could make it. We didn't have the resources for all of us to go to college. They placed a big bet on me. I was able to get my teaching certificate from Texas A&M. Now I want to help other families and other kids."

If Houston's African American and Hispanic young people are not getting the education they need to succeed in today's economy, it is demonstrably not because they and their parents do not value that education or recognize its importance. It is because these minority communities are far more likely than Anglos and Asians to be living in areas of concentrated disadvantage, in overcrowded, underfunded inner-city schools, with all the additional out-of-classroom barriers that poverty imposes on a young person's ability to succeed in the public school system—the decaying neighborhoods, the constant threat of hunger and homelessness, the unmet medical and dental needs, the continuing disruptions as impoverished families keep moving in search of more affordable places to live.

The survey respondents have also been asked over the years if they thought the public schools in the Houston area generally have enough money, if it were used wisely, to provide a quality education; or whether they believed instead that, in order for the schools to provide a quality education, significantly more money will be needed. As seen in Figure 5.4, during the mid-1990s, when the question was first asked, decisive majorities, by 54 and 55 percent to 38 and 37 percent, were clear in their belief that the schools have all the money they need to provide a good education. During the ensuing ten years, from 1999 through 2009, the respondents were evenly divided in their assessments of the adequacy of school funding.

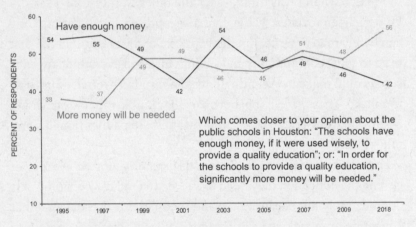

FIGURE 5.4: *The adequacy of funding for the public schools in Houston (1995-2018)*

We came back ten years later to ask that same question again. In the 2018 survey, a solid majority of area residents (56 percent compared to 42 percent) were now clear in their view that the schools will need significantly more money in order to provide a quality education. The findings underscore a potentially consequential shift among area residents in their understanding of the urgent need for larger and more sustained investments in public education if Houston is to succeed in the new economy.

Also in 2018, area residents were asked directly, for the first time in these surveys, if they were in favor or opposed to increasing local taxes in order to provide universal preschool education for all children in Houston. By 67 to 30 percent, Harris County residents were in support of this proposition, with four out of ten indicating that they were strongly in favor. This is a remarkable degree of consensus for a population that is so well-known for its opposition to increasing taxes for almost any purpose.

"But," counters Shattuck, who's seen her fair share of promising circumstances fall apart when put to the test, "will the politicians be brave enough to act on this? Will we put people in power who see it as a priority? Houstonians may believe this when asked about it in their homes, but will they act in the public arena to make sure that it happens? That said, I think if the people of Harris County really had the opportunity to vote for putting more of *their* public dollars into high-quality early education, I think they would vote 'yes'!"

The realities seem undeniable. As educators well know, one of the "moments of truth" in public education is third-grade reading: If you're not reading at the third-grade level in third grade, if you haven't made the transition by then from "learning to read" to "reading to learn," you are four times more likely to drop out of high school. The single most powerful predictor of the ability to read at a third-grade level in third grade is: Did you start kindergarten ready to learn to read?

Rich children in Houston and across America generally enter kindergarten one and a half to two years ahead of poor children. The achievement gap begins there and inevitably grows larger from that point on. "When I was a child," Algenita Scott Davis says, "I had a vision problem. My mother spotted it and so I was able to read at an accelerated pace [once it was corrected]. But my sister, who has a different mother, she wasn't so lucky. They didn't figure out that she had the same problem until she was eight. By then, it was too late for her to catch up. She still couldn't read. She started having children at fourteen years old. She has seven. None had the same kind of opportunities I had." And none of them is participating in the economy. When people like Algenita's sister drop out of high school, economic opportunities have diminished, and the ripple effects profoundly impact families, neighborhoods, and future generations.

Though once an opponent of Houston's no-zoning, no-planning approach to growth, Mayor Annise Parker now celebrates the role it has played in building a community with affordable housing, where one in five residents is foreign-born. "Oil brought a global community here. If you're a magnet for the best and brightest, that's a good thing," Parker says. "If the culture celebrates the risk-taking entrepreneur with a wildcatter mentality, that's also great. But if we don't educate our own kids to compete in the new economy, we are setting up for a train wreck. We recognize the importance of early education and of improving Houston's inner-city schools, but we aren't willing to pay for them. We are instead creating a permanent underclass. We are a center of gravity for charter schools, some of the most dynamic anywhere. But the kids who graduate are exported to college. Meanwhile, who will build buildings? Who will work in manufacturing? That's the yawning gap."

"Education is the civil rights issue of our time," says Sylvester Turner, mayor in 2019, echoing President Obama. "It's our job to provide kids with life skills and tools, not just the ability to pass tests. We need to give them a sense of community. That's why I fight for neighborhood schools. When you take kids out to another community, you disconnect them instead of providing additional life-support skills. It's one thing to pass a test; it's another to pass through life successfully. We want them to pass the life tests. Their connection to the community, the neighborhood, is everything."

Houstonians seem increasingly to agree with these imperatives. The question is, when will private opinions get translated into effective public policy?

CHAPTER 6

The Moral Core of a Paradoxical City

Houston is a city of conveners, not a city of kingmakers.

—Mustafa Tameez[55]

Harris County is the death penalty capital of America. This "liberal" city, under America's first openly gay female mayor, rejected an ordinance guaranteeing equal rights for members of the LGBTQ community when the proposition was put on the ballot in 2015. The choice to terminate a pregnancy has been increasingly restricted in Texas, and on any given day, the women's clinics in Houston have both guards and protesters posted at their entrances. In a city with at least thirteen billionaires and private foundations with some of America's largest endowments, Houston's public schools are filled with a majority of children in poverty who will graduate without the skills needed to succeed. And yet the city's network of nonprofits is among the most robust in the nation; the number of heroic individuals who step up to create positive change is staggering; and the views expressed by the majority of the survey participants point in quite a different direction from the policies that are currently being enacted by state and local governments.

Religious conservatives today dominate the agenda in the Texas legislature, working tirelessly to impose more restrictions on abortion, gay rights, voting rights, and immigration, while they block environmental regulations. Meanwhile, Houston-area residents themselves have not only been increasing their identification with the Democratic Party; they are also less likely to say that they are affiliated with any organized religion. And yet, throughout Houston's history, progressive movements for civil rights and social justice have originated with the city's prominent clergy.

Tom Cole paints a vivid picture of Houston in the 1950s and 1960s as a traditional Jim Crow Southern city, much like Montgomery, Birmingham, Selma, or Little Rock, suddenly confronting a robust and growing civil rights movement.[56] The reason you don't remember seeing or hearing much about Houston's activism during this period is that the owners of the local TV, radio, and newspapers—most of which were controlled by Jesse Jones's nephew and heir, John T. Jones—conspired to suppress any coverage of the protests.

The Reverend Bill Lawson, then a young chaplain from St. Louis, newly installed at Texas Southern University in 1959, welcomed Martin Luther King Jr. at his newly founded Wheeler Avenue Baptist Church, despite warnings from J. Edgar Hoover. But when several students at TSU asked for his blessing and guidance as they prepared to engage in the city's first serious civil rights protests, he resisted.

"Their parents had worked so hard to get them into this school," Lawson explained at breakfast one morning, the day after his eighty-ninth birthday, still recovering from recent hip surgery. The room was festooned with metallic balloons left over from the party the night before. "If the kids were arrested, they'd get kicked out of school. I was afraid the dogs and fire hoses would be brought in. I was sure they'd get beaten, or worse. I didn't want anything to happen to those kids."

Eldrewy Stearns, a TSU student-protester who had been beaten by police to within an inch of his life, was one of the leaders. "'Reverend,' he said to me," Lawson continued, "'we are going to go ahead with or without your blessing.'" So when Jones and others from the Houston business community approached Lawson with a strategy they hoped would minimize the likelihood of the kind of violence that had occurred in other Southern cities, Lawson offered his support; their plan was to engineer a media blackout on the imminent civil rights protests.

The coverage across the American South of police violence and the actions of the National Guard had outraged the rest of the country. The whole region was being portrayed as brutal, frightened, and backward. If Houston appeared to the rest of America to be no different from the other racist Southern towns, opined John T. Jones, that would be bad for business. It would mean fewer first-rate doctors willing to work at the burgeoning medical center; fewer professors wanting to teach in the area's universities; fewer scientists willing to work at NASA; fewer skilled workers coming from other parts of the country; fewer corporate headquarters relocating to Houston.

So, just as his uncle Jesse before him had brought the banks together during the Depression and convinced them to act collectively out of enlightened self-interest, John T. Jones called on the business community to accept the inevitable. His message: None of us wants this change. But if we don't desegregate on our own, the federal government will force it on us just as they forced it on Little Rock. If we actively try to prevent the desegregation of our shops, restaurants, and theaters, Houston will be seen as just another dying Southern town desperately clinging to the old ways in the face of inevitable change.

The message was heard. With the collusion of the local media, the student protests, the marches, the sit-ins, and the beatings were given virtually no coverage. Houston's business community quietly desegregated the lunch counters and movie theaters, off-camera and outside the reach of local and national media.

That successful effort to desegregate public accommodations did very little to improve the quality of life in Houston's black communities. It didn't improve the segregated public schools. It did nothing to stop the refineries and industries from continuing to dump their toxic wastes in black neighborhoods.

Among the most significant and paradoxical consequences of desegregation were the changes it brought to the inner-city neighborhoods themselves. Wealthy blacks would now be able to move out of middle-class areas like Pleasantville into more affluent, traditionally Anglo neighborhoods. The vital social capital available in these inner-city communities, the support networks that are so necessary for upward mobility, would begin to dissipate when a lawyer was no longer living down the block from someone who owned a shoe-shine stand.

The class divide hit African American neighborhoods early and hard. Residents who had been successful in previous generations pulled further ahead and moved to whiter pastures. Those who were left in the impoverished neighborhoods, in pockets of increasingly concentrated disadvantage, their children stuck in overcrowded, underfunded, inner-city schools, would fall further behind. The fear of integration on the part of Anglo Houstonians had solidified and widened the gap.

Reverend Lawson's fight for social justice, however, wouldn't end there.

If you begin a sentence, "A priest, a rabbi, and a Baptist preacher . . . ," Houstonians will roll their eyes at the familiar opening, while nonresidents will probably think you are about to tell a joke about what happens when the three of them walk into a bar. Archbishop Joseph Fiorenza, Reverend Bill Lawson, and Rabbi Samuel Karff still aren't sure how they connected, but two of the Three Amigos agree that it was in the efforts of their churches and synagogues to help people who were falling off the economic grid, as Houston's oil economy began to shed jobs. Soul mates, as they refer to each other, they were successful in working together to knock down some of the major barriers that were blocking pathways to opportunity and that had long resisted more rational and compassionate policies in the city's criminal justice system.

Fiorenza, in black shirt, black jacket, and white collar, stands behind his desk at the diocese on the edge of downtown Houston, a little wobbly on his feet at nearly ninety. The retired archbishop has been in Houston for almost sixty years, arriving after participating in the march from Selma to Montgomery. "To be involved in that epic social movement," he said, "was what was required of us as people of faith. I grew up in Beaumont next to an African American neighborhood. We kids all played together. I never understood why we could play with each other but not go to the movies together. It was wrong. In Selma, I could feel the hate coming from the state troopers, and I began to understand what African Americans were experiencing in the South.

"It was homelessness, I think, that first brought Sam and me together," Fiorenza recalled. People who had arrived in Houston in the late 1970s hoping to find work in this booming metropolis would lose their jobs when the bust came in 1982, and many would end up living on the streets. Fiorenza and Karff spent a memorable night wandering the encampments in lay clothes, looking for a place to sleep, trying to understand more fully what it felt like to be homeless and why people were building tent cities underneath bridges instead of seeking the services offered in city shelters.

"We tried to bring awareness. We passed a five-million-dollar bond under Mayor Whitmire," Fiorenza said of the effort to help people get off the streets and back into jobs and homes, "but nothing seemed to change. They say the statistics are better now." He is referring to the data coming out of Central Houston, Inc., run by Bob Eury, who was leading the effort to end homelessness in Houston. "But I don't see it. Thirty years later, the encampment we visited is still there. They gather people up and take them to shelters once in a while, but it comes right back." The archbishop is speaking about the perennial tent city that arises from the concrete and weaves its way among the pylons supporting the US 59 overpass at Wheeler

Avenue in Third Ward. Residents of the encampment are from time to time taken to shelters. The tents disappear for six months or so. They pop up right away somewhere else and eventually come back to the same encampment.

The Three Amigos may not have been able to end homelessness, but though there are still many problems, they succeeded in their efforts to reform Houston's criminal justice system. Until November 2010, Harris County was the only major metro area in America without a public defender's office. In the nation's fourth largest city, criminal justice was handled through the courts and the district attorney's office, which were responsible for assigning private attorneys to serve indigent defendants. Poor people, many of whom would eventually be found to be innocent, languished in jail, their lives wrecked by lost jobs and housing, at the mercy of a system that had no incentive to speed up the process. No one was looking out for the interests of the criminal defendants themselves.

Lawson had assembled a panel of black religious leaders to discuss the need for reform in the justice system, but he got nowhere. "Those in power could say no to me," said the tall and elegant Baptist preacher. "But they couldn't say no to all three of us. So I called Sam and Joe, and together we succeeded in getting a public defender's office and in raising the age at which you can be tried as an adult.[57] The three of us have the same picture of what church and synagogue ought to be fighting for," continues Lawson. "We share a deep concern for human justice."

"It was Bill who brought us together on the issue of the public defender," says Fiorenza. "We felt it was crazy that an area this size didn't have a program of that sort. But despite our efforts, the courts and the DA still tend to bypass the public defender's office and go straight to the legal panels. That's something that still has to be addressed. I don't know how to make it happen without a complete overhaul of the system."

In an effort to interrupt the school-to-prison pipeline, "Sam pulled us in hard on the issue of how old young people have to be before they can be put in jail as an adult. Right now it's sixteen," says Lawson. "But Sam is fighting for the minimum age to be eighteen. He argued that a young kid who stole some candy bars or was caught driving without a license ought not to be sent to jail and have his or her life ruined. We agreed."

"We introduced a bill in the state legislature, raising the minimum age for incarceration, but it didn't go anywhere," adds Fiorenza. Yet they never gave up.

Tall and still strong at eighty-five, Rabbi Samuel Karff arrived in Houston in 1975 from Chicago, where he'd been a rabbi at Sinai, the oldest congregation in Chicago, and taught at the University of Chicago Divinity School. "It was a tumultuous time," he said when I asked him about Chicago in the late 1960s. Looking back at me across his home's mid-century furniture, and leaning over a low, brown wooden coffee table, he continued, "There were so many assassinations. So many riots in Grant Park. And then came the Democratic Convention."

He grew disillusioned with the various authorities after that disaster, when students were brutally beaten by police in riot gear during the protests against party leaders who shifted their delegates straight to Hubert Humphrey following LBJ's decision not to run. Though 80 percent of the Democrats were anti-war, the very popular anti-war candidate, Eugene McCarthy, was denied the nomination, even though Humphrey had not participated in a single primary. And the anti-war plank was removed from the platform. It left people in the city feeling helpless and enraged. At that same moment, Karff reports, he too was growing restless. "The congregation was aging rapidly, and young people had moved out to the suburbs, so when they called me with an offer from Beth Israel in Houston, I was ready to go."

Though Sam has retired from his post, he's still working on bail reform with Joe and Bill. "We aren't interested in big public protests,"

Lawson says about their efforts. "We are interested in heading off some of the most critical issues that are emerging in Houston's vast and growing underclass by enlisting the help of those with power." Their next target is the development of a geriatric hospital in the Texas Medical Center, the first of its kind in the world.

"Houston has a lot of people who step up," Lawson reminds me as I express some concern about the general lack of progress on social-justice issues. "We are the place that can undertake aggressive projects like the Astrodome, the first fully enclosed air-conditioned stadium. There are so many things like that, something that could only be dreamed of in Houston. That is why we remain optimistic about this city."

I remarked to Fiorenza that I've heard others express that same sense about Houston, that people so often respond in a positive way to big, compassionate ideas. "Yes, but getting from idea to reality always seems to be a problem," he responds. "There isn't enough of a sense of urgency in pushing through the obstacles to completion."

"We need to be sure that there is someone to speak up for those who can't speak up for themselves," says Lawson. "And because the three of us do it with one voice," adds Karff, "we've been able to open doors for others. We all three wanted there to be societal dimensions to our denominational work. Each of us had a firm belief in the role religion could play in strengthening human and civil rights and in advancing spiritual values and goals in the wider society."

"This is what I mean," says Mustafa Tameez, "in saying that Houston is a city of conveners, not a city of kingmakers." Tameez, a communications expert and one-time political operative, was one of the key players in helping to reelect Houston's first African American mayor and former Clinton appointee, Lee Brown, in his race in 2001 against Cuban American Orlando Sanchez, who was backed by George W. Bush. Tameez was the first in Houston to create mailers and doorknob flyers in many of the native languages spoken in this diversifying city.

His communications campaign is credited with bringing many new voters to the polls.

That effort was collaborative, working hand in hand with community leaders across the area. "To get anything done in New York," says Tameez, "you needed to kiss a lot of rings. But not in Houston. It's all about who to call in order to gather enough people to get something done for the city." This is still true, but in earlier years, it was easier to do. As long as corporate headquarters and business interests were tied to the success of the city, local investment in the community made direct economic sense. It went back to Jesse Jones and his firm belief that if Houston didn't succeed, neither would he. Houston real-estate developer Ed Wulfe said that this collaborative, wide-open society is what made it possible for him to succeed as a Jewish developer in the 1950s. As for why so few people outside Houston know about the good things being done here, Wulfe commented, "Houston is too busy doing to talk about itself."

★

It is also in this economically segregated, formerly black/white Southern city that the national effort to roll back affirmative action came to a stop in the mid-1990s. Around the time Bob Lanier took office, affirmative action policies were under attack across the country: In 1996, California, under pressure from the national anti–affirmative action movement, voted to end the state's affirmative action programs. On the heels of that success, the movement launched a petition drive to force a vote on a similar proposition in Houston.

Lanier recognized that if Houston was unable to preserve the city's modest use of affirmative action for women and minorities in determining the way it allocated municipal jobs and city contracts, it would be facing another image crisis, much like the one it narrowly averted during the civil rights era. "Let's not turn back the clock to the days when guys who look like me got all of the city's business," Lanier was famous for saying repeatedly during the campaign over Proposition A, the ballot initiative that called for an end to the city's affirmative action program. He worked hard to make sure the language on the ballot was clear, forcing a change in the wording of Prop A that would have otherwise made it look as if it were a vote for nondiscrimination in assigning city contracts.

In Houston's minority communities, pastors, grassroots leaders, and local radio stations joined Lanier in mounting a concerted and spirited campaign. Blacks went to the polls in unprecedented numbers, and by nine to one, they voted against the proposition, as did almost three-fourths of Hispanic voters. Meanwhile, in a powerful expression of the city's black/white divide, the Anglo precincts were voting by two to one in favor of ending the city's affirmative action contracting program. On November 4, 1997, the final tally was 45 percent in support of Prop A, and 55 percent opposed. Affirmative action held.

Houston had taken a progressive position on a deeply contentious issue, showing that a majority of area residents were committed to redressing the discrimination that women and minorities have long experienced in its municipal hiring practices, and more generally to welcoming a much more diverse workforce. The anti–affirmative action campaign had been overturned in Houston, Texas, of all places,[58] led by a mayor who looked like just another rich white guy. After the decisive defeat in Houston of Proposition A, the movement lost momentum and the national efforts to topple affirmative action programs ground to a halt, if only temporarily.

The groundswell of support that Lanier had relied upon to carry Houston to victory in upholding its affirmative action policies was effective in part because of the earlier efforts by the Three Amigos, by the partnerships they helped to create among both the secularly motivated and the spiritually motivated.

★

In all the thirty-eight surveys, Harris County residents have been asked to indicate their religious preference: "Is it Protestant, Catholic, Jewish, some other religion, or no religion?" As indicated in Figure 6.1, the proportion of area residents who answered "none" or "no religion" has increased significantly, as it has in most national polls as well. The proportion of survey participants who claimed no religious affiliation grew from just 6 or 7 percent in the early years, to 18 or 19 percent in the more recent surveys.

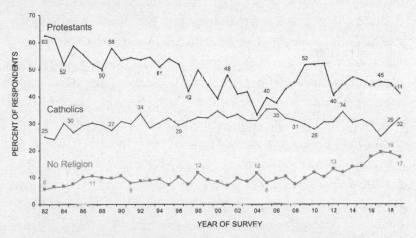

FIGURE 6.1: *The distributions of Protestants, Catholics, and "Nones," from 1982 to 2019*

Among the religious, there has been a slight rise in Evangelicals, and a decline in mainline Protestants; the number of Catholics has held steady, fueled primarily by the influx of Hispanics, Filipinos, and Vietnamese. And the proportions of Muslims, Buddhists, and Hindus have grown from tiny numbers into measurable proportions of 7 or 8 percent in recent years.

The rise of the "nones" does not necessarily mean that religious or spiritual sensitivities are declining. Six out of ten (59 percent) of all area residents in 2019 said that "religion is very important in my life," a number that has remained essentially unchanged across the thirty-eight years. What it does suggest is that the kind of closed-minded, church-based, socially conservative religiosity, the kind that fuels the state's right-wing politics, is gradually diminishing among residents in the Houston area, as it is (perhaps more slowly) across the country as a whole.

City leaders have said repeatedly that Houston is a faith-driven city, and that activism and engagement often come from a spiritual motivation. That may be true, but with the influx of so many different traditions, the way religion manifests itself has changed. No longer is it exclusively centered in specific church denominations. The region's many interfaith and nondenominational organizations are playing increasingly important roles in working to reduce inequalities, to welcome immigrants and refugees, and to bring more inclusion, beauty, and justice into Houston's varied communities.

For many years, Interfaith Ministries for Greater Houston has been organizing dinners to encourage people of different faiths to get to know each other. "What's unique and special and why you love Houston despite everything," Andrea White says, "is the people, their openness, how welcoming they are, a sense that all of us are in it together." As first lady of Houston ten years earlier, White had a front-row seat to what happens when a city like Houston chooses to open its doors to neighbors in distress.

It was the end of August 2005 when Americans watched in horror as the giant category 5 hurricane, the strongest in recorded history to make landfall in the United States, took aim at New Orleans. It was big. It was wet. It had winds at speeds no one had ever measured in a hurricane. It devastated the city. Though evacuation warnings had been given, many lacked the means to leave. During the storm, many of the poor were stranded on rooftops, in hospitals, trapped in attics, swept away by a storm surge that blasted through neglected levees.

People cried out from their homes, tried to rescue loved ones in rowboats, saw the elderly and sick evacuated from hospitals that were without power. The nation watched helpless and guilty as Anderson Cooper brought in the CNN cameras, wading through chest-high water to prove that too many had died because they had no money, no car, and nowhere to go; no possible way to heed the evacuation warnings that might have saved them.

Emory University professor Frans de Waal is celebrated for his pioneering research on primate social behavior, including analyses of conflict resolution, cooperation, inequity aversion, and food-sharing. He has dedicated his life to making the case that primates have generous and empathetic instincts that are just as strong as the negative instincts for dominance and the hoarding of resources. De Waal opens his 2009 bestseller, *Age of Empathy: Nature's Lessons for a Kinder Society*, with the grim story of Hurricane Katrina and quotes a headline from the morning paper he picked up while in Alabama to give a lecture: "Why have we been left behind like animals?"[59] It was the cri de coeur of a survivor stuck in the Louisiana Superdome for days without sanitation or food.

"I took issue," De Waal wrote about this comment, "because animals don't necessarily leave one another behind." He mentioned that there was an outpouring of sympathy, and left it there. He concluded his book without returning to the story, and without acknowledging the most empathetic event of all that took place during one of the largest displacements of human beings in American history.

De Waal failed to mention the city that sent a fleet of air-conditioned buses to collect tens of thousands of evacuees. He said nothing about the city that, in one day, created a massive hospital and shelter in a famous sports stadium. He ignored the city that opened its doors, its public housing, its medical center, and its private homes; the city that took in 150,000 people, fed them, clothed them, got their children into school, made sure they had a network of support to help them get settled. He took no notice of the city that sent a message to evacuees from New Orleans that they were welcome to stay for as long as they wanted, even for the rest of their lives.

A massive wave of compassion, bigger than a storm surge, brought an extraordinary mobilization of resources, driven by Houston's mayor and first lady, Bill and Andrea White, along with civic and business leaders and the nearly full-time engagement of more than 5 percent of the city's entire population. This was four years after Enron, the biggest breach of trust Houston had ever known. Thirteen years after Katrina, Andrea White is still overwhelmed with emotion, unable to complete the sentence, "What these people did, they showed up . . . I still can't talk about it."

"I was aware of what could occur with the breach," says Bill White, the former Clinton appointee and businessman who would go on to lose the race for governor of Texas to Rick Perry. "Houston was the largest city next to southern Louisiana; many Houston residents, including my wife, were born in Louisiana. So we have friends and roots in Louisiana. It wasn't a matter of telling people where to go when landfall hit. A large number of evacuees had already arrived in Houston by landfall. There was nothing else to do but bring everyone here, where we had the resources. We had firefighters pre-positioned for rescue operations."

The decision was made overnight. Mayor White convened his team, and he knew they in turn would convene others. It's how he operated, making sure there was a chain of responsibility and competency. "Bill White never took personal credit for anything," recalled Nancy Kinder, one of Houston's most influential philanthropists. "When we came to him with the idea of building parks along the bayous, he sent us immediately to all the people who could help us get it done, and he said to call him if we needed him. He stepped out of it and let everyone do their jobs."

The same would be true with how Houston's response to Katrina was organized. Air-conditioned buses were sent to New Orleans, with enough capacity to empty the Superdome. Elena Marks, director of Health and Environmental Policy under Mayor White, was charged with converting the George R. Brown Convention Center into a hospital prepared to treat illness and injury, dehydration and hunger. "We started working on it at seven a.m. I had until eleven p.m. to get it set up." That's when the evacuees would begin arriving after their six-hour bus trip. "And we did it. It isn't that I'm so smart, it's that I knew who to call." It's another example of why communications expert Mustafa Tameez calls Houston "a city of conveners, not kingmakers." The convention center would be, for the two weeks it was in operation, the tenth largest hospital in America, when you counted the number of beds and physicians gathered in one place.

By 11:00 p.m. on the night the first evacuees arrived, the Astrodome had been converted into a shelter. The entrance was lined with volunteers handing out water and supplies to the evacuees as they arrived. One woman burst into tears upon receiving her package. "You actually want us here," she cried. Angela Blanchard, who was part of the effort, cried along with her. BakerRipley, which Blanchard led for thirty years, would go on to impact the lives of at least twenty thousand of the Katrina evacuees.

"The message I delivered at the time that resonated," says White in an early-morning conversation in his Memorial Park–area home, "is that we would treat our neighbors the way we would want to be treated. For the evacuees, I said they could look forward to the future, to being in apartments, near transit and schools, to be in a position to obtain self-sufficiency, not having to live indefinitely in tent cities or remain in shelters. Their job was to keep their kids in school and to find work. We don't believe in handouts to the able-bodied. People responded to that. The Astrodome," White reminded me, "was empty ten days later. We made sure it was a place people would pass through on their way to resuming their lives—it was never going to be a place where people would be housed long-term."

Mayor White called on business and civic leaders for logistical support. "I asked them to take over areas of the city and assign families to their employees who would make sure that basic daily needs were met—food, medicine, diapers, baby formula, getting their kids into school and help with contacting relatives. I didn't manage the process. They were all professionals, and they all understood responsibility and accountability.

"I called executives at El Paso [Oil Company], at CenterPoint, and many other local corporations," says Bill, "and asked their employees to adopt one or two motels or large apartment complexes where the evacuees had moved in. After they'd registered at the Astrodome, we were able to get them the medical treatment they needed, and we quickly implemented a voucher program to get them placed into apartments. Competent employees from well-organized businesses showed up, and I asked them to take care of the basic needs. Until the evacuees got into apartments with utilities, furniture, stipends, and job training, the employees were responsible for helping them.

"One corporation set up a back-office company to procure furniture for the apartments. Some of the very large churches with professionals in executive-level positions in their normal lives set up a warehouse system with forklifts, 18-wheelers, inventory management to distribute items donated by Houstonians. We had more clothing than the 150,000 evacuees could ever use. The warehouses were so full with donated items that we loaded large amounts later that year into military aircraft to provide relief in northern Pakistan after a massive earthquake there left seventy thousand homeless."

"I went out to the Hong Kong City Mall," says Hong Kong native Mandy Kao, talking about the unofficial capital of Houston's sprawling Chinatown. "I found Asians sleeping on the floor there." As a partner with her husband in real-estate investment, Kao had seen some tough conditions in the neighborhoods where they have owned apartment buildings in Las Vegas, Phoenix, and now in Houston. "We cleared out as many apartments as we could in our buildings and invited the evacuees to stay in them until they could get back on their feet. We had afternoon tutoring and hired out-of-work teachers to give lessons to their kids."

Among the 150,000 evacuees were an estimated fifteen thousand Vietnamese. With little attention from the media, they found their way not to the Astrodome or the convention center shelters, but to the Hong Kong City Mall in the middle of the great Houston Chinatown that spreads for miles along the Bellaire Strip. There they were quietly absorbed by the more than sixty thousand Asian families in the city. In the 2006 survey, a remarkable 23 percent of the Asian respondents, compared to 5 percent of all Houstonians, answered yes when asked if they had ever had an evacuee staying in their home. Many of Kao's apartments were trashed by evacuees. "She never asked for a dime from the city to clean them up," adds Andrea White.

The 2006 survey also documented the widespread willingness among ordinary Houstonians to help out. Among the questions we included that year was the following: "Did you donate any money, any food or other items, or any volunteer time to help the evacuees?" Of all the survey participants, 85 percent answered in the affirmative; 55 percent said they had personally interacted with one or more of the evacuees, and 5 percent said they had an evacuee actually staying in their home.

Peggy and I were among those who hosted a Katrina evacuee for several days while she tried desperately to get back to New Orleans. It wasn't an easy experience, but we were glad to have been able to help at least a little. People from all over Houston were coming from unexpected corners to do whatever they could to be of assistance.

"A woman I know," says Andrea, "who is as right-wing crazy as they come, hopped into a minivan and went down to the Astrodome. She picked up the first family she saw and said, 'You're coming home with me.' I heard stories like that every day."

The rapid absorption of 150,000 Katrina evacuees inevitably took a toll on the city, generating ambivalence and mixed emotions among many area residents. Of the 2006 survey respondents, 97 percent agreed that the Houston community really came together to help the evacuees. At the same time, 74 percent concurred with the suggestion that helping the evacuees had put a considerable strain on the Houston community, and 66 percent believed that a major increase in violent crime had occurred in Houston because of the evacuees.

"Crime did go up in the short term," said Bill White, "but we took steps in our policing to deal with it. After about six weeks, the gangs that had come from New Orleans were able to find each other. In areas where we knew they were gathering, we blanketed them with officers, gave citations, stopped everybody for minor traffic violations, did whatever we could within the bounds of the Constitution to show we meant business. We established an aggressive zero-tolerance policy. It took about six months of intense activity focused on the crime hot spots to make sure that the people who preyed on others were either in jail or had returned to New Orleans. Within nine months, our crime rate had returned to normal just as crime in New Orleans went right back up. But the vast majority of people who came to Houston stayed here. And overall, it was of great benefit to the city.

"You are tested in a situation like this," Bill continued. "The aftermath of Katrina was a significant benefit to our city, but I never talked about that until years later, after I left the job as mayor. I didn't want to crow at a neighbor's expense. Many of Louisiana's businesses and professional firms and employers relocated permanently to the

Houston area. That is indicative of the fact that Houston's ultimate success is determined by the way you would measure the success of any city. Do free people want to move there, or do they want to move out? The cities that journalists and urban planners hold up as models often seem to be cities people don't want to move to as quickly as they move to Houston. They are voting with their feet, and it's hard to find another major city in America since World War II that has been as successful."

"What I saw," continued Andrea, "was a basic goodness in all of Houston's communities, and I feel like that would be the case across the U.S., but if you don't have the leadership to bring out the best in people, all that potential gets lost. Bill brought out the best in people. You could trust him. He was a uniter. He never used fear of the other to make himself important."

We wondered if the respondents in the February 2008 survey, two and a half years after Katrina, would have wanted the city to respond any differently. Specifically, we asked, "If a hurricane like Katrina happened again in 2008, do you think the Houston community should respond to the evacuees with about the same level of assistance, more assistance, or less assistance than was offered in 2005?" Only 28 percent called for less assistance; 25 percent said more assistance; and another 46 percent, despite their misgivings, said the city should respond with the same level of assistance as in 2005. More than 70 percent of Houston-area residents, despite all the difficulties they felt the Katrina experience had imposed on the city, said they would do it all over again.

"Because we have such a strong faith-based community," Bill White suggested, "a situation like this appeals to our better angels."

"I learned during this time," says Andrea, "how much good is out there in people. People want to be led to share what is good in them as opposed to being led by fear and division. Katrina was a way to do that. You just have to stand in front of that parade, call for unity, give people a role to play, and they will come through. Bill said the hardest job he had as mayor during Katrina was finding good roles for all the volunteers who came forward, enabling them to really make a difference. When people are given meaningful projects and are let loose to do them, they love it. There has to be effective leadership to make this possible."

The perception of Houston at the time among many outside observers was that the city was remarkably compassionate in responding to the events brought about by Katrina. People were surprised by the generosity being demonstrated in this oil and gas capital, by its seeming willingness to help so many. This perception may have generated a momentary shift in how most Americans perceive this city, but as the flood waters receded, so did the softer image of this southwestern metropolis.

★

Among the U.S.-born non-Hispanic whites, those who do not identify with any organized religion consistently express more progressive views on the survey questions than do those who claim a religious affiliation. In the 2019 survey, for example, 80 percent of the unaffiliated Anglos believed that Houston's burgeoning ethnic diversity is a good thing for the city, compared to just 56 percent of the religiously affiliated; 73 percent agreed that government has a responsibility to help reduce the inequalities between rich and poor in America, compared to 37 percent of the affiliated.

One of the most striking shifts recorded in all the history of American public opinion research is seen in the consistently growing support for the rights of gays and lesbians during the past quarter century. In the Houston surveys, on virtually all the relevant questions we have asked over the years, support for gay rights has steadily increased. Three of the questions are depicted in Figure 6.2.

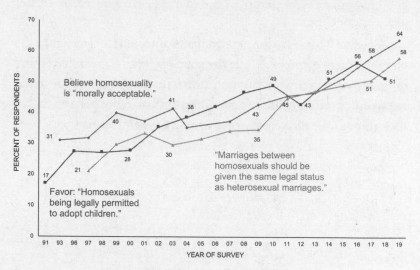

FIGURE 6.2: *Support for gay rights among Harris County residents (1991–2019)*

Across the thirty-eight years, the survey respondents have consistently said that they disapprove of abortion. At the same time, they are decidedly pro-choice in their defense of abortion rights. In the 2019 survey, 56 percent of Harris County residents said they believed abortion is morally wrong, but 64 percent were *opposed* to a law that would make it more difficult for a woman to obtain an abortion. The figures have changed only slightly from the time the same two questions were first asked back in 1999.

Social psychologists have posited for decades that when a broad shift in public attitudes has occurred, it is usually the result of cohort succession, as younger generations supplant older ones and come into adulthood with different experiences and different beliefs. In attitudes toward Houston's ethnic diversity, the surveys found that the public's growing support for the demographic shifts is primarily due not to people actually changing their minds over the years, but to younger generations who have come of age in a different world and are embracing different views than those espoused by earlier cohorts.

But when it comes to the determinants of support for gay rights, the picture is more complex. While the younger cohorts are indeed more progressive in their views of homosexuality, Figure 6.3 shows that members of the baby boom generation have actually been changing their minds over the years with regard to gays and lesbians.

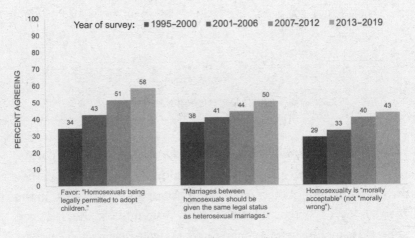

FIGURE 6.3: *Support for gay rights in four successive periods among Anglo baby boomers*

At the same time, each new generation of Houstonians is coming into the public arena with a much stronger commitment to protecting the rights of the LGBTQ community than the earlier generations they are replacing. In light of the growing support for gay rights among Americans of all ages and generations, it seems clear that it will be difficult for conservative legislatures, however much they may feel impelled by religious convictions and zealous constituencies, to reverse the court decisions on gay marriage or to enact laws that discriminate against homosexuals.

★

Backed by the Ford Foundation, Fred Baldwin and Wendy Watriss came to Texas from New York and San Francisco in 1972 to do a documentary on rural poverty in the state. In 1983, they would start Houston's Fotofest, a biennial exhibition of photography that has become one of the largest in the world. "We are old WASPies," Fred says, as the couple describe the elite families and societies they grew up around. "I had just come back from Europe," he continues. "Texas was exotic to me, but we got along great with rural Texans. If you're interested in somebody, the suspicion melts. And we became a photographic service for the community. We took pictures at every wedding, funeral, all the churches. We made it all available and gave it away. People were open about inviting us everywhere, and about talking to us."

The Dalai Lama speaks frequently about his religion being based on kindness and on the understanding that all human beings "are just like me" in their desire for happiness and their wish to avoid suffering. That the feeling of connection and common humanity might change the way we think about one another is clearly evident in Houston's, and America's, increasing support for a group of people whose behavior as recently as 2003 was deemed to be illegal. It is evident as well in the ability of artists like Watriss and Baldwin to use rites of passage and the art of photography to build bridges of connection across communities.

THE DIVERSITY REVOLUTION

★

CHAPTER 7

The Black/White Divide

Houston won't get to where Steve Klineberg wants without moving from a love affair with the idea of diversity to actual pluralism. We need to figure out how to live with each other in a pluralistic society. All human beings should count simply because they are human beings. No labels. No categories. We should get over the idea of tolerance, which was coined in the 1950s: I don't have to like you; I just have to tolerate you. I tolerate roaches, ants, mosquitoes, and heat. I won't put a human being on that level. How do we move to the acceptance of each other simply because we are all humans? What is the threshold level on which we want all human beings to exist? We have to establish that bar.

—Larry Payne[60]

It took more than two years after the Emancipation Proclamation for Major General Gordon Granger to arrive with his troops in Galveston and to enforce the order that all slaves in the Confederate States were now free. His announcement on June 19 of 1865 has been celebrated ever since as Juneteenth. The first freed African Americans settled off the southern bank of Houston's Buffalo Bayou, just west of downtown, which became known as Freedman's Town. Fourth Ward grew around it. Third Ward and Fifth Ward were historically black neighborhoods as well. (And if you try to insert an article, "the" Second Ward, "the" Fourth Ward, you will be gently scolded for not being sensitive to the history of the neighborhoods, for not knowing that natives never say it that way.)

During Reconstruction, there were three African American aldermen. As part of reparations, African Americans were given land, but as soon as the Union army left, recounts former Harris County judge Ed Emmett, the land was taken away. African Americans were confined to segregated neighborhoods, and the Jim Crow laws took over the South.

At the same time, heroes like Jack Yates fought back. Born into slavery in 1828 in Virginia, Yates got himself educated despite the law against teaching slaves to read. He founded the school that became the historically black college Texas Southern University (TSU), and he organized the purchase of Emancipation Park, when blacks were finally allowed to live in Third Ward. A walkable neighborhood, a complete community, was populated by the relatively wealthy African Americans who moved into the neighborhood in the 1920s with the establishment of TSU.

Judson Robinson III, president of Houston's Urban League, comes from one of Houston's most prominent African American families. His grandfather, Judson Robinson Sr., was the first in the family to graduate from college. Under Jim Crow laws, there weren't many career opportunities open to educated blacks, so he went to work for the railroad, became president of the black porters' union, and after that, started business as a Realtor.

"There were no black mortgage companies in those days," says Robinson. "My grandfather had to form everything from scratch to support black home buyers. He was the first lender approved by HUD to make loans to black families. He worked with housing authorities to manage huge properties that were in segregated areas. Mack Hannah was the banker for Blacks. My dad was the real-estate guy. Chase was the architect. Coleman was the doctor." They were chosen, according to Robinson, by the white community as the "trustworthy" blacks with whom one could do business.

Judson Robinson III grew up in the segregated middle-class neighborhood of Pleasantville, in the northeast part of the city, a joint venture between a Swedish developer and Judson's grandfather. The neighborhood had affordable apartments where families could live within their means, while they saved up enough to buy a home, of which there were also different sizes and different price points. The goal was to create a generation of African American homeowners. "My grandfather made it possible for so many to buy homes," remembers Robinson, as he pushes back from his desk with a youthful vigor that belies his almost sixty years. "My grandparents made a lot of dreams come true, and they were loved by the community."

Pleasantville was, by Judson's account, a great place to grow up. "The black community grew rapidly in the sixties because of the oil boom. People came here to make money," Robinson says at Houston's Urban League headquarters. There were lots of families, lots of hardworking people, who could live comfortably close to the Anheuser-Busch plant, Cameron Iron Works, the docks at the nearby ship channel, and the oil refineries. They were excluded from unions but were able to form their own labor organizations.

The Urban League is housed in one of the few remaining ornate small buildings in downtown Houston. It is the site of a former Federal Reserve Bank, with neoclassical columns marking the entryway and three floors of balconies ringing the square atrium, off of which are the offices. "My grandfather lived across the street from us. My mom was the first black RN at Anheuser-Busch, where she worked until she joined my father in the family business. Everyone worked. There was dignity and pride. You could make money back then even with just a high school diploma."

Pleasantville was an economically diverse neighborhood, with working-class people, a strong middle class, and a few wealthy families like the Robinsons, the Colemans, and the Davises all in one place. "Segregation was all we knew, and in some ways, it created and sustained the black middle class," says Judson.

The community's social capital remained in one place, creating the networks that opened opportunities; helping people dream of a different way of living, options you could actually see playing out in your own neighborhood. "It was a complete community," says Judson. "I went to school where I lived. Everything was there in the neighborhood. The social realities are as important as the economic ones. When we have the community resources, we succeed."

Riverside Terrace, along Braes Bayou in Third Ward, had been a predominantly Jewish neighborhood until TSU was established. As soon as African Americans started moving in, Jews started moving out, and Riverside Terrace would become the neighborhood for the more affluent blacks. Reverend Bill Lawson, TSU's first chaplain, has lived there since he came to Houston from St. Louis in 1955.

Algenita Scott Davis grew up in Fifth Ward, just northeast of where she works now. As she talks about her early years, she remembers that the neighborhood had a thriving business community and a growing middle class; professors and postal workers alike were among her neighbors. Her grandmother grew up there, and for generations they all went to the same schools. Desegregation had its familiar negative effects on Fifth Ward, but that was only part of what destroyed the neighborhood.

In the 1960s, as America continued its many great postwar infrastructure projects, the Houston freeway that was to become the widest highway in the world, I-10, was progressing eastward from California to its terminus in Jacksonville, Florida. Fifth Ward was directly in its path, the Texas Department of Transportation (TxDOT) did nothing to redirect it, and the agency's former head, Mayor Bob Lanier, welcomed the freeway. "We knew for twenty years it was coming," said Algenita. "When I-10 came through at Grand Street, it wiped out five of our relatives' homes. It cut off all the streets that connected us to the routes heading downtown—Hazard, Mandell, and Dunlavy. It shut down Lyons, which was our major thoroughfare. I-10 killed Fifth Ward." This was one of the places that in the 1980s Robert Bullard would show was also targeted for the dumping of the city's municipal wastes.

Meanwhile, Texas 288 was bisecting Third Ward, which stretched from Riverside Terrace to east of downtown, and I-45 would drive up the middle of Freedmen's Town, the historic site in Fourth Ward that was settled by Houston's first freed slaves. The highway cut off a significant portion of the neighborhood from Houston's downtown, amplifying an exodus that had started with the increasing number of Anglo developments sprouting up around it in the 1940s. And US 59/I-69 was running through the eastward side of Third Ward, an area in which one of the city's most infamous shootings would take place on July 26, 1970.

Some remember Black Panther member Carl Hampton as a drum major and friend from high school. Others remember him as the founder of People's Party II, a black revolutionary group modeled after the Black Panthers. Hampton had established the group's headquarters in one of the most dangerous, crime-ridden areas of Third Ward, on the 2800 block of Dowling Street, now renamed Emancipation Avenue. Judson recalls that when neighborhoods desegregated, a lot changed in the black areas. "We didn't foresee the drugs and poverty that would come in." Third Ward was deteriorating rapidly. Carl Hampton's mission was to provide the residents with much-needed social services and to protect the community from rampant police brutality—it was seven years later that the death of José Campos Torres would expose what the national media labeled an "out-of-control police state" in Houston.

On that summer day in 1970, snipers from the Houston police force's Central Intelligence Department were stationed on top of the buildings surrounding the Party's headquarters. Hampton was wanted on a weapons charge stemming from an armed standoff with police a few days earlier, in which no shots were fired. When the armed members of the People's Party II realized they were pinned down, they rushed back into their headquarters. Eyewitnesses said the shooting began from above; the police claimed the shooting was started by Party members and they fired back in response. None of the Houston police officers was indicted by the grand jury, even as the jurors acknowledged that policing practices in the black communities needed to change. "Carl Hampton was assassinated," said a former classmate. Many believe the twenty-one-year-old activist was specifically targeted by the police.

Mayor Sylvester Turner grew up in Acres Homes, just outside the I-610 loop that encircles the sprawling center of the City of Houston. Turner is the youngest of nine, his father died early, and his mother was left alone to care for the family, working as a housekeeper at the Rice Hotel a few blocks from his current office in city hall. Turner, of medium stature and always impeccably tailored, describes the many ways the community would step in to make sure promising kids like him were supported. Elders like Evelena Moldrew would hand a tightly wadded five-dollar bill to the teenager on Sundays at church, telling him that she saw his promise and that everyone was betting on him. "That five-dollar bill was a lot to them. I felt its weight." Friends who were experimenting with drugs would ace him out. "Not you, Sylvester," he told me they said. "Don't let Sylvester have any of this stuff."

When the schools were desegregated, Turner was bused thirty-six miles each day to what had been an all-white school; he and his classmates were accompanied on the bus by thirteen teachers from their neighborhood whom they'd known their whole lives. "Those teachers were our continuity. They kept supporting us. Without them I don't know what would have happened to us." Turner went on to the University of Houston, Harvard Law School, the Texas State Legislature, and as of this writing he's just been elected to a second four-year term as mayor of Houston.

Algenita, the third generation of women in her family to graduate from high school, was the first to leave Houston in all the years since her grandmother had been brought to the city on a pillow when she was one month old. Attending Howard University in Washington, DC, was a revelation. "I walked into Hecht's department store and saw black people on the sales floor. I had never seen black people in those positions in Houston. In DC, the mayor at the time [Walter Washington] was black and the city actually functioned. I had always gotten the message that we couldn't be in charge and still have the water run. I had to leave Houston to find out what we are capable of. When you go to Howard, they tell you it's your responsibility to change the world."

Melanie Lawson, longtime news anchor for the local ABC affiliate, had a similar experience, being not only one of the first African American women at Princeton but also one of the first women. She now serves on its board of trustees. "I didn't know anything about Princeton," she said with the directness of the investigative reporter she is, "until Momma and Daddy drove me up there and kicked me out of the car. The difference between who we met in Houston and who I met at college was dramatic. In the North, there were generations of black people who had been educated in integrated schools and colleges, and who owned property. The first time I went to Martha's Vineyard and realized black people owned property there for hundreds of years, it was a revelation.

"There are some wealthy blacks in Texas, of course, my mother and father were both college educated, but Jim Crow stopped it from growing. In other parts of the country there was a black intelligentsia and black affluent communities that we didn't know anything about." Similarly, her youngest sister, Roxanne, lights up when she talks about her time at Spelman. "I had no idea how competitive it was. And it was a revelation being on a campus like that."

"When we first came to Houston in 1955," says Reverend Lawson, seated in a wheelchair, in a conversation at his home with three generations of his family, "it was back-of-the-bus days. The basic fight then was just to be able to go to Foley's department store and buy a pair of shoes. We fought for school desegregation in 1960–61, to let black kids go to white schools. It was just as simple as that. My kids were attending black schools near home, of course. But I had to ask myself, *How will they live in a desegregated world if they stay in exclusively black schools?* So I had to send them out of the neighborhood, and it was hard on them. It was as if they had been dunked in cold water."

Melanie and her sister Cheryl, superintendent of the Lawson Academy, founded by their mother, Audrey Lawson, were two of the roughly eleven black children to attend Poe Elementary in the first years of busing. The school is situated near Rice University between the parallel North and South Boulevards at their westernmost edge, in one of the city's oldest and most exclusive live-oak-lined neighborhoods. In her first year there, Cheryl was the only black child in the entire third grade. By the time Roxanne Lawson, the youngest of the three daughters, now division manager in the City of Houston's Housing and Community Development office, got there eight years later, there were four or five black children in her second-grade class.

Melanie remembers "fancy, lovely homes on either side of Poe. All the owners of the homes were white, so we were the interlopers who had been bused in. And we were not welcome. You had to have a thick skin. Until that time, we had never experienced this kind of animosity. We had lived our whole lives pretty much within five miles of where we were sitting," which, at that moment, was in the living room of the Riverside Terrace home in which the Lawson children grew up.

"We knew of the hostility," continues Melanie. "I had been on marches with Daddy. I remember Martin Luther King Jr. coming to our house with Jesse Jackson and Andy Young. I would sit on the staircase and listen to the whooping and hollering downstairs, as they considered different protest strategies. We were kids and didn't understand what it was all about, but we knew we were in the eye of whatever kind of storm it was. Daddy feels guilty for making us take the brunt and putting up with what we put up with. We don't feel that way."

"Did the exposure to whites when you were young make you feel more comfortable living in this multiethnic world?" I wondered.

"I don't know if you ever feel comfortable," Melanie replied. "But we all became more familiar. I went to a white girlfriend's house to play, and the black maid who worked there pulled me aside when she saw that I heard the N-word being used. She told me, 'It's just how they are. Don't let it work you up.' I thought if she could put up with it, then I could too."

Sylvester Turner remembers the tension and fights that marked the first years in his desegregated high school. "Blacks and whites were meeting each other for the first time. An all-white school was suddenly ten percent black. It was like cold air rushing to meet hot. We had no history of being in classrooms with each other. The only history we had is what we'd seen on TV or what our parents told us about whom we were about to meet. It was really rough at the beginning.

"There were fights in the hallways. The police were called in a number of times. When the adults, the parents, stopped talking into the ears of their children, we found a way to get along. As time went by, and the walls started coming down, we discovered we had more things in common than not. By the time I graduated, things were better. We worked through it. I was elected president of the student body, voted in by a school that was ninety percent white.

"Kids," Turner reminds me, "don't come into the world knowing how to hate. When you get them away from the influences that teach them to hate, they find ways to get along with each other. And we did." But he also credits the help of those thirteen teachers who rode on the bus with them. "They encouraged us. They helped us learn how to cope."

Desegregating public education often meant closing longtime schools that were central to their communities. "When I was a kid," Mayor Turner says, "and they closed my elementary and junior high school, it made you wonder, *What's wrong with my school, with my neighborhood, that I have to leave? Why don't they bring the other kids into my neighborhood instead of making me go somewhere else?* I believe every neighborhood is important. I'm still living in that same community. I am a person of color from that world. I remember being embarrassed about buying food with food stamps; I would run away from the grocery store when my friends came in. You hear all the time about people on welfare, but you don't hear about the many others who are struggling to make it, who would much rather work than rely on food stamps.

"So how can I build a dynamic city for the future if I don't educate the children?" Turner asks, addressing data from HISD showing that fewer than 8 percent of African American students graduate from high school with test scores indicating that they are college-ready. "How can we not prepare them for the workforce? So I have established a new position as city director of education. Houston City Council now has a permanent subcommittee on education. We are working to create a new nonprofit that will bring in philanthropists and others who care deeply about education but are unwilling to contribute big dollars to HISD the way it is currently operating.

"But the system needs money and it's not going to get more from the city, nor has the state been willing to raise the amount it's allocating

to the school system." (This was true at least until the 2019 legislative session, when considerably more money was finally allocated to
education.) "We are looking at the example of the LA United School
District, through which the LA mayor was able to attract fifty million
dollars. Ours is called the Coalition for Educational Excellence and
Equity. We have to develop a skilled workforce. Education is *the* civil
rights issue of our time."

★

A big part of the attraction of conducting research in the social sciences, particularly the kind I've been able to practice over these
thirty-eight years, is not only in being able to watch the mind of a
city emerge out of the careful analysis of objective data; it's also in
being able to measure across the years the way the mind of a city
changes in response to new realities. Houston, like much of Texas
and the South, was essentially a good ol' boy, blue-collar, redneck
city during most of the twentieth century, and, like much of America, this has produced cultures of intolerance and the persistence of
profound inequalities.

But the city has continued to evolve, and many of its attitudes
have changed in the process. Rice had desegregated in 1968, just four
years before I joined the faculty. Activism was everywhere. The baby
boom generation, the hippies, thought they were going to change the
world, my colleague Jenifer Bratter reminds me. They were going
to finally desegregate the neighborhoods, and everyone was going
to live happily ever after together. And there has surely been some
movement over time in that direction.

As the years of systematic surveys have made clear, area residents
are increasingly committed to protecting civil rights and rejecting
discrimination. We have been asking identical questions of successive
representative samples of Houston-area residents over the course of

almost four decades, and we have watched the city gradually opening its arms and heart, more prepared today than in earlier years to help build a more just and welcoming multiethnic society.

Transformations of this sort are inevitably uneven. No long-term demographic trends as profound as the transformation of Houston from a black/white Southern town into the country's most diverse metropolitan region will be experienced without setbacks, conflicts, anxieties, and anger. Every change in life entails a loss, as nostalgia for a receding past slowly gives way to an uncertain acceptance of the new. One area in particular has been slow to change, despite the general embrace of the region's growing diversity: The surveys show clearly how difficult it has been for Anglos to change their attitudes toward blacks when asked about living with these groups as neighbors. Houston's profoundly segregated communities continue to reflect the underlying biases that keep the groups apart.

When any of us are choosing where we would like to live, where to raise our children, where to spend our nonworking hours, we generally pay close attention to neighborhood characteristics such as education, safety, and property values. Many sociologists have argued that practical concerns like these, reflective of social-class preferences and interests, were pretty much all that went into making the decisions about where to live, and that racial considerations were not in themselves responsible for the continuing segregation the nation was experiencing. While some national surveys were suggesting that this was the case, I and many other researchers were pretty sure that race was still a key factor in and of itself in determining neighborhood preferences. We needed a clearer way to separate out the effects of the racial composition of neighborhoods from the other characteristics homebuyers care about, such as crime rates or school quality.

We examined these questions through a set of survey items

included first in 2004 and then again in 2016 and 2017. The respondents were asked to imagine that they were looking for a house and found one they liked much more than any other house: "It has everything that you've been looking for; it's close to work and within your price range." Because crime rates and poor schools are often cited as reasons for not wanting to live in an area with many racial minorities, the question went on to say, "Checking on the neighborhood, you find that the schools are of high quality and the crime rate is low."

This introductory spiel was followed by one of six randomly presented statements, specifying further that the neighborhood was composed of 10, 30, or 60 percent of one of the other two major ethnic communities and that the inverse proportion of the neighborhood was made up of the respondent's own ethnicity. So, for example, one-sixth of the Hispanic respondents were asked about a neighborhood, with good schools and low crime rates, that was 40 percent Hispanic and 60 percent Anglo; one-sixth of the Anglo respondents were asked about a similar neighborhood that was 10 percent black and 90 percent Anglo. Anglos were asked about a black-Anglo neighborhood or a Latino-Anglo neighborhood, blacks were asked about neighborhoods with different black-Latino or black-Anglo ratios, and Hispanics about Latino-Anglo or Latino-black neighborhoods. After being presented with one of the six randomly designated vignettes, respondents were asked, "How likely or unlikely do you think it is that you would buy this house?"

The findings in Figure 7.1 make it clear that, while blacks and Latinos seem equally happy to live with each other and with Anglos in all the ratios described in the vignettes, Anglos, in contrast, are significantly less willing to buy a house in a neighborhood that is 60 percent black or 60 percent Latino, even when informed that the local schools are excellent and the crime rates are low.

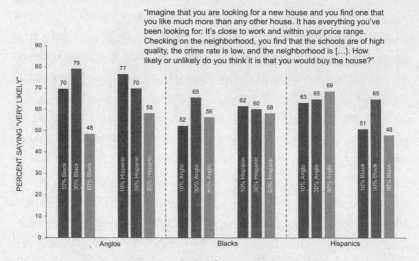

FIGURE 7.1: *A neighborhood's racial composition and the likelihood of buying a house (2016-2017)*

When asked in the combined 2016–2017 surveys how likely they would be to buy that house, 79 percent of the Anglo respondents said they would be very likely to move into an otherwise desirable neighborhood that was 30 percent black, but the percentage drops to less than half (48 percent) when the proportion of black families reaches 60 percent, and (again) this was after being told that the schools are of high quality and the crime rate is low. A similar, but less dramatic, falloff, from 70 to 58 percent, occurs when the neighborhood changes from 30 to 60 percent Hispanic.

Moreover, despite clear evidence of their overall positive and improving assessments of ethnic relationships in Houston and their increasing embrace of the region's burgeoning diversity during the intervening years, Anglos were just as resistant in 2017 as they had been in 2004 about moving into an integrated neighborhood. The percentage of Anglo respondents in that earlier survey who said they would be very likely to move into a neighborhood with low crime rates and good schools dropped from 73 percent to 49 percent when the neighborhood went from 30 to 60 percent African American, and from 81 to 58 percent when it changed from 30 percent to 60 percent Hispanic. The firm resistance among Anglos to living in a neighborhood where the residents are majority black or Latino had not changed at all in the course of those fourteen years.

Figure 7.1 also indicates that the neighborhood's racial composition has no consistent impact on the housing preferences of either Hispanics or African Americans. The far greater comfort among blacks and Hispanics with the idea of moving into a fully integrated neighborhood was found in the 2004 survey as well. It seems undeniable that Houston's continued high levels of residential segregation are at least in part a reflection of the continuing resistance to neighborhood integration on the part of Anglo Houstonians themselves.

A more elaborate series of questions along these same lines was asked in 2003 and 2005, and again in 2013 and 2014, when we varied randomly the quality of the neighborhood's schools, crime rates, and property values, and went on to specify eleven different ethnic compositions, ranging from 100 percent made up of the respondents' own ethnic group to 100 percent composed of one of Houston's other major ethnic communities, this time including Asians. This complex design provided a more rigorous test of the importance of the ethnic composition of the neighborhood, separate from the effects of all three of the commonly cited reasons people give for not wanting to live in an area with many residents of a different ethnicity from their own—concerns, ostensibly having nothing at all to do with race, but with high crime rates, poor-quality schools, and declining property values.

Sophisticated computer analyses of the responses, rigorously isolating the effects of the neighborhood's racial composition from its other attributes, confirmed the findings from the more compact questions we asked in 2004 and again in 2016-2017. The data showed clearly that Anglos are significantly less likely to buy an otherwise desirable house as the proportion of either blacks or Hispanics in the neighborhood increases, whereas the proportion of Asians in the neighborhood had no effect on the Anglo preferences. The responses of the black and Hispanic respondents were once again unaffected in any systematic way by the ethnic composition of the neighborhood.[61]

Part of the explanation for these consistent findings may lie in the difficulty people have in separating their racial stereotypes from the neighborhood characteristics we described in the vignettes. When informed that a predominantly black neighborhood has low crime rates and good schools, Anglos may simply find that hard to accept. To Anglos, living in neighborhoods with high percentages of blacks and Hispanics seems like an inherently bad idea, yet they have no problem living with Asians.

The attitudes reflect and reinforce the stereotypes. Anglos don't see the gangs and the poverty that exist in some Asian neighborhoods. They see their Indian doctor and their Chinese colleague. Houston, like all of America, still has a long way to go in the effort to transcend a racist past, with its deep-seated assumptions about intergroup differences; the survey findings strongly suggest that the continued high levels of residential segregation in Houston reflect the underlying persistence of racial prejudice in the residential preferences of Anglo Houstonians themselves.

To the extent that African Americans and Hispanics are able in the years ahead to move into the middle class, those prejudices and stereotypes will diminish. But that hasn't happened to a sufficient extent, at least not yet. Anglo reluctance to move into a neighborhood with a majority of black or Latino families was just as strong in 2017 as it was in 2004. Will the attitudes change eventually? They surely will, but probably not until we manage to reduce significantly the remaining intergroup inequalities.

The continuing pervasive segregation in Houston, and indeed in all of urban America, helps to perpetuate the misconceptions and misunderstandings that keep Anglos and blacks in their separate worlds, with striking differences in their everyday life experiences and in the attitudes and sensitivities they develop. The surveys underline these distinctive differences. Figure 7.2 compares Houston's four major ethnic communities in their beliefs about equality of opportunity and the realities of discrimination. On questions asking about the structural barriers to economic mobility in American society, the sharpest differences by far are between Anglos and blacks.

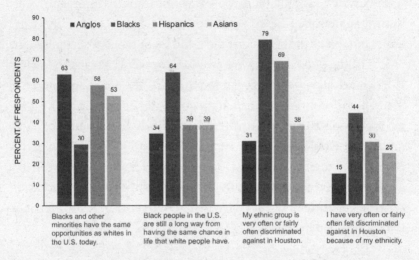

FIGURE 7.2: *Differences by ethnic communities in beliefs about equal opportunity and discrimination (2009-2019)*

Almost two-thirds (63 percent) of the non-Hispanic whites, but only 30 percent of African Americans, agree that blacks and other minorities have the same opportunities as whites in the U.S. today. Conversely, 64 percent of blacks, but just 34 percent of non-Hispanic whites, concurred with the alternative view, that black people in the U.S. are still a long way from having the same chance in life that white people have.

The intergroup differences were also striking when respondents were asked about their personal experiences with discrimination. As seen in Figure 7.2, African Americans are far more likely than Anglos, 79 to 31 percent, to assert that members of their ethnic community are often discriminated against in Houston, and, 44 to 15 percent, to report that they themselves have often personally felt discriminated against. Note also that Hispanics are much more likely than Asians, 69 to 38 percent, to indicate that their ethnic community is often discriminated against in Houston.

A question asked in the 2006 survey, six months after Hurricane Katrina, underlines the different worlds that blacks and whites generally inhabit as they consider the realities of racial discrimination: "Most of the people who were stranded in New Orleans following Hurricane Katrina were African Americans," the question stated. "If instead, most of the victims had been white, do you think the government would have responded more quickly to the situation, less quickly, or would that not have made any difference?" Among the Anglo respondents, 71 percent insisted that race played no role in the government's response, but fully 70 percent of the African Americans said the government would have responded more quickly if most of the victims had been white.

★

Ed Emmett is blunt about what he sees as the reasons for the unchanging biases. "Watch the nightly news when there is a shooting. The media overwhelmingly reports black-on-black crime. The homeless they depict on our streets are overwhelmingly black. So it's not surprising that biases remain, or that people are unwilling to move into minority neighborhoods. There is no way to sugarcoat these perceptions."

John Guess, CEO of the Houston Museum of African American Culture (HMAAC) and a descendant of one of the few African

American families in Houston that have been able to acquire multigenerational wealth, is not at all surprised by these preconceptions. He's a friend and frequent critic of our surveys. "Houston is a much more deeply racist town than the surveys reveal. You see it in how blacks were granted the right to eat at the lunch counters only because whites wanted to make sure their businesses wouldn't die. You see it in how Judson's grandfather and others of that generation basically had to ask permission from whites to do business in the black communities. You see it in the mushrooming wealth gap.

"You see it in how hard it has been to secure the donations needed to sustain this museum. We have an impressive board of credentialed and qualified black people, but Houston's money goes to organizations with more whites on the boards. Blacks have the same degrees from the same institutions; we work in the same financial companies, but what we do is discounted. My degree from Johns Hopkins isn't worth the same as a white person's degree from Johns Hopkins."

It's difficult to ignore the continuing blight of racism, the persistence of the black/white divide even in this, the most diverse metro area in America. "The city has come a long way," counters my friend and longtime Houston resident Travis Broesche. "It's hard for me to acknowledge the docile acceptance of the racist culture here in the 1950s," he says, looking back at the Jim Crow days and at a day in 1953 when he tried to give his seat in the front of a crowded bus to a black woman.

"The bus driver curbed the bus and stopped," Travis recounted. "'Hey, boy,' he shouted. 'What do you think you are doing?' To the woman, he yelled, 'You, get the hell up and get to the back where you belong!' I was terrified; my heart was pounding. 'You pull that again and I will kick you off this bus,' the driver yelled at me."

While Anglos may feel we are far away from that time, many African Americans are unimpressed by all the recent changes. Raised in Queens, New York, with stints in Los Angeles and Florida, Houston resident Denise Hamilton described what it was like to live in her well-heeled mostly white Upper Kirby/River Oaks neighborhood. "My neighbors say hello to my white husband, but they won't talk to me, my mother, or my daughter." When she first moved into the neighborhood, she found dog feces on the door handles of her late-model Mercedes, and again in the days following the 2016 election of Donald Trump.

Not long after that, she was driving home when someone who looked like a police officer pulled her over just blocks from her house. "I was shaking like crazy. I was trying to decide whether or not to reach for my phone and record what was happening, but I was afraid the officer would shoot if he saw me reaching for something in my bag. I really didn't know if I would survive the encounter. Sandra Bland had just died in a Waller-County jail (near Houston) after being stopped for a minor traffic violation. That was on my mind." After she had provided proof of residence in the area, the officer told her he was hired to work as a private security guard to make sure the "wrong kinds of people" were kept out of the neighborhood.

What happened to Denise is not so different from the event that Travis witnessed in 1953, except there was no COLORED sign written in vertical letters clearly demarcating the line beyond which blacks were not allowed to stand or sit or drive. While some recently arrived wealthy African Americans say they've had fewer "Driving While Black" episodes in Houston than in other parts of the country, the Houston surveys found that affluent blacks are slightly *more* likely than middle-class African Americans to report that they have often felt discriminated against in Houston. In fact, the wealthiest and poorest blacks are the most likely to report experiencing prejudice in this city, compared to other African Americans.

"I was sitting at the outdoor café of a posh uptown hotel," said one of Houston's most prominent African American journalists in 2017. "I was waiting to meet someone. So were several other people. There were white women alone at various tables and one other black woman also alone at a table, all of us clearly waiting for friends to join us. The white women were offered water or iced tea while they waited. The waiters never came near my table, nor that of the other black woman."

Communications expert Mustafa Tameez has been offering diversity training to the Houston police department for many years and has trained five thousand officers. In one of the sessions, a white policeman said he couldn't understand why African Americans were afraid of the Houston police. An African American sergeant who had been on the force for decades responded by telling the story of what happened when his son, who was in his early twenties, got pulled over by police for no obvious violation in a neighborhood he'd just moved to. His hands were shaking so badly he couldn't get out his license and registration.

"In the following days, every time he got back in his car to drive, he started to shake again. So the sergeant brought him to the local precinct of his son's new neighborhood and introduced him around. This kid had grown up around his father's colleagues," Mustafa told me, describing the episode, "so he knew all the cops in his neighborhood. But he didn't know any of them in the area to which he was moving. He was so scared that he asked his dad to go with him to his new local precinct and introduce him around. 'So if *my* kid was scared,' the sergeant told the white cops in the room, 'imagine what everyone else is feeling.' It was a powerful moment."

One of Tameez's training sessions takes the form of a mock town hall in which seventy officers are divided into tables of ten. Each table is made up of officers from different ethnic backgrounds. I sat in on a diversity training session and watched as the police were asked to role-play the participants in various crime scenes, all of which were situations that had actually occurred, many of them involving police brutality. The officers were asked to take on the roles of victim, victim's family, victim advocacy group, reporter, police on the scene, elected officials, and more. As the scenarios played out, they came to understand more fully the motivations of others at the scene, so that if faced with a similar situation they might be able to react more sensitively than their colleagues had. "The goal," says Tameez, "is to build empathy. The only way to see the other side is to feel what it's like to be in the other person's shoes."

The session went well, but after it was over, several African American and Latino officers said off the record that while this was a useful experience, the police force itself was still deeply segregated. "We will go back to our precincts," said one participant in a private conversation, "and the Anglos will continue to keep themselves separate. The real diversity training should be in getting the police to socialize with each other across ethnicities."

★

"Was it easier to make progress on social issues during the time of your father and grandfather?" I asked Judson Robinson.

In a way, he says, it was. "For years after the civil rights bill was passed and King was killed, there was a lot of energy around this. The government had funded a great study on the obstacles facing black schoolchildren. It was the Kerner Report: 'Our nation is moving toward two societies, one black, one white—separate and unequal.' There was a lot of data and passion at that time. But now, with all the negative stereotypes in the media, it's hard for us to get the message of our successes out there. The report showed that we have made gains in education and health. We made more progress recently, due to Obama-era changes and the Affordable Care Act. For the first time, blacks are living almost as long as Anglos."

"And now how would you sum up the current condition of blacks in Houston?" I wanted to know if anything else was changing from his perspective.

"Better for some, worse than ever for others," Judson continued. "The underclass is growing faster. There is an inability to respond to the daily disasters of being poor. People are overwhelmed by societal factors. And then on top of everything, Houston has to deal with worsening floods and storms. So if you lost your car in a flood, chances are you lost your job, too, because you had no way to get to work."

The surveys show clearly that the only ethnic group for whom economic success does not predict a lessening of support for government programs is the African American community. As Hispanics, Anglos, and Asians become more affluent, they come to believe that if you haven't succeeded it's most probably because of your own lack of effort or talent. African Americans, in contrast, continue to acknowledge, no matter how wealthy they become, that poverty is most often the result of circumstances people can't control, and that government programs are needed to help people get back on their feet. But Judson Robinson and John Guess tell me that they are not seeing this sensitivity play out among wealthy African Americans (where "racial solidarity" is thought to trump class interests); they are not seeing that much generous support from affluent blacks for their organizations.

"My big donors are not the wealthy African Americans," says Judson. "They are not on our board. They can do business on other boards, so they join those boards. They might buy a table at our gala, but they don't invest in the black community like my grandfather did. They don't sponsor a kid through the whole Urban League program. We have a fifty-year history in Houston, and they don't invest in their own people. Black businesspeople don't do business in Houston. They got their shot somewhere else," because they had to—it wasn't available to them in the South. In those days, African Americans had to leave the state of Texas to get graduate degrees.

"So how diverse and inclusive are we? There's a lot of rhetoric, but most of it isn't real. It's classism that keeps rich blacks from helping our Urban League kids."

★

Houston used to be an 80/20 white/black city. Now the power-wielding non-Hispanic whites make up just 35 percent of Harris County's demographic mix. W. E. B. DuBois said that the story of the twentieth century would be the story of the color line. It will inevitably be an important part of the story of the twenty-first century as well.

"And I have to give you this, Steve," says John Guess. "Increasingly, in every white family, you will see black people who have become part of the family, and in black families you will see white people who have become part of the family. There is hope in that."

CHAPTER 8

The Demographic Transformations

Texas was, for most of my life, a foreign land—a place and a culture far from the one I knew, growing up in New York City and suburban New Jersey.

And I will shamefacedly admit that for most of those years, I entertained the same lazy prejudices and assumptions about what Texas was like—and who, I believed, lived there.

But judging from Houston, it ain't like that at all, is it?

Houston is, in fact, about as multicultural a city as exists in the country. Houston has been, from what I experienced, particularly if not more welcoming to immigrants and refugees from all over the world than most other cities I know.

Our show focuses on some of those communities and on those stories, of people who looked to America as a refuge, as an ideal, as a place of opportunity—and who found it in Houston.

Yes, I took subversive pleasure in opening the show with an American flag—and then spending an entire episode in an America that is non-white, non-Anglo-Saxon, non-cowboy—and entirely devoid of the usual tropes: barbecue, Tex-Mex, big hats, and big oil.

Houston is far, far more—and more interesting than that.

—Anthony Bourdain[62]

At 6:00 a.m. on May 16, 2018, the lines snaked around both sides of the giant arena at Aldine High School, the early-morning sun rising on the celebratory confusion pervading the parking lot. Arriving at the front of an hour-long line to gain entry, families and friends were separated. "Guests of those who are being sworn in as citizens need to go around to the other side of the building"—where another hour-long line had formed. It would take nearly two hours to get the three thousand visitors seated for the naturalization ceremony. Sweat from the hot, rising sun was blasted away in the air-conditioned arena. Concessions sold water and small flags. There were nervous smiles all around as those about to become citizens tried to find their family members and friends who had come with them. By 8:00 a.m., everyone was in place, when an announcement was made that the judge would be there by 9:30 or 10:00 a.m.

Yes, the organizers knew the crowd would be annoyed by the long wait. But because of regulations set by immigration policies, when the doors closed at 9:00 a.m., no one else would be admitted. Anyone still outside would have to apply for another swearing-in date and that could take a while. The naturalization process had gotten so backed up under the Obama administration that many of those attending that day had waited years longer than normal for this day to arrive. Nobody was taking any chances under Trump's administration, as growing uncertainty prevailed.

The African American judge in his fifties arrived at a door just behind the basketball court on which his "bench" was set up, flanked by tables filled with officials on either side. He looked out at the crowd that morning as he took his seat at 10:00 a.m. Filling the steep risers of the enormous U-shaped arena was a packed sea of color, skin, textile, and design: batiks, headdresses, saris, kurtas, churidars; bright colors from the Caribbean, the Pacific Islands, Africa, and every part of Asia; Andean costumes from South America and the brightly woven fabrics of Central America; the delicate floral patterns and gilded fabrics of east Asia. The judge confirmed that the twenty-three hundred people who had made it through a rigorous yearslong process in order to become naturalized American citizens represented 118 nations and spoke an even greater number of languages. The young Mexican-born Texas State legislator who addressed the group touched on how he dealt with the bigotry they too were bound to face: by ignoring it and working extra hard to succeed.

Every month in Houston, the ritual is repeated, with more than two thousand at a time becoming American citizens, having arrived in the metro area from virtually every nation on the planet. Immigration has been the primary source of population growth in this city and nation since the early 1980s, and the face of America is changing rapidly. Harris County, which was nearly 80 percent Anglo in 1960, looked like this in 2019: 42 percent Hispanic, 31 percent non-Hispanic white, 19 percent African American, and 8 percent Asian or other.

The business leadership has generally embraced the change. "Immigration has been fantastic for Houston," says Patrick Jankowski, senior vice president of Research at the Greater Houston Partnership. "When the overall economy in America is weaker, Houston gets more domestic migration. But even when the Houston economy isn't going as well as the rest of America, international migration holds steady. This has been true for forty years. International migration has been the foundation of the region's population, employment, and economic growth.

"You hear the same comments from pretty much everyone," Jankowski continued. "Nobody really wanted to come here, everybody has heard the bad press about Houston, and they expected to hate it, but this is where the jobs were, so they figured they'd suck it up for their family, do their time, and then leave. But to a person, they almost never leave, unless work or family obligations take them somewhere else."

"I didn't think I'd stay so long," says Hong Kong native, commercial real estate developer, and Sugar Land resident Mandy Kao. "We came here in 2000 for an investment opportunity after living in Vancouver and Phoenix. When I saw how big Houston's Asian community was, I thought, *Hey, we can make this work.*" Kao, who has become a leader in strategic philanthropic giving circles, found a welcoming city.

It's an important part of what brings, as Jankowski's numbers show, so many foreign companies, so much international investment. "If we can persuade company officers to visit, they get it immediately. It's a place where they know their people will feel comfortable. They'll be accepted and embraced." It's part of the reason most of the investment in Houston is still coming from overseas. When Annise Parker was asked what she learned as mayor that surprised her the most about Houston, she spoke of how international it is: "Every language of business spoken anywhere in the world is spoken in Houston by native speakers with global connections."

This city has never had the rigid social hierarchy of older American, and particularly Southwestern, cities. There's a saying in Houston that nobody cares who your daddy was, and you can get in to see anyone here once. If you have a good idea, and we can make money together, let's talk some more. It's that kind of openness to new people and new ideas that is a continual draw.

"I had two job offers when I graduated from law school," says water expert and oil and gas executive Amanda Martin Brock. "I had arrived in New Orleans from Zimbabwe for college with two hundred dollars in my pocket. I was nobody there without the proper pedigree. The firm in New Orleans that wanted to hire me said that by working for them I would be allowed entry into New Orleans society. The firm's name would give me the clout. But Houston, I saw, accepted me for who I was, regardless of where I came from or

THE DEMOGRAPHIC TRANSFORMATIONS

where I worked. So I moved here in the eighties. And I'll probably never leave."

"Everyone is from somewhere else," says former mayor Bill White. "I wasn't born here. My wife, Andrea, wasn't born here. So how can we be snobby about newcomers?" That attitude has surely helped to encourage the continuing globalization of the region's population. During the past thirty years, no metro area in the country has been changed by immigration as completely, as suddenly, as irreversibly, as Houston, Texas.

Between 1492 and 1965, 82 percent of all the human beings on the face of the earth who came to American shores came from Europe. Another 12 percent were African Americans, who were originally brought here as slaves to serve the Europeans. A handful of Chinese and Japanese were working as farmers and laborers in California and Hawaii; a very small number made it to Houston in the early 1900s, such as this city's famous Gee family, settlers in its original "Chinatown," just east of downtown Houston. This nation was to be a melting pot almost exclusively of European nationalities—deliberately so.

Figure 8.1 provides a vivid summary of U.S. immigration history. Scholars usually distinguish four historical streams of immigrants to America. The first wave (1600–1820) was composed of the early settlers who fought the War for Independence and who came primarily from Great Britain, along with some from France, Holland, and Spain. The second wave (1820–1880) brought the Irish fleeing the potato famine, and then the Germans and Scandinavians. The third wave, arriving on these shores between 1880 and 1924, comprised the largest number of immigrants up to that point in recorded history: More than twenty-five million were pouring into this country, most of them to work in its urban factories, coming mainly from southern and eastern Europe in a stream composed primarily of Poles, Italians, Greeks, Slavs, and Jews.

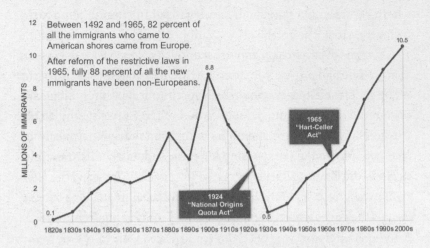

FIGURE 8.1: *The number of documented U.S. immigrants, by decade (1820–2010)*
Source: U.S. Department of Homeland Security, Office of Immigration Statistics

The typical reaction of Americans to each of these waves has been ambivalent at best, and more often downright hostile. U.S.-born European Americans have generally believed that the previous wave of immigrants was great for America, but the current wave is destroying the country. That's how U.S. citizens reacted when the Irish and the Germans came in the mid-nineteenth century, and they especially felt that way with regard to the massive numbers of third-wave immigrants.

The third wave was predominantly European, to be sure, but they were not from northern Europe. And they weren't Protestants: They were Catholics and Jews, along with Arabs and the "yellow hordes" from Asia. They had no history of democracy, and they were threatening to take American jobs and to undermine American culture, bringing foreign customs and resisting assimilation. Those concerns grew into a virulent, anti-immigrant, racist backlash, a nativist movement that pushed Congress to enact the most restrictive immigration laws in American history, culminating in the 1924 National Origins Quota Act.

The new laws were explicitly designed to limit immigration to the "superior stock" of northwestern Europeans. They made use of the new science of psychology and its recently developed IQ test to assert that science had proven that there are three distinct subspecies of the white race: the Nordics, who were supposedly superior biologically and intellectually to the Alpines, who in turn were superior to the Mediterraneans. And all members of the white race were presumed to be superior to the Jews, Arabs, Africans, and Asians. The new laws codified the Chinese Exclusion Act of 1882 in California and the Gentlemen's Agreement with Japan in 1906 to declare in the 1924 act that Asians in particular were an inferior subspecies of humanity. Asians were banned entirely from coming to America—the only group ever to be specifically targeted for exclusion based purely on their ethnic identity.

The 1924 law ushered in a forty-year immigration hiatus, which lasted through the Great Depression into World War II and its devastating aftermath and refugee crisis. The restrictive laws of the 1920s permitted unlimited immigration exclusively for northwestern Europeans, including those who had fled to South America and were seeking entry from there into the U.S.

The civil rights movements in the 1950s and 1960s put a spotlight on the racist underpinnings of the 1924 act. The immigration laws were also becoming an international embarrassment and a major impediment in the cold-war rivalry with the Soviet Union, complicating American efforts to win over the hearts and minds of the newly independent nations in Africa, Asia, and the Middle East. The 1924 act simply could not survive these shifts of consciousness.

In a speech to the Anti-Defamation League in 1963 on the occasion of that organization's fiftieth anniversary, President Kennedy said, "We are the descendants of forty million people, who left other countries, other familiar scenes, to come here to the United States and build a new life to make a new opportunity for themselves and their children." He had been pushing for immigration reform since he took office and was revising his 1958 book, *A Nation of Immigrants*,[63] a passionate celebration of how much immigration has contributed to this country throughout its history; he was assassinated before he could finish it. The following year, partly in tribute to him and in the knowledge that it was time to get this embarrassing legislation off the books, Congress changed the law.

The Immigration Reform Act of 1965, also known as the Hart-Celler Act, established a new system of preferences, based no longer on ethnicity or national origin, but on family reunification and on professional qualifications; later legislation would also open the door to refugees with proven vulnerability to persecution. The thinking was that an emphasis on reuniting families would help ensure that America's ethnic mix would be unchanged and the emphasis on professional qualifications would attract more British doctors and more German engineers. It seems never to have occurred to anyone during the congressional debates in the 1950s and early '60s that there were going to be African doctors, Chinese scientists, Indian engineers, and Filipina nurses, who would be able for the first time in the twentieth century to come to America.

From 1924 to 1965, a total of about seven million immigrants, overwhelmingly white Europeans, had come to America. In the 1960s alone, 3.2 million newcomers arrived, and just 34 percent of them were from Europe. There were five million immigrants in the 1970s, of whom only 18 percent were Europeans. During the 1980s, 1990s, and 2000s, almost ten million immigrants per decade were coming legally to America, and fewer than 11 percent were from Europe.

Of all the new immigrants who were part of the nation's fourth and largest wave of immigration, 88 percent were coming from Asia, Africa, Latin America, and the Caribbean. Mexicans and Central Americans were arriving in large numbers with low levels of formal education through the family-reunification provisions of the Hart-Celler Act. There were highly educated Russian and Chinese defectors, and large numbers of Vietnamese refugees; there were waves from South Africa, Mali, Nigeria, Ethiopia, Egypt, and India.

The United States was rapidly, if unintentionally, becoming a microcosm of all the world's peoples. The country was turning into the first truly "universal nation," the first nation in human history that can say, "We are a free people and we come from everywhere."[64]

★

There was excitement in Houston's early, tentative opening to other cultures. In 1960, 0.3 percent of Harris County's population was Asian. "It was probably all the Gee family," jokes Rogene Gee Calvert, whose father came from Canton in 1925, after the Asian Exclusion laws were enacted. "He was a 'paper son,'" Rogene tells me during a conversation at the Kinder Institute's Main Street offices in the southern corner of the Rice campus and across from the Texas Medical Center. She is describing how her father came over as a teenager with false papers, claiming he was the son of another family, one that had successfully immigrated. Otherwise, he would never have been permitted to enter.

"My parents came to Houston in 1941." Rogene laughs. "There was no air conditioning, and hardly any other Asians. My mom had a rough time. The old Houston Chinatown, east of downtown, wasn't walkable like it is in San Francisco and New York. Everybody worked there, but they didn't live in Chinatown. They moved west to the suburbs, to the Gessner corridor, to Katy and Sugar Land where the schools were better."

It was the Vietnam War that would diversify Houston's Asian population and bring new opportunity to inner-city areas. When the U.S. pulled out in 1975, the first wave of Indochinese refugees, mainly professionals, politicians, and officials in the defeated American-backed governments, fled the country and were sent to designated resettlement centers, primarily in Orange County, California, and in Harris County, Texas. The next wave of refugees were the Vietnamese boat people, who arrived in the 1970s and 1980s, and were sent in large numbers to Houston because its warm humid climate resembled Vietnam's and because of its proximity to the familiar shrimping and fishing industries in the Gulf of Mexico.

In 1979, the Houston Ballet, through the efforts of its British director Ben Stevenson, was the first American company to tour China, and the first to bring back a dancer for a summer internship in America.[65] Many will remember the dramatic rescue from the Chinese Consulate of Li Cunxin from the movie *Mao's Last Dancer*, but they may not remember that it played out in Houston, with the involvement of famed local immigration attorney Charles Foster and then vice president George H. W. Bush.

The defection was covered by the national media. President Reagan and Deng Xiaoping talked directly in an effort to defuse the situation, and finally Li Cunxin was allowed to remain in Houston, to continue to perform with the company, and to begin a new life in the West. Despite the resentments the incident caused, Li Cunxin's internship in Houston marked the beginning of the many rich exchanges, which would include Chinese scientists working alongside Americans in the Texas Medical Center, for example, on the innovations in genetic treatments for cancer and other diseases.

When I first arrived in Houston in the 1970s, the Anglo population comprised more than 70 percent of Harris County's total population, and many of them were actually the descendants of the "Hispanos" from the Spanish and Mexican Empires. Some Mexican soldiers defected and fought alongside Anglo troops in the Battle of San Jacinto, which established the Republic of Texas. But the relationship between the two groups was fraught with mutual suspicion and animosity. When the Texas War for Independence ended, Mexican prisoners of war, for the most part, had to work as indentured laborers and were not allowed to return home.

Records show that in the mid-1800s, there were no more than twenty or so Mexicans living in Houston.[66] The city was decidedly hostile to residents of the former enemy country, and most were run out of town. The predominantly Hispanic communities were farther west and south, remaining below the invisible line that stretches from Corpus Christi through San Antonio to El Paso.

Houston native Dorothy Caram traces the Mexican side of her family's roots back three hundred years to the time of Emperor Maximilian. With every revolution in Mexico, her ancestors fled to Texas and later Houston, and then returned to Mexico when the dust had settled. She has been a major force in the preservation of the history of Mexicans in Houston. And she remembers the bigotry. "Oh yes," she says in her home filled with museum-quality antiques and a giant miniature crèche that stays assembled throughout the year. "We were second-class citizens."

Around 1900, as the railroads improved and as things got worse economically in Mexico, migration north began in earnest. Some made their way to Houston, settling into Second Ward ("El Segundo Barrio"), and then fanning out across the northern and eastern parts of the city, segregating into Spanish-speaking enclaves. Anglo Houstonians turned on the Mexicans during the Great Depression, accusing them of causing much of the economic hardship and cutting them off from the public assistance that was being granted to Anglos during the Depression years. While the worst of the economic downturn mostly missed Houston, in part because of the efforts of Jesse Jones to keep the banks afloat, what job losses there were inevitably impacted the less affluent residents the most.

In the late 1960s, as the economy in Houston was booming, and as the new laws opened the country to immigration once again, large numbers of Hispanic immigrants came legally through family reunification, or as undocumented workers looking for opportunity. By the 1970s, the trickle turned into a wave, and Houston's independent school district began classifying Latinos for the first time as a race separate from whites; during the earlier years of segregation in the 1950s and '60s, Hispanics had attended the white schools. The new classification would change the officially reported demographic mix forever as the state worked to find a way to respond to court-ordered desegregation without requiring non-Hispanic whites to attend the same schools as blacks.

Harris County's population grew by 17 percent in the 1980s and by 21 and 20 percent in the ensuing two decades. The black population grew by about 18 percent in each of these decades, keeping pace with the population growth overall, fueled both by African and Jamaican immigration and by the "Great Remigration," the return to the South of middle-class blacks from northern cities.[67] Meanwhile, after the collapse of the oil boom in 1982, Harris County's Anglo population stopped growing altogether, and then declined by 6.3 percent in the 1990s.

U.S.-born Hispanics, who had typically stayed south of an invisible line stretching from Corpus Christi through San Antonio to El Paso, were now heading north in large numbers to take advantage of the new opportunities as Houston's economy recovered, with its continued abundance of inexpensive apartments and unfilled jobs in construction, restaurant work, and personal services. At the same time, highly educated Asian and African immigrants were drawn to the professional opportunities in Houston as scientists and doctors in the Texas Medical Center, computer programmers at NASA, and engineers in the resurgent petrochemical industries, with their feedstocks of oil and gas now much cheaper than before the bust.

Houston's economy became increasingly intertwined with the neighbor to the south. Mexico was America's third largest trading partner, with many of the transactions happening through Houston's port, and the city was a shopping hotspot for Mexico City's wealthiest. With everything you'd find on Madison Avenue or Rodeo Drive, those with means would spend between five thousand dollars and a hundred thousand dollars in a day. The impact on Houston's restaurant scene is undeniable. The hottest tables in the city are at those offering haute Mexico City and regional cuisines: Hugo's, Caracol, Xochi. You won't find burritos on any of these menus. But you will find mole tastings, tequila flights, lobster, and sautéed crickets.

★

As you travel away from Central Houston on Westpark Tollway, heading toward Missouri City in Fort Bend County, you will encounter along the Beltway 8 service road a variety of small warehouses and areas filled with industrial and construction equipment. But turn down South Garden Street, and near the end on the left, you will find one of Houston's very few landmarked Victorian homes, a structure that, even in this minimal government/lax regulation environment, is prohibited from being altered or torn down. "The property was on the market for years," says the young Tibetan spiritual master, Gala Rinpoche. "Nobody wanted the house. But we did."

Rinpoche, a title that means "precious one," was born in central Tibet in 1975. "I was left, when I was ten years old, to be educated in a school started in India by the Dalai Lama." He was sixteen when he was recognized as a *tulku*, the seventh reincarnation of a particular spiritual master who returns again and again to help people transform their suffering. When the monastery opened a branch in Atlanta, Gala Rinpoche became a resident teacher there and assistant program director. Now the founder of the Drepung Loseling Institute of Texas, the forty-four-year-old Rinpoche tends to an almost entirely Vietnamese flock. "There was a big Buddhist community here in Houston. I wanted to bring more study and practice into it," says Rinpoche over a home-cooked Vietnamese feast, prepared by one of his students, who owns a local restaurant.

With the help of his benefactors, Rinpoche has been buying up the land surrounding his Buddhist temple. "The older generation is being separated from the younger. The elders are more traditional, but their kids are becoming Americanized. The families aren't living together and caring for each other as they used to. I want to build a retirement home next door," he says, gesturing to the empty lot he had acquired for that purpose. How did it all happen so fast? "I just showed up and people started contributing," he says of all the various organizers—Vietnamese architects, NASA engineers, business owners—who helped make this happen.

A few miles away, closer to Bellaire Boulevard, where the street signs are in both Vietnamese and English, we come to another large Buddhist compound. A statue of Kwan Yin, the female Buddha of compassion, floats above a large, artificial pond just behind the entry gate, in front of the main temple with its pagoda roof. Inside the Jade Buddha Temple, an exquisite wood-carved shrine stands at the front of the main hall. The space resounds with a plaintive chant calling for blessings from the Buddha and Kwan Yin before their resident teacher begins his lessons in Chinese.

Around the back of the hall is a smaller temple, host on Sundays to their English-speaking Dharma Group. Members from both Asian and Western communities gather to hear a guest speaker, who usually follows their morning meditation. They trade stories of their involvement in Buddhism, of how they came to Jade Buddha, and gently correct each other's pronunciation in their respective languages. The temple was constructed in 1989; its founders also started an agency that would help other Buddhist organizations form their own nonprofits. They have connected with western Buddhist centers such as Dawn Mountain, founded by Rice religion professor Anne Klein and her psychotherapist husband, Harvey Aronson.

Drive back to the northeast from Fort Bend into Houston and you'll find, near the square with a large statue of Mahatma Gandhi, Parivar Grocers, which not only has an abundance of lentils, rice, large chunks of ginger, and freshly ground spices, but all the necessities for Hindu rituals. Here at the square and across Northwest Houston, you'll find clothing and fabric shops of varying quality, suitable for every occasion. Drive south and you will arrive at the Ismaili Center with its many surrounding mosques.

In an interview with the *Houston Chronicle*'s editorial page, Ali Zakaria talks about taking driver's ed soon after arriving in Houston from Pakistan. He describes being intimidated at the age of fifteen by the cowboy-boot-wearing good-old-boy instructor and the other Anglo teenager in the car. Upon discovering that the other kid was from New York, the instructor motioned for Ali to take the front seat, saying with a smile, "Any Pakistani is welcome over a Yankee." He felt immediately accepted, but after some hesitation he follows with, "And then came Trump."[68]

Many Asian immigrants talk about how accepted they felt in Houston. Nihala, who is married to Ali Zakaria's brother, Shaukat, worked in communications for Mayor Bill White and was head of Asian outreach during White's campaign for governor. She expressed concern over whether her children in today's climate would find the same kind of welcoming culture she experienced. After the 2016 election, many Muslims stopped wearing head scarves and were more discreet about praying during the day.

The rapid and sustained growth in Houston's Asian communities has had an enormous impact on the region as a whole, in a wide variety of areas, notably including the region's reputation as one of the best restaurant hubs in the country. In much the same way that everyone has their own favorite barbecue joint, Houstonians are unlikely to agree on the top Vietnamese restaurant, or which one makes the best pan-fried flat noodles.

Asian fusion has gripped Houston's celebrated restaurant scene. Underbelly, which won the James Beard award in 2014, sports Korean goat dumplings, Vietnamese flank steak, and grilled shrimp with soba noodles. Anita Jaisinghani, from Gujarat, India, exploded onto the Montrose neighborhood in 2001 with Indika, which quickly became one of Houston's most popular restaurants. She opened Pondicheri in an open-air apartment and shopping complex, with some of Houston's most expensive retail outlets. In the restaurant and the bakery lab on the upper level of the shopping area, Jaisinghani delights and tortures guests—a mix of Western and Indian patrons—by constantly changing the menu, pushing Meatless Mondays, offering outrageous new concoctions and removing favorites permanently, seemingly deaf to customer protests. Her daughter has exported the philosophy to the Pondicheri Café in New York City, near the Flatiron Building on West Twenty-Seventh.

★

The influx of immigrants was changing the face of Houston's metropolitan region. Harris County was 75 percent Anglo in the 1960s, while the number of Hispanics, which had doubled in the 1960s and doubled again in the 1970s, expanded by another 75 percent in both the 1980s and the 1990s. The Asian population grew by 129 percent in the 1980s and by 76 percent in the 1990s.

The Geographic Information System (GIS) maps presented in Figures 8.2 and 8.3 illustrate the remarkable transformation that Houston has undergone. In the U.S. Census of 1980, the tracts in Harris County that were majority Anglo overwhelmingly predominated. The majority African American census tracts were largely confined to what was known as the "Black Corridor" along the eastern side of downtown, primarily in Third and Fifth Wards. The predominantly Latino tracts were concentrated in the "Segundo Barrio" along the Houston Ship Channel. There was a smattering of census tracts along the Beltway surrounding downtown in which there was no majority.

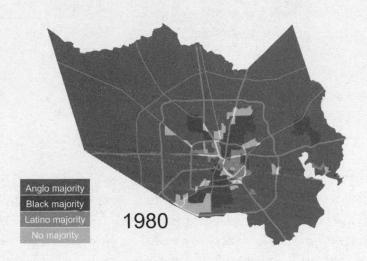

FIGURE 8.2: *The ethnic distribution across Harris County in 1980*
Source: Outreach Strategists, LLC

Virtually all the net growth of Harris County's population since the oil-boom collapse in 1982 is attributable to immigration from abroad, as well as to new births, primarily the children of earlier immigrants and of U.S.-born Hispanics, Asians, and African Americans. In the population estimates for 2016, the census found that almost 4.5 million people were now living in Harris County, and just 31 percent were non-Hispanic whites. The county's population, by these estimates, was now 42 percent Hispanic, 19 percent African American, and 8 percent Asian or other.

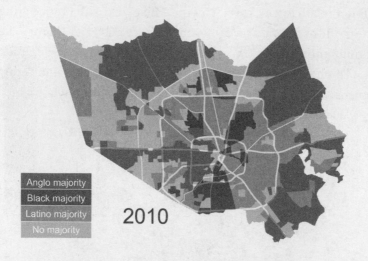

Anglo majority
Black majority
Latino majority
No majority

2010

FIGURE 8.3: *The ethnic distribution across Harris County in 2010*
Source: Outreach Strategists, LLC

Figure 8.4 compares the nine-county Greater Houston Metropolitan area with the seven other most diverse large metropolitan regions in America. The data show clearly how the new immigration has been transforming the ethnic composition of the most successful urban centers throughout America. The figures also justify the claim that Houston is indeed among the most diverse metro areas of all. One of the standard measures of ethnic diversity is the "entropy index,"[69] asking how close a given population comes to having equal fourths of Asians, blacks, Hispanics, and Anglos. By that measure, the Houston region is virtually tied with the New York metro for the diversity crown. Los Angeles, as measured by the "entropy index," has too few African Americans; Chicago has too many non-Hispanic whites; Miami has too few Asians.

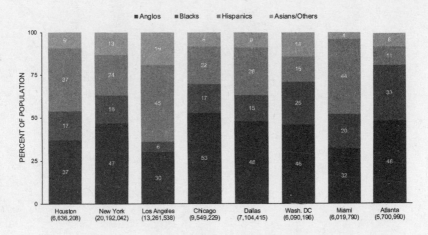

FIGURE 8.4: *The demographics of the most diverse large metro areas in America*
Source: U.S. Census, American Community Survey (2013-2017)

All Houston-area residents are now minorities; all are being called upon to build something that has never existed before in human history: a truly successful, inclusive, equitable, and united multiethnic society, made up of nearly all the ethnicities and all the religions of the world, gathered together in this one remarkable place.

CHAPTER 9

The New Face of Houston

As Hispanics go, so goes Houston.

—Laura Murillo[70]

There are twenty-seven different cultural traditions in Asiatown. I know they call it Chinatown, but it should be called Asiatown.

—Rogene Gee Calvert[71]

From the twenty-eighth floor of a Houston high-rise overlooking the tree-lined colonnaded fountains and gazebos of Hermann Park, you can get a front-row seat to the daily photo shoots in Houston. Circling them on any given afternoon are teenaged girls in boldly colored, formal off-the-shoulder dresses, sporting tight bodices and full skirts. Perfectly coiffed, they are flanked by their best friends in minidresses of the same hue, and by five to ten male escorts often in vaquero dress. On the weekends, the surrounding streets line up with pink Hummer limos; photographers direct the movements of the parties.

Later in the day these groups, led by the quinceañera—the fifteen-year-old debutante—parade through the Galleria shopping mall, soaking up the admiration of onlookers. The tradition has given rise to a major industry in Houston, with dressmakers, event planners, special venues, musicians, photographers, and limo companies dedicated to the birthday party, which more closely resembles a wedding. "I didn't have one," my friend Maria said when I asked her. "My mom said I could have a party or a car. I took the car." And, as the thirty-year-old American citizen confirmed, this was not the decision that most of her friends have made.

"I'm Latina and I love color," says Laura Murillo, when she greets me in her office wearing a bright yellow, curve-hugging dress with a large ruffle of the same lemony hue lining the neckline. "This is how I dress, and they are just going to have to learn to deal with it," and her track record gives her the right to proudly be herself. "I was born here, but my parents crossed the Rio Grande from Mexico with a second-grade education," she says when I ask her about her early life.

"I'm the youngest of nine kids. I grew up working in our family's restaurant in the East End. I was the first in my family to apply to college. I got into the Ivies, but I stayed home and went to the University of Houston, and I'm glad I did. I met incredible people and got introduced to a network of Latino leaders. When I worked in fundraising at Memorial Hermann [hospital], it was the first time I had ever worked with non-Latinos."

Murillo, who had been on the board of the Hispanic Chamber since she was twenty, was tapped by the chairman of the board to put together a gala in three months. She broke records and was hired away from Memorial to be CEO of the Chamber. "I could have stayed at Memorial Hermann. But I wanted to have a more direct impact in the Hispanic community."

Murillo has been a controversial leader, demanding that she be allowed to function as a real CEO—"not an assistant to the board. We changed governance. We made the Chamber more diverse. The board had been all Mexican American. Now it's as diverse as Houston itself: just 40 percent Hispanic. Because shame on us if we can't get rid of ethnic silos."

The Chamber continues to grow. In 2019, there were more than three thousand people at the annual luncheon, "and we can do that with no keynote speaker," Murillo adds, emphasizing that it is now the largest business luncheon in Houston. But fundraising is still a major challenge for the organization. "It's not at the same level as the other businesses and far behind the Greater Houston Partnership. It's really hard to get grants from the big foundations. We get tiny grants. We live donation to donation."

Her concern for the community is focused primarily on economic mobility. "The needle hasn't moved much for us in either politics or business. We still don't have the board representation in the major companies, on school boards, the big nonprofits. We still have less than 2 percent representation. We are also facing a growing poverty and inequality gap, and a massive technology gap. The education gap is daunting."

The generally low levels of formal education among Latino immigrants in Houston mask significant differences by country of origin. Figure 9.1 makes it clear that immigrants from Cuba and South America, unlike those from Mexico and Central America, are coming to Houston with considerably higher levels of education than most Latino immigrants, and higher than most U.S.-born Anglos as well. Almost four out of ten (39 percent) of the Cubans and South Americans who participated in the surveys, and 41 percent of those coming from Europe, have college degrees, compared to just 22 percent of all U.S.-born Latinos, and 40 percent of the non-Hispanic whites.

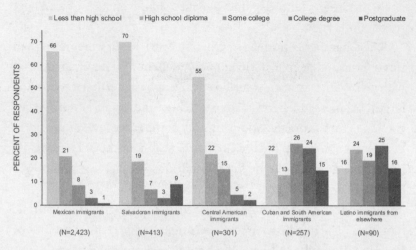

FIGURE 9.1: *Education by national origin among Hispanic immigrants, aged twenty-five or older (1994–2019)*

It is important to acknowledge these differences by country of origin, but it is equally important to recognize that the highly educated immigrants coming from Cuba, South America, and Europe comprise fewer than 10 percent of the total Hispanic immigrant population in Harris County. The vast majority of Hispanic immigrants are coming to Houston with striking educational deficits. The percentages of adults who do not have high school diplomas reach 66 percent among Mexican immigrants, 70 percent for Salvadorans, and 55 percent for immigrants from elsewhere in Central America. And that is inevitably impacting economic progress.

Figure 9.2 compares three groups of Hispanic immigrants based on the length of time they have lived in America, along with the two groups of U.S.-born Latinos, on some key indicators of socioeconomic status. Since education is generally completed after age twenty-five, it is not surprising to find little progress across the three groups of immigrants in the proportion who have obtained at least some college education.

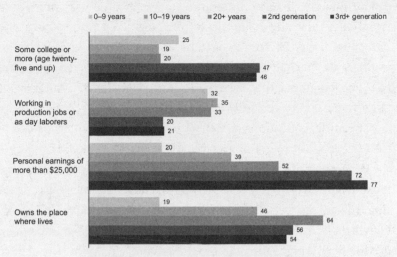

FIGURE 9.2: *Socioeconomic status among Hispanics,*
by time in the U.S. and by generation (2009–2019)

More surprising and more concerning, however, is the finding that there has been virtually no advance in educational attainment at all between the second and third generations of U.S.-born Hispanics: No more than 47 and 46 percent, respectively, report that they have ever attended a college class, and this is at a time when more than 60 percent of all the jobs that currently exist in this country require completion of a program certifying at least one or two years of education beyond high school.

Figure 9.2 also underlines the general lack of occupational mobility among Latino immigrants regardless of how long they have lived in this country. The foreign-born Hispanics who have been here for twenty years or longer are just as likely as more recent immigrants (at 33 percent, compared to 35 and 32 percent) to be working in low-level production jobs or as day laborers.

However, when asked about their personal earnings in those jobs, a more optimistic picture emerges. The longer they have been in this country, the more they are working their way out of poverty. The proportion of Hispanic immigrants reporting earnings of more than twenty-five thousand dollars grew from 20 percent among those who had been in the U.S. for fewer than ten years, to 39 percent for the immigrants who had been here between ten and nineteen years, and to 52 percent among those who had been in Houston and America for twenty years or longer.

The critical questions for Houston's future rest with the fates of these Hispanic immigrants and their children, for they will constitute the largest part of the city's future workforce. Will they continue to be locked in poverty, fueling the growth of a new underclass, as educational disadvantages effectively prevent them from moving forward? Or will they be able eventually to work their way into the middle class, gradually improving their circumstances and expanding the chance for better jobs for themselves and their children?

"Yeah, this is on me, and people like me. We didn't mentor enough," says attorney Michael Treviño, now approaching his seventies, when I ask him why there isn't a much deeper bench of Latino leaders in Houston. Treviño was born in San Antonio but raised in Mexico. Seated around a large stone table in the conference room in his office in River Oaks, Treviño is dressed in the Texas businessman's uniform: a beautifully tailored dark suit and tie and expensive cowboy boots. He prefers ostrich. He and his wife, Ileanna, are leading figures in Houston society. But that's not at all where he started.

Treviño's trajectory is not typical. Given Houston's historical hostility toward Hispanics and the difficulty so many Mexican Americans face in climbing out of poverty, I wondered how Treviño was able to achieve such high levels of civic and social leadership. "It's been a struggle," he said. Like many people of color in Houston, his major complaint is a stifling politeness that stops productive conversations from ever getting started. Treviño saw this firsthand at an early leadership forum sponsored by the Center for Houston's Future, which was founded by Gene Vaughan in 2000.

Vaughan's purpose in starting the organization was to help build a deeper bench and wider circle for civic leadership, to bring people together from different walks of life, all of whom were rising stars, leaders like Sylvester Turner. Vaughan wanted to make sure people like Turner, Treviño, and Murillo would get to know legislators like Ed Emmett. The hope was that the interactions would lead to proactive, collaborative initiatives that would help shape Houston's future. But the early meetings of the leadership forum proved to be nearly disastrous.

"People weren't being honest," recounts Treviño. "It was awkward, and nobody was talking openly. And then a white woman who worked for a search firm admitted that she was afraid of getting into elevators with African American men. And the black men were like, 'My God, how can you say that?' All hell broke loose. But you can't fault the attempt at honesty. We were there to confront the facts. If you can't talk openly about racial fears, you can't talk about what really matters."

The communication dam broke, and Treviño found himself next in the hot seat. "I was working in oil and gas, and the next issue that came up was air quality and its adverse impact on the health of those living near the refineries, the environmental racism of it all. We were trying to get a bunch of old white guys to understand that this was a different world. They didn't want to hear it. And they still don't want to acknowledge the incidence of disease along the Ship Channel [a.k.a.: Cancer Alley] or the terrible gaps in educational attainment. But at least we broke the tension and we could start talking more honestly about it."

"Michael, I still have one big question." I managed to squeeze in the comment during a gap in Treviño's stream of consciousness. "Forty-three percent of the entire Harris County population is Latino. Fifty-one percent of everyone under twenty is Latino. With a community that big and growing that fast, why are there so few Latino leaders?"

Treviño barely hesitates in his answer. "It forces me to accept some of the blame for not cultivating more leadership. So I am doing it now. I'm taking kids in as interns. One is at Northwestern, one at

Columbia, one at Fordham. My job now is to get more people in the room where the conversations about power are happening. Ileanna has a charity, Cherish Our Children, which looks after the kids of incarcerated parents. It was started by a parole officer, and fifty-nine kids have graduated high school because of it."

Laura Murillo has also developed programs for cultivating future leaders that may well have a long-term impact on Houston. "The Chamber has been a leader on so many issues. We've been on pension reform; we've been on the committee for establishing the downtown University of Houston campus; we've been bringing students to the Chamber and the annual luncheon to begin getting connected when they're still young. We have ninety partner organizations, we work with the rodeo, we are starting new Latino PACs, and we are encouraging new candidates for political office. We are supporting women who, despite pressure from family to marry and have kids, have opted for Lane A in oil and gas [focusing on their careers instead of marriage and children]. We connect them with senior female leadership to help them further their careers."

The Chamber has raised over two million dollars to support its mentoring initiatives and has graduated over two hundred young professionals. Murillo expects them eventually to run for mayor and city council. "They have to be the future leaders of Houston," she says. "So we are sending them into leadership positions at BakerRipley and United Way. We are building a base of key leaders who we are developing and vouching for. And they all have to work together, not just Hispanics, but Anglos, African Americans, Asians, Africans, everyone."

Young Latinas in Houston are certainly on the rise. In the 2018 election, twenty-seven-year-old Lina Hidalgo knocked Republican Harris County judge Ed Emmett out of his twelve-year stint in office by the narrow margin of about 1.5 percent of the vote.[72] Emmett blames his loss on the Democratic wave that resulted from Beto O'Rourke's race to unseat Senator Ted Cruz. "Without the straight-ticket voting," he told me, "this would never have happened." Hidalgo credits her win to a fifteen-month ground game to get out the vote. "This didn't happen by accident," she said during her speech accepting victory.

Born in Colombia, Hidalgo and her family fled the drug wars of the early 2000s. She attended high school in Houston, then Stanford, Harvard's Kennedy School of Government, and New York University Law School. She's the first woman and the first Latina to hold the position of Harris County judge.

Not long into her tenure, in the middle of March 2019, a disastrous chemical fire broke out on the Houston Ship Channel, at Mitsui's ITC, releasing deadly toxins into the air and into the Ship Channel, forcing the closure of one of the world's busiest ports for nearly a week. Hidalgo was slammed for her performance at the first press conference, where she appeared uninformed and a little frightened. A neighboring county commissioner, Mark Tice, was angry when he heard her speaking in Spanish. "This is not Mexico," he tweeted, demanding that she speak in English.[73]

Only a few months earlier Tom Brokaw, former NBC News anchor, had accused Hispanics of not trying to learn English, not wanting to assimilate. Both had to apologize. An editorial in the *Houston Chronicle* responded to Brokaw on January 31, 2019, citing evidence from the Houston surveys documenting the rapid assimilation of Hispanic immigrants into the mainstream of American society.

Hidalgo was using her bilingual skills to answer questions in English and then translate the questions and answers into Spanish. About one-third of Houston's Hispanic population speaks mostly Spanish. She was delivering crucial information about air quality and shelter-in-place instructions, and she wanted to make sure that everyone understood what she was saying.

The surveys provide no support for the claim that Latino immigrants and their children are unwilling to learn English, or are devaluing education and purposely resisting cultural assimilation into the American mainstream. Today's Hispanic immigrants are becoming "Americanized" in ways that parallel the experience of the third great wave of immigration (1880-1924), when similar concerns were being expressed about the newcomers from eastern and southern Europe. The United States has once again become "a nation of immigrants," and the traditional American story of successful immigrant assimilation is very much in evidence.

Figure 9.3 gives one of the many indications of that progressive assimilation. The longer Hispanic immigrants have been in this country, the more likely they are, in beautiful linear fashion, to say that they have close personal friends who are Anglo, black, or Asian. The survey findings also confirm that Hispanic immigrants are managing over time to improve their economic well-being and to move their families out of poverty. The longer they have lived in this country, the more likely they are to own their own homes and to have health insurance for themselves and their children. The longer they have been here, the more fluent they become in English and the more likely they are to think of themselves as primarily Americans.

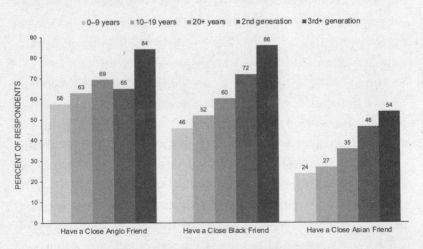

FIGURE 9.3: *Interethnic friendships among Hispanics, by time in the U.S. and by generation (2009-2019)*

As with all previous immigrant waves, those who manage to make it to America are not random samples of the populations in their countries of origin. Laura Murillo's parents came on foot across the Rio Grande. Caravans of people from Central America are walking for thousands of miles, and according to President Trump, creating a national emergency as they attempt to seek asylum across America's border. These are not ordinary people who pack up their belongings and carry their children across thousands of miles to find refuge.

Researchers at the University of Texas School of Public Health have identified what they call the "healthy migrant effect" or the "Hispanic health paradox."[74] Newly arriving Latina women, typically living in abject poverty, with all the stress that poverty imposes, are giving birth in area hospitals to full-term, healthy babies, whereas African American women in similar circumstances are more likely to have low-birthweight babies with serious problems. How is that possible? The answer is part of the great American story: Who braves the immigrant journey, with its substantial physical and emotional demands? Only the healthiest. Only the most self-confident. Only the most committed to the belief that hard work will eventually bring success.

When the survey participants in 2019 were asked if they agreed with the classic Houston assertion that "If you work hard in this city, eventually you will succeed," Hispanic immigrants (at 92 percent) were by far the most likely to concur with that confident assertion. Their health advantages and the social support their communities provide will surely be important factors in helping Latino immigrants cope with the barriers they face and work their way into a better future.

The data show that Hispanic immigrants are indeed doing better the longer they are in this country, making more money at better jobs, and the U.S.-born Latinos of both generations are doing much better than first-generation immigrants as a whole. But advancement stalls among the U.S.-born Hispanics. Members of the third generation are not obtaining substantially more education, finding better jobs, or making more money than those in the second generation. As a group, the U.S.-born Hispanics closely resemble native-born blacks on measures of socioeconomic well-being, suggesting that these two communities are facing many of the same barriers of poverty and discrimination that hamper their efforts to succeed in today's economy.

When the "third wave" of immigration at the turn of the nineteenth century (1880–1920) brought some twenty-two million largely unskilled newcomers into this country, there were plenty of blue-collar jobs that required few language or technical skills and offered many upward rungs on the ladder of mobility. This was particularly the case during the broad-based prosperity of the 1950s and 1960s, when the third-generation descendants of the Europeans who came early in the century were entering the labor force. The classic formula for successful assimilation envisioned three or four immigrant generations to progress from low-wage entry-level jobs, to semi-skilled and skilled blue-collar work, and finally into postsecondary education and mainstream America. And that accurately described the lived experience of most descendants of the third-wave immigrants.

In today's increasingly unequal, two-tiered economy, most of the intermediate rungs on the occupational ladder have disappeared. Increasingly, the economy now provides low-wage, low-skill personal service or production jobs on the one hand, and well-paid technical or professional positions requiring college educations on the other. With their parents working at two or three jobs yet unable to lift their families out of poverty, and with very little education themselves and not much understanding of how to help their children succeed in America's inner-city public schools, impoverished Hispanic and black high school students are facing daunting challenges in their efforts to obtain the postsecondary educations they know they will need in order to qualify for decent jobs.

★

The Asian population faces stereotyping of a different sort, in the prevalence of the "model minority myth," but not all Asians have had the same access to education and social capital. One-fifth of the Vietnamese respondents in the three Asian surveys (conducted in 1995, 2002, and 2011) said they were high school dropouts, compared to just one-tenth of all the other Asians in Harris County. Only 30 percent of the Vietnamese have college or professional degrees, but this is the case for more than 50 percent of all Asians.

An article in the *Houston Chronicle* in March 2019 tells the story of a homeless teenager named Derrick Ngo who slipped through most of the cracks.[75] In a speech he made before going off to college, Ngo speaks about how he survived for two years, beginning in tenth grade, without anyone realizing he was living on his own. His mother was on the lam, warrants for her arrest the side effects of a gambling problem. He was one of six kids; the others were either dropouts or incarcerated or both. The apartment he lived in was full of mold from the leaky roof that gave way during Hurricane Harvey. The air burned his lungs and he had to ration his food, sometimes going for days without eating. He evaded authorities such as Child Protective Services by having learned to ask officials for warrants before opening the door or just not answering at all.

Ngo had attended twelve different schools between kindergarten and eighth grade, and he realized that if he were going to succeed in high school he needed to stay in one place. So he applied to the Energy Institute, a new magnet school with a focus on helping underprivileged students to acquire the skills they would need in the new economy. He worked hard and was invited to participate in a program called EMERGE, which targets high-performing, low-income students. Participants in the program have been admitted to top colleges around the country. Ngo was the valedictorian at the Energy Institute; he was accepted at Harvard and was welcomed into the family of his Asian mentor, whom he met through EMERGE. He's had a safe place to live ever since.

★

The most compelling question for the Houston (and the American) future lies in the interconnection of ethnicity, age, and access to good schools. The aging of America has turned out to be as much a division along ethnic and socioeconomic lines as it is along generational lines. Figure 9.4 shows the striking relationship between age and ethnicity in Harris County today. As the 790,000 predominantly Anglo baby boomers in Harris County (those born between 1946 and 1964) move inexorably through their lives, it is only among the area residents today who are over the age of sixty-three that non-Hispanic whites still constitute a majority of the population. At each younger age group, the percentage of Anglos plummets and the percentage of Hispanics surges, with stable shares of African Americans and Asians across the various ages.

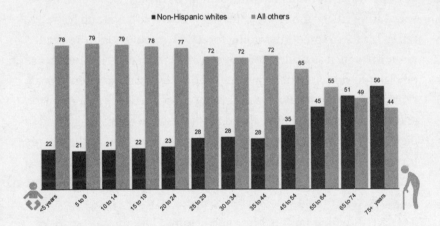

FIGURE 9.4: *The current population of Harris County, by age group and ethnicity (ACS, 2013–2017)*
Source: U.S. Census, American Community Survey (2013-2017)

Of all the 1.4 million residents of Harris County who are under the age of twenty, 51 percent are Hispanics and 19 percent are African Americans; 9 percent are Asians, and 22 percent are Anglos. In 2018, 62 percent of the more than 214,000 students enrolled in one of the 284 schools in the Houston Independent School District were Hispanic and another 24 percent were African American. Just 9 percent were non-Hispanic whites, and 4 percent were Asians. Moreover, three-fourths (75 percent) of all the children in HISD schools qualify for free or reduced-price lunch programs. And we know what concentrated poverty does to a child's ability to succeed in the public schools.

The coming together of two fundamental transformations has redefined the challenges and opportunities of our lifetimes. Today's economy is generating growing inequalities predicated above all else on access to good schools and colleges, and America is in the midst of an extraordinary transition in the ethnic composition of its population. Nowhere are these two trends more clearly seen or more sharply articulated than in Houston today.

Even as the current administration in Washington tries to halt immigration and block all asylum seekers on the southern border, help-wanted signs continue to mushroom across restaurant windows and at construction sites in Harris County. One construction magnate in particular has been trying hard to keep the immigration doors open so that the area's economy doesn't collapse.

Way out past the inner loop, the ring of highway I-610 that defines the center of Houston, stands developer Stan Marek's steel-and-glass mid-rise building, looking much like many other buildings along the energy corridor in this industrialized part of Northwest Houston. It is distinguished only by the large parking lot full of trucks, dumpster equipment, and big machines. The Marek Brothers Company, just in the last two years, built Atlanta's Mercedes-Benz Stadium, the Massachusetts Museum of Contemporary Arts, the James Turrell exhibit on the Rice campus, Houston's Marriott Marquis hotel, and San Antonio's Henry B. González Convention Center, among many other projects. "We like big, tough jobs," says its energetic CEO. And for projects like that, you need a lot of construction workers. Finding the best people and keeping them in America has become his central challenge and mission.

Born in 1947, Marek is the grandson of an immigrant Czech farmer who settled near Houston and lost everything during the Great Depression. "My grandfather became an alcoholic, lived in a shack, and ate possum and armadillo. We grew up poor in Aldine," to this day one of the least-affluent regions in the Houston area. "Most everyone here is from Mexico," he says as we breeze through the lobby of his headquarters. "I've worked hard to make sure they speak English and have a full-time job with benefits. It isn't easy—so many of the contractors have gone to 1099 piecework, and that means the workers are making a lot less money."

Most of the companies, Marek contends, are working with subcontractors who are exploiting the vulnerability of their undocumented workers, though they claim otherwise. "The jefes may tell me they are paying each of them twenty-five dollars an hour. But nobody knows what they are actually paying. In this climate, things are getting much worse. None of us contractors can find enough people anymore. You can expect some construction costs in the area to triple over the next five years," he continues.

Marek has been lobbying Washington for comprehensive immigration reform for decades. He's met with three presidents, many Speakers of the House, and prominent members of Congress. He's even lobbied the IRS to improve their auditing of construction companies in order to reveal their exploitative labor practices, since they are the cause of so many of the injuries and deaths among undocumented workers. "If you audit one company, the message gets sent and eventually these practices will stop. Then it will force us to enact real immigration reform."

Seated behind his desk, Marek reminisces about a time when Mexican workers crossed the border daily, illegally, for work. Everyone, from migrants to border patrol officers, knew each other. "They knew the IDs were fake, but nobody asked questions," Marek said. The workers made union wages, and for those who could join, the unions had apprenticeship programs that turned out generations of people with skills. "But the unions became corrupt, and companies were pushed toward the merit-shop model and piecework." This focus on hiring independent contractors as non-salaried workers, Marek argues, is part of what opened the door to both exploitation and labor shortages. The problem is now exacerbated by the current climate of intimidation and fear.

"So," I challenged him, "what about offering some of that training in the high schools? What about hiring more African Americans? There must surely be other options besides relying so completely on undocumented Latino immigrants, aren't there?"

"Yes, of course. You try to help African Americans to get these jobs, but they were historically forced into taking construction jobs and they don't want them anymore. They'd rather get the training to be a plumber, electrician, or something mechanical. Those careers are more sexy and not so physically demanding. But to be a roofer? A framer? To work outside in the Houston summers, mixing and pouring concrete? It's hard, it's hot, and nobody wants to do it, no matter how good the pay is, if they have any other choices."

Think of what it takes to cross deserts, oceans, and mountains, to survive unspeakable violence and the harshest conditions. There is nothing lazy or fearful in a human being who flees the threat of death on the chance for a new life. There was nothing indolent or lacking in courage in the people who risked their own lives and their children's lives on the chance of not being killed by violence and poverty in Ireland, Italy, and eastern Europe during the late 1800s and early 1900s, in Europe during the two World Wars, in China during the Communist Revolution, in Africa, the Middle East, and in the gang and drug violence that the United States has helped to generate in Mexico and Central America.

Ronald Reagan, in a campaign speech in 1980, had this to say about the wave of immigrants at that time: "These families came here to work. They came to build. [They] came to America in different ways, from other lands, under different, and often harrowing, conditions, but [Ellis Island] symbolizes what they all managed to build, no matter where they came from or how they came or how much they suffered. . . . They didn't ask what this country could do for them but what they could do to make this refuge the greatest home of freedom in history. They brought with them courage, ambition, and the values of family, neighborhood, work, peace, and freedom. They came from different lands, but they shared the same values, the same dream."[76]

One particular force of nature, a renowned expert in helping refugees, disaster recovery, and building resilient communities, would have agreed wholeheartedly.

"I don't know why they gave me a handheld mic," said Angela Blanchard as she took the floor at BakerRipley headquarters, at the beginning of a conference on immigration she was hosting for a group of similar organizations around the world. "I'm Cajun. I talk with my hands, and I curse a lot," says Blanchard, who's from Beaumont in East Texas. After a little confusion, a lavalier mic was quickly attached, her hands now free to bolster her words.

"The story people expect to hear," she says in almost every address, "is how people are the problem. How people are broken. But it's the wrong story." A welcomer of the shipwrecked, whether from across the world or across the railroad tracks, Blanchard spent more than twenty years as CEO of the BakerRipley centers, helping thousands of newly arriving refugees to "learn, earn, and belong."

She asks all of us to think about poor people differently. "The story we usually tell is about crime, hopelessness, lacks, gaps, needs, and broken stuff; we think about their diseases, their skills gaps, their lack of education, and we focus so much on these problems, on trying to help with those problems, on what's missing, that we begin to think of people as the problem. You can't build on a broken foundation. Nobody ever asked you to fill out an application telling them everything you're lousy at," she said in a TEDx talk in Houston in 2011.

As the CEO of BakerRipley centers, "I saw so many people like my parents, living in poverty, trying to create a new life out of their own imaginations." As head of an organization with a $275 million budget funded by forty different grants and donation streams, Blanchard made sure that new and different questions were being asked of the refugees fleeing the suffering in Syria, Iraq, Pakistan, and Central America, as well as in neighboring cities and states. Instead of asking what can we fix for you, she asked of the people who fled their homes with almost nothing: What are you bringing with you? Who do you know? What do you need to succeed?

"Even after fleeing disaster, when you ask them these questions, they brighten and sit up straighter. They can see the outlines of the first steps on a path to a new story." The answer is not "money"; the answer may be: "We need to learn English"; "We need safe schools for our children"; "We need to transfer our job skills." Every six months, BakerRipley asks the questions over again, and they adjust their services to evolving needs.

"We find amazing strengths and resiliency in every neighborhood every time. We have a brand-new story to tell about extraordinary people who come thousands of miles to build a new life in a city where you can do that more readily than any other city in America. We embrace you for what you can do. When you work with people around something that matters most to them, you don't have to motivate them. When you stand side by side with them, working with their strengths, and seeing them for the brave passionate people they are, they are inspired."

Located in the Gulfton neighborhood, the new BakerRipley headquarters—pristine, brightly colored buildings situated on a four-acre open campus—brims with the energy of engaged adults and children from every part of the world. Its genesis in 2010 shows another quality of its leader: doing something that everyone else told her wasn't possible. "I bring in all kinds of supporters," says Blanchard. "When they see what's happening here and they meet the people, they say, 'I get it. These people are just like me and my family.' And then I tell them that if they just voted the right way, they wouldn't have to write such a big check."

The energy on the campus is palpable. Kids are in class. Adults are learning English. Lawyers are helping with immigration issues. And in the midst of this supposedly dangerous neighborhood, there are no gates, no fences, no barred-up windows, and not a speck of graffiti in sight, whereas everywhere else in Gulfton, as they say, if it isn't moving, it's tagged. "The VIP parking is over there," says Blanchard as she points to the curb along the street. So many people have been helped at the BakerRipley centers that Gulfton has become famous even as far away as Pakistan.

Syed arrived at BakerRipley from Lahore in 2011, fleeing two murder attempts by his extended family.[77] His relatives practiced an extreme form of Islam that to his mind was consumed with hatred. He thought that Islam was all about love, yet he saw acts of violence everywhere. When he converted to the Ahmadi sect, whose motto is "Love for all; hatred for none," the other members of his extended family issued a fatwa, an order for him to be killed as an infidel. Syed was caught, stabbed multiple times, his legs broken, as were most of the bones in his body. He was dumped out of a car onto the side of the road and left for dead. His wife and children were taken away.

He survived somehow and fled to Lahore, where he began to hope again and to think about the future. He remarried, had children, and thought he was safe at last. But in the middle of prayers in May 2010, the mosque he was attending was attacked by terrorists with automatic rifles and suicide bombs. "My clothes were drenched in the blood of my friends," he said in the short film that was made about his journey, titled *These Bones of Mine*. The next Friday, a group of assassins came again. This time, they left a message: "We've found you, and we won't stop until we kill you."

Syed and his new family, along with ninety-six other members of the Ahmadi sect, sought asylum in Thailand. Upon arriving, the families were separated and thrown in jail, where they remained for six months. The Ahmadi community in the U.S. lobbied to have them released and brought to America. Part of the community had already settled in Houston, having come through Gulfton. The word was out in Lahore: If you want to go to America, go straight to Gulfton, in the city of Houston, in the state of Texas.

Seven years later, Syed and his family are thriving. BakerRipley helped them find suitable housing. Their kids started school, and his wife was able to resume her college studies. They are grateful for the open air, the warm weather, the green trees, the lawns, and parks. Most of all for the chance to dream again.

Gulfton is full of stories like this, of people coming from almost every country on the planet, bringing an indomitable will to survive and a determination to succeed. Blanchard has commissioned several films describing the lives of people who have come through BakerRipley because, as she says, "I want everyone to know why we are so lucky they chose to make this region their home. Houston is full of stories of people who came with nothing," Blanchard continues. "What makes a great city is one where you can come with nothing and make it to the top. We don't share a past," she concludes. "We share a future."

Throughout its history, Houston was essentially a black/white Southern city, dominated and controlled by members of the white male business elite. In 1960, 74 percent of the 1.24 million residents of Harris County were Anglos and 20 percent were blacks. Just 6 percent were Hispanics, and less than one-half of one percent were Asians.

The surveys document the gradually increasing embrace of the new diversity among the U.S.-born Anglo respondents. In the 2018 survey, almost half (48 percent), up from 36 percent in 2000 and 30 percent when the question was first asked in 1994, thought that immigrants to the U.S. generally contribute more to the American economy than they take. The proportion who believed that the increasing immigration into this country today mostly strengthens (rather than threatens) American culture increased to 49 percent in 2019, up from 42 percent in 2007 and from 33 percent in 1997. And the percentages who said that Houston's ethnic diversity will eventually become a source of great strength for the city, rather than a growing problem, increased from 59 percent in 1998 to 70 percent in 2019.

Comparable changes have been occurring among the U.S.-born African Americans and Hispanics. In alternating years since 1995, we have asked the respondents whether they thought the United States should admit more, fewer, or about the same number of legal immigrants in the next ten years as were admitted in the past ten years. In all three of Houston's major ethnic communities, the trends are similar and compelling. The fear of being overwhelmed by all the new immigration has faded dramatically in cities like Houston, where the changes are the most profound, and the benefits of immigration are the most apparent.

But challenges remain. Black/Asian tension is a common experience in almost all major American cities, when Asians, such as Rogene Gee Calvert's family, open small produce shops in inner cities. Asians tend to hire other Asians, and their offerings are inevitably more expensive than in the big-box stores—because they are smaller and unable to buy in bulk. Blacks think they're being ripped off and the Asian store owners and employees are afraid the blacks will rob them. We've seen the tensions reflected in the surveys over the years: When participants are asked to rate the relationships between their group and each of the other three major ethnic communities, the lowest ratings of all are given by blacks and Asians to black-Asian relations.

For a number of reasons, there's relative peace in Houston despite the tensions. "We don't pick up a rock," says Rogene, "we pick up the phone when there's a problem."

It's true that Houston has had far fewer race riots than most big cities in America—but we both know that part of the reason there is less overt racial tension in Houston is because of its sheer physical size. Ethnic groups in Houston rarely live that close to one another and as a result, the different ethnicities are less likely to feel that their neighborhoods are being encroached upon as much as in denser urban areas. Across the thirty-eight years of surveys, Anglos tend to give more positive ratings to race relations overall, while the other three ethnic groups are more likely to see the problems and the strain. African Americans are the most sensitive to the tensions inherent in Houston's interethnic relationships, and they generally give lower ratings than other groups to the relations among ethnic groups in the Houston area.

"And this is part of what bothers me about this city," Rogene says gently, though her concern is apparent. "We talk about how great it is that we live in the most diverse city in America. We tell each other it's the great strength of Houston. But we are all so segregated. We don't really live it. We don't really get to know each other. We just talk around it. To me, this is where we are failing."

If Houston had not turned out to be such a powerful destination for the new immigration of the past thirty years, this city would have lost population. It would have had the same fate as other important American cities that may be wonderful urban places, but they are gradually losing their status as major cities because, for more than three decades, they have stopped growing: cities such as Philadelphia, Baltimore, Pittsburgh, St. Louis, Detroit, Cleveland, Cincinnati, and Buffalo. Instead, Houston is one of the most vibrant, rapidly growing metropolitan areas in America, with a vigorous entrepreneurial economy, thriving primarily because of the tremendous energy, vitality, and commitment to hard work on the part of immigrants who have been pouring into this city from Africa, Latin America, Asia, and the Caribbean.

Asians, and most Africans as well, were able to come to America because they came with high levels of education and the specialized skills that were needed in this country. The only pathways to legal immigration open to Africans and Asians after 1965 were by obtaining refugee status (e.g., the Vietnamese), by qualifying as professionals of exceptional ability (e.g., the Indians and Pakistanis, Chinese and Taiwanese, Nigerians and other Africans), or by having occupational skills that were sorely needed and in demonstrably short supply in the United States (e.g., Filipina nurses). The unprecedented socioeconomic disparities across today's immigrant communities reflect the history of American immigration policy.

The contrasts in educational attainment depicted in Figure 9.5 make it clear that Asians have been relatively successful in Houston and America mainly because so many of them have come from families in their countries of origin whose educational and occupational achievements far exceed the average for U.S.-born Anglos. When asked in the 2002 survey what occupation their fathers had when they themselves were sixteen years old, four out of ten Asian respondents (39 percent) said their fathers were doctors, lawyers, professors, engineers, corporate executives, or other professionals. Family backgrounds of this sort were reported by only 32 percent of the Anglos, 17 percent of African Americans, and 12 percent of Latinos. At the other end of the spectrum, just 22 percent of Asians said their fathers were employed in low-paying production jobs or worked as agricultural or day laborers, but this was the case for 45 percent of Anglos, 63 percent of blacks, and 74 percent of Hispanics. There are, of course, important differences within the communities by their countries of origin.

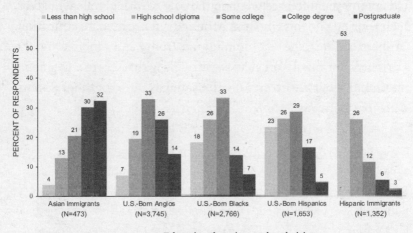

FIGURE 9.5: *Educational attainment by ethnicity, among all respondents aged twenty-five and up (2009–2019)*

The surveys indicate further that only 12 percent of all the Asian respondents were working in low-paid production or day-labor jobs; yet this was the case for 26 percent of the Vietnamese. The latter were also the most likely of all the Asians to have completed the surveys in their native language rather than English, to have no health insurance, and to report that they had difficulty paying for the groceries they needed to feed their families. Clearly, many Vietnamese in the Houston area are facing major challenges, and they may be less likely to receive the assistance they need, in a language they can understand, from a wider community that generally believes that all the Asians are doing fine.

Meanwhile, the African American population has continued to

grow since 1980, keeping pace with the Harris County population as a whole. The growth is fueled primarily by immigration from Africa and the Caribbean. As indicated in Figure 9.6, the immigrants from Africa (mostly Nigeria and Ghana) have come with educational levels that are at least as high as those of most Asians. Well more than half (60 percent) of all the African immigrants who were reached in the past twenty-five years of Houston surveys (1994–2019) had college degrees, including 20 percent who had obtained a postgraduate education. In sharp contrast, the black immigrants from Latin America and the Caribbean (primarily Jamaica) are arriving with levels of educational attainment that are essentially the same as those of the U.S.-born African Americans.

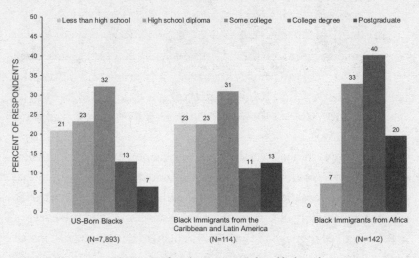

FIGURE 9.6: *Education among U.S.-born blacks and in two immigrant communities (1994–2019)*

When asked what it was that brought them or their parents to this country, 56 percent of the Vietnamese respondents said they immigrated because of political persecution, as a result of war, or in search of freedom. Only 11 percent of the Chinese gave political reasons of this sort, and virtually none of the Indians/Pakistanis or Filipinos did so. They have come with different religions—from Catholicism to Islam, from Hinduism to Buddhism, Baptist to atheism enforced by government edict.

According to the 2010 U.S. Census, a total of 253,032 residents of Harris County checked an Asian nationality on the "race" question and an additional 27,309 checked "Asian" in combination with one or more other races, for a grand total of 280,341 Asian-origin residents. This represented an increase of more than 45 percent from the 193,059 Harris County Asians who were counted in the 2000 census; and the 2000 figures constituted a growth of 76 percent from the 1990 numbers.

Sugar Land, in neighboring Fort Bend County, has absorbed more immigrants from South Asia than any other area in the region. Nihala's parents came in the late 1960s from Hyderabad, in northern India. Her father is an engineer and her mother a psychiatrist. "And I'm in PR, not something my parents are particularly proud of. They would have rather I become a scientist or doctor like them." Nihala lives in one of the most diverse counties in America. Formerly a company town for the sugar growth and processing industry, Fort Bend's population represents a more even distribution among America's four major ethnic communities than anywhere else in the nation, except perhaps Alameda County, across the bay from San Francisco, and the borough of Queens in New York City.

Though backgrounds and experiences are diverse, as Rogene says, "there is a lot of intermarriage"; and Asian Americans are the most likely of all the major ethnic communities to marry across ethnicities. Rogene herself is married to an Anglo. "And we get along across the ethnic lines," she goes on to say. "Of course there is always some tension, but the Asian numbers aren't big, and we know we need to work together. We have looked to the Jewish community for ideas about how to increase our influence. In forming our Asian PACs, we see their 80/20 ratio as a model: If you can get a bloc of 80 percent to agree on any one issue, you can influence public policy."

The growth in the population of Asian and Hispanic adults in Houston and America today is no longer due primarily to the arrival of new immigrants. It is attributable instead to the coming of age of the U.S.-born children of immigrants from the 1990s and early 2000s. The three successive Asian surveys document this social dynamic: Just 10 percent of the Asian adults who were reached in the 1995 survey said they were born in the United States. The proportions of U.S.-born Asian Americans grew to 15 percent in 2002 and to 31 percent in 2011. [78]

The surveys indicate further that the U.S.-born Asian Americans are doing even better economically than the first generation of Asian immigrants. Second-generation Asians are even more likely than the foreign-born to have graduated from college, and they are far more likely to have continued their formal education beyond high school. Despite being younger and thus at an earlier stage in their careers, the U.S.-born generation is already earning significantly higher salaries.

It will be fascinating to watch the continuing rise of the new generation of Asian Americans, born in this country and coming generally from highly privileged backgrounds, young people who are 100 percent American, yet with deep connections still to their countries of origin.

★

Houston-area residents have now experienced several decades of living in a city that has become a major immigrant destination. When, as an Anglo Houstonian, you meet more people who are looking less like you, speaking other languages and celebrating different customs, the strong initial resistance tends to give way to an appreciation of the many ways that Houston benefits—in the revitalization of decaying inner-city neighborhoods, in the celebrated new restaurants sprouting up all over the region and winning more national and international awards, and in the enrichment of the arts and culture and festivals in this increasingly global city.

The increasing presence of young adults who are U.S.-born Asians and Latinos changes everything. The concerns are no longer: Will the new immigrants ever learn English? Will they ever become truly American? Are they going to remain in their co-ethnic enclaves, keeping with their foreign ways, and refusing to assimilate? Those fears have faded in this new world of thriving interethnic friendships and increasing rates of intermarriage.

Also in play is what is known in social science as "the psychology of inevitability,"[79] the human tendency to make the best of things that you know are virtually certain to occur. As the seventy-six million members of the predominantly Anglo baby boom generation (aged fifty-five to seventy-three in 2019) move inexorably into senior status and continue to shrink in numbers, the United States as a whole will become a progressively more multiethnic society. The young people throughout America are disproportionately non-Anglo. The multiethnic future of Houston and America is inevitable, and recognition of that destiny may be another force that is helping to move the general public toward a growing acceptance of the new diversity.

By around 2042, non-Hispanic whites will be a minority across the entire country and all of America will be in the same boat as Houston. Figure 9.7 gives the projection from the U.S. Census of the distributions by age and ethnicity of the American population as a whole in 2050. The projections assume very little additional immigration during the next thirty years and build almost entirely on the actuarial tables that reflect the age differences among the nation's ethnic communities. In 2050, as indicated in Figure 9.7, all of America will look very much like Houston today.

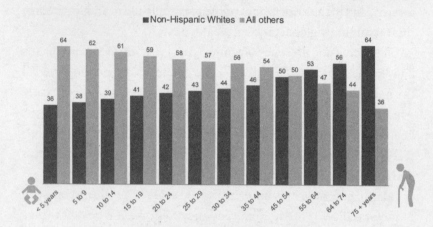

FIGURE 9.7: *Projected population of U.S. by age and ethnicity in 2050,*
assuming no change in immigration
Source: *U.S. Census, 2012 National Population Projections*

Out of all this comes a new understanding of what it means to be Hispanic, Asian, black, or Anglo in this city and nation. By now, most non-Hispanic whites in Houston recognize that the future workforce of the city will be predominantly black and Hispanic, the two groups that have been the least well served historically by the region's educational and social-service organizations. The residents of this famously anti-government, anti-tax Texas city surprised even us in their responses on the 2018 survey, when 56 percent said the public schools will need significantly more money, up from 48 percent in 2009, and when 67 percent said they were in favor of raising local taxes in order to provide universal preschool education for all children in Houston.

If the Houston community as a whole can summon the political will to make the needed investments in educational opportunities and social support systems, it will have taken a big step toward building the foundations for sustainable prosperity. And in the process, it will be making real progress toward true equality of opportunity for all American citizens and toward closing the gaps in earnings, income, and eventually in generational wealth as well.

COMING TO GRIPS WITH
THE NEW REALITIES

★

CHAPTER 10

Generational Divides in a Time of Transition

This country will not be the greatest country in the world if Houston is an example of what the entire country will be like in 2050. I won't be here, but my kids will, and I do not want to leave them a country that looks like Houston. I hate what Houston has become. The inclusion of this liberal ideology that America is here for anyone that wants it is to blame. They need to close the borders and they need to make immigrating to America an extreme privilege. Even at that, there will be many who want to change America to the America they want it to be and not the America that my ancestors have created. I am not a bigot, and I am not a hater. I am an American who wants and deserves to preserve this way of life for my kids and their kids.

—Larry W., Houston resident[80]

That's an excerpt from one of many messages that have appeared in my inbox in recent years, expressing deep concerns about Houston's burgeoning diversity. Sentiments of this sort are not surprising. No transition of this magnitude can occur without generating social conflict and feelings of anxiety and loss. Too many Americans, especially older non-Hispanic whites, and especially among the less educated, have found their lives to be profoundly disrupted by the economic engines of globalization and automation, in a country that seems to be ignoring their plight while opening its doors to foreign immigrants and paying disproportionate attention to the needs of people of color.

Tom, who retired as an oil and gas offshore mechanical engineer in 2008, lives in The Woodlands, some thirty miles north of downtown. It is in Montgomery County, one of the region's least diverse (and most Republican) areas. The Woodlands was developed by fracking pioneer George P. Mitchell in the 1970s to be an environmentally sensitive unincorporated urban township, built from East Texas timber, with a nature preserve within the municipality's limits. Mitchell's vision was for the town to be an inclusive, mixed-income, and diverse community, but Anglos today comprise close to 70 percent of the population, with a median income of more than $100,000. The natural setting is lush, and the homes are large and well separated from neighbors. Residents walk or bike in their cul-de-sacs for exercise, but to get to work, schools, or shops, you need a car.

A native of Houston, Tom shares the views of Larry W., and that was part of what pushed him to move out to The Woodlands in the first place. Things are growing tense with his son, Dave, these days. A graduate of the University of Texas at Austin, Dave is living in Houston's Midtown and working nearby for a solar energy start-up. At twenty-five, he shares a town house with three friends. Dave gave up his car after graduating, preferring the Metro light-rail or an Uber, "especially on the weekends, because then I don't have to worry about drinking," he says. When it's not pouring down rain, he walks or bikes to work.

His girlfriend, Roxanna, is Latina and Irish. She has one more year to finish her MBA at Rice's Jones Graduate School of Business, and they have been talking about moving in together. They want to live close to a rail line either in Midtown or in EaDo (East of Downtown, in the gentrifying Second and Fifth Wards); and they would like to be able to walk to restaurants, bars, and shopping.

In the seven years from 2012 to 2018, the Houston research was expanded to include surveys in Fort Bend and Montgomery Counties, the second- and third-largest counties in the metropolitan area. Fort Bend County, at 21 percent Asian, 24 percent Hispanic, 20 percent

African American, and 34 percent Anglo, is one of the most ethnically diverse counties on this planet, in sharp contrast to Montgomery County's homogenous population.

Comparing responses across the three counties, the surveys find that the respondents from Montgomery County are more inclined than those in Fort Bend or Harris Counties to reject government programs designed to reduce inequality. They are less in favor of federal health insurance to cover the medical costs of all Americans. They are more likely to believe that government is trying to do too many things that should be left to individuals and businesses, and less likely to assert that government should do more to solve our country's problems. They more often claim that people who receive welfare benefits are taking advantage of the system, and that such government handouts encourage poor people to stay poor and dependent. They are more likely to be Republican, and more anti-immigrant.

As America's baby boom rapidly ages (the seventy-six million predominantly Anglo babies, who were born between 1946 and 1964, aged fifty-six to seventy-four in 2020), the young people across the country are disproportionately non-Anglo. The new generations from all ethnic communities are more used to living in a multiethnic world; they are falling in love with each other, marrying across ethnicities, having children, and feeling increasingly at home in this multiethnic world.

The math is pretty simple. No matter how many undocumented immigrants are deported, no matter how high a wall you try to build, and even if immigration comes to a complete halt and the nation slams its doors on all refugees seeking asylum, the actuarial tables alone make it clear that no conceivable force is going to stop this city, state, or nation from becoming more Latino, more Asian, more African American, and less Anglo as the twenty-first century unfolds. The demographic transition is a done deal. Houston is America on demographic fast-forward. Where this metro area is today along the path of transformation is where all America will be within twenty-five to thirty years.

Tom voted for Trump. Dave leans toward Bernie Sanders but says he votes a straight Democratic ticket. He was vehement about opposing his father's views and about wanting to change the world for the better, but he became a little evasive when I asked how he had actually voted in the past few elections and what the experience was like.

The most powerful predictors, regardless of ethnicity, of whether or not registered voters actually make it to the polls are age and education. In Harris County, which has one of the lowest voter turnouts among all large American metropolitan areas, the discrepancy is even more pronounced. "My mom's always yelling at me to vote," Maria says of her sixty-year-old mother, who came to America with an accounting degree from Mexico. Her mother was a devout Catholic, and that's how Maria was raised. But she recently broke with her family to find a more accepting church. "My new pastor encourages people to use contraception and not to have babies they can't afford. Nobody likes abortion, but he doesn't tell people that abortion is always morally wrong. He also really encourages people to get engaged in the community and in politics and to make sure we vote."

When you look at the changing ethnic makeup not just of Houston, but of the state of Texas as a whole, and you watch the public's attitudes becoming more progressive and tolerant, it looks as if the state might soon become purple, if not solidly blue. Wendy Davis, famous for her eleven-hour filibuster to block a strict anti-abortion bill (SB5) in the Texas State Senate, observed during her failed run for governor against Greg Abbott in 2014, "Texas is not a red state; it's a nonvoting blue state."[81] There have been some close calls recently, as in Beto O'Rourke's challenge to Ted Cruz for Senate in 2018, but Texas still hasn't elected a Democrat to statewide or federal office since 1994.

"I know you guys are going to be quick to blame Houston's low voter turnout on apathy," says a recent San Francisco transplant, "but when I got to Houston I was shocked by how hard it is to get an ID, to find out when elections are being held, and even what the election is about, unless it's a national election." Having lived in New York as well, this Generation X, U.S.-born, well-educated Anglo woman continued, "In coastal states you get reminders in the mail from the Board of Elections. If you don't vote in New York or California, it's probably due to apathy, since it's impossible *not* to know when elections are being held there and what's being voted on.

"But when I moved to Texas," she continued, "for the first time in my life I had to research elections online just to get a ballot date. The only communication I've gotten was when they sent me my voter registration card. I had to keep digging to find out about candidates and propositions. After asking around, I saw that most people used League of Women Voters' information, but they didn't cover the judicial races. For that I had to subscribe to the *Houston Chronicle*.

"So I thought, *If it's this hard for me, with all my resources, then it must be practically impossible for people without these resources.* I see a huge difference in attitude about this kind of thing between those who've lived in Houston or in Texas for most of their lives, and people who have arrived here from bluer states in the past ten years."

The impact of the state's low voter turnout, which skews the electorate to the right, can look like this: During a single day in March 2019, the Texas legislature passed an anti-LGBTQ bill; they changed the execution protocol so that spiritual advisors were no longer allowed in the chamber; and they had to acknowledge the inadequacies in the state's petrochemical regulations and monitoring, after toxic emissions and serious illnesses were reported in the Ship Channel area; typically, it was clear from the legislative response that nothing significant was going to change. As one of my students asked when we met in my office, "Why do we see so much individual kindness in this city, and so much collective neglect and indifference?"

"It has a lot to do," I suggested, "with who is actually voting, whose views politicians need to care about." The gap so clearly revealed in the surveys between public opinion and politically effective opinion is about voter suppression, the impact of concentrated wealth, a relatively moribund Texas Democratic Party (at least until recently), and single-issue voters who are deeply motivated to stop specific policies, such as abortion or gay rights, or the efforts to strengthen gun laws or to find alternatives to the death penalty. But things are happening in Houston and in Texas today that might well be pointing to a different future.

★

Phyllis Frye has been a judge on Houston's Municipal Courts bench since Mayor Annise Parker, the country's first openly gay mayor of a major city, appointed her in November 2010. She became the nation's first openly transgender judge. This happened in Houston. Not San Francisco. Not New York. Not Los Angeles. In Houston, Texas.

This is also the place where, after the city council enacted the "Houston Equal Rights Ordinance," making it illegal for city agencies to discriminate on the basis of sexual orientation or gender identity, the city was forced by an organized opposition to put the ordinance on the ballot in November 2015. The motivated minority turned out in droves, and by 61 to 39 percent, Houston voters decisively rejected the ordinance that sought to expand the basic rights of gays and lesbians.

Did that vote signal a reversal among area residents in their growing opposition, as seen in the surveys, to discrimination against homosexuals and transgendered persons? Or was the election skewed by a much higher voter turnout among those who were the most motivated by religious conviction to go to the polls on this single issue, and above all by the framing of the proposition as a "bathroom ordinance" that would have allowed "gender-confused" men to enter women's restrooms?

Three months after that decisive electoral defeat of the proposition, the 2016 survey asked city residents how important they thought it was for Houston to pass an Equal Rights Ordinance that would protect people from discrimination. Fully 70 percent said that enacting such an ordinance was very important, another 16 percent said somewhat important, and just 14 percent thought it was not very or not at all important. Clearly, it would be a mistake to infer that the actual votes on propositions of this sort are faithful reflections of the policy preferences of the population as a whole.

The loudest voices in the media and in the Texas legislature are generally anti-gay, anti-immigrant, and pro-death penalty, even though most Americans (and most Houstonians), when interviewed in the privacy of their homes, take decidedly more progressive positions on these and other issues. The political rhetoric may be anti-immigrant, but members of the general public have clearly been growing more comfortable over the years with the ethnic and cultural diversity of their communities.

The election of Donald Trump in November 2016 gave powerful evidence of the social and political fissures that divide Americans along the lines of geography, race, income, education, gender, and religion. The most critical division of all, laid bare in that presidential election, is between those who are feeling okay in the new economy, in a position to benefit from the processes of globalization and automation, and those who have not yet found their place. Some Americans are coping well in the face of the economic and demographic transformations; others like Tom and Larry W., not so much.

Houston has the dubious distinction of being one of the most segregated cities in America, but more so by income than by ethnicity. Americans generally prefer to live in neighborhoods made up of

"PLUs" (people like us), and some are genuinely discomfited when having to share public spaces with diverse others. "You really take the light-rail?" Tom asked his son, Dave, his voice tinged with concern about the number of homeless and low-income riders he envisioned. Unlike in New York, where the subway mixes all ethnic and socioeconomic groups, Houston has never had that kind of democratization of public spaces, and many area residents continue to resist such mixing.

As area residents continue to feel more comfortable with Houston's diversity, and as most will have no more than one or two children, this will further reinforce their growing preference for smaller homes and more walkable urban living. Houston's developers are beginning to respond to the changing demands, building more highrise, multifamily structures, and developing more transit-oriented communities—not just in downtown Houston but also in the densifying town centers that are sprouting up throughout this far-flung multicentered metropolitan region.

In this respect as well, Houston is reinventing itself in response to the new realities of life in the twenty-first century. "Yes," says Bill Fulton, the Kinder Institute's director and an expert on urban development. "It's happening, to a degree. But if you're in Town and Country," he says, referring to an open-air, walkable, mixed-use development where I-10 and Beltway 8 intersect on the far west side of town, "you have to drive across the street to get to a grocery store, a clothing store, or a school because you're trapped by one of the widest and busiest highways in America.

"The problem is that Houston does walkability through the lens of a car-obsessed culture," Bill continues. "Because I have some vision problems, I much prefer to live in a walkable neighborhood and near public transportation. So I'm in Midtown near the Metro line. But have you ever tried to cross Travis, or Milam, or Elgin during rush hour? Cars are doing sixty trying to connect to US 59 or I-45 to get out to the suburbs. Even with all the lights and crosswalks, drivers show little respect for the rights of pedestrians. Houston has more bicycle and pedestrian fatalities than any other big city in America. We are creating density without urbanism," he concludes, "and we still haven't figured out how to integrate walkability into this sprawling, car-dependent metropolis."

★

During the year 2014, nearly fifty thousand unaccompanied children, mostly from Central America, arrived at the U.S. southern border seeking asylum. They had been sent off alone by their parents to escape from the death threats of the gangs, hoping the United States would grant them asylum and help them find a better life. The sheer numbers overwhelmed the Obama administration.[82]

I wondered at the time if the rest of the nation noticed which of the states experienced the most virulent protests against the entry of the refugee children, and in which were volunteers showing up in the largest numbers to help care for them. Of the nearly forty-three thousand unaccompanied children who were arrested at the Texas border that year, only a few thousand showed up in California. National outlets broadcast multiple images of Anglos in the state blocking buses full of desperate children. White protesters were holding signs reading GO HOME, STOP ILLEGAL IMMIGRATION, and ILLEGALS OUT. The protests were not happening in South Texas or in Houston where most of the kids ended up. They were concentrated in Southern California, just north of San Diego, where protesters were blocking the children's access to a border patrol station.[83]

If views such as those expressed by Larry W. and Tom are widely held in the cities most directly undergoing the demographic shifts, the Houston surveys would find that the region's burgeoning diversity is making area residents more fearful and angry. But drill down into the attitudes of representative samples of Harris

County residents, follow the changes in their views over time, and a different, more complex, and more hopeful picture emerges. The thirty-eight years of Houston surveys reveal a general public that, albeit gradually and inconsistently, is clearly growing more optimistic about the impact of the new immigration, and are more at ease with the ongoing changes.

On virtually every relevant measure of attitudes and beliefs, Harris County Anglos have been expressing more comfort with the region's burgeoning diversity and more support for the new immigration. While these more open and tolerant views are tempered by reservations and contradictions and are sharply divided by age and education, the strong early concerns about the impact of undocumented immigrants in the region are fading rapidly. For example, the proportion of U.S.-born Anglos who said they were in favor of granting illegal immigrants a path to legal citizenship if they speak English and have no criminal record grew from 56 percent in 2010 and 60 percent in 2012 to 65 percent in 2016 and to 71 percent in the 2019 survey, two full years after implementation of the Trump administration's anti-immigration policies and rhetoric.

Area residents are also increasingly rejecting the calls to restrict immigration from Muslim countries and to turn away refugees seeking asylum in America. In the 2016 survey, 64 percent agreed that refugees who are in danger in their home countries because of their beliefs or their ethnicity should always be welcome in Houston. Support for that view increased further to 75 percent in 2018.

No matter how the questions about immigration are worded, the surveys show that attitudes expressed by non-Hispanic whites have become markedly more favorable over the years. The proportion of U.S.-born Anglo respondents who believed that immigrants generally contribute more to the American economy than they take grew from 30 percent in 1994 to 48 percent in 2018. The numbers asserting that the increasing immigration into this country today mostly strengthens, rather than threatens, American culture grew from 33 percent in 1997 to 49 percent in the 2019 survey. The percentage of U.S.-born Anglos who thought that Houston's diversity will eventually become a source of great strength for the city, rather than a growing problem, increased from 59 percent in 1998 to 70 percent in 2018.

The fear of being overwhelmed by a continuing "invasion" of undocumented immigrants has dissipated as the actual net number of undocumented immigrants has declined precipitously in the past several years. More recently, there have been large numbers of refugees, predominantly mothers and children, fleeing terrible conditions and desperately trying to make their way to America seeking asylum, but far fewer undocumented immigrants are being apprehended by the border patrol.

★

"My mom has already moved back," Maria confirms when I ask if she's worried about her mother-in-law's undocumented status. "And she figures if they want to deport her it's not a big deal. Our family still has homes in Mexico. And while here my mom cleans other people's houses; over there, she has people who clean hers."

The many years of Houston surveys provide a rare opportunity to ask more precisely why it is that Anglo attitudes have been changing. We can track the views of the baby boom generation, whose members were interviewed with identical survey questions when they were in their prime working years during the 1990s and 2000s, and on into middle age and into their seventies in the more recent surveys. The data can tell us whether minds have actually changed within this generation during the years since the questions were first asked in the early 1990s. We can also compare the answers given to these identical questions by members of three successive generations of

Anglo Houstonians, when all three were twenty-five to thirty-five years old. Over the course of the surveys, we can determine whether people are actually changing their minds over time, or whether the changes in attitude are primarily a consequence of generational replacement.[84]

Figure 10.1 shows the attitudes expressed in four different time periods by members of the same cohort of Anglo respondents, all baby boomers born between 1946 and 1964. The surveys find little change over time on these questions. Members of the baby boom generation were giving much the same answers when the questions were asked in the mid-1990s, in the early and mid-2000s, and in the most recent years (2012 to 2018). Across the twenty-five years, virtually identical percentages have agreed on two of the three questions—whether immigration strengthens or threatens American culture, and whether immigrants are contributing more to the American economy than they take or taking more than they contribute.

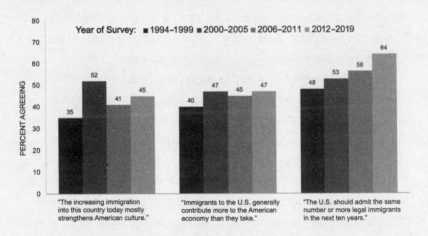

FIGURE 10.1: *Immigration attitudes in four successive periods, among Anglo baby boomers (born 1946-1964)*

On the third question, however, when asked about the number of legal immigrants the U.S. should admit in the next ten years compared to the past ten years, the respondents were clearly calling for less restrictive policies in the more recent surveys, as the actual numbers of new immigrants coming to America have continued to decline. The percentage of Anglo boomers urging the United States to admit the same number (or more) legal immigrants in the next ten years as were admitted in the last ten years grew systematically from 48 percent when the question was first asked in the 1990s, to 53 and 56 percent in the first decade of the twenty-first century, and to 64 percent in the 2019 survey.

Immigration has slowed in recent years, and as the baby boom generation retires with fewer young Americans available to replace them, many low-skilled jobs as well as high-tech professional positions need more qualified workers. Stan Marek has been warning anyone who will listen that the impending shortage of skilled workers will cause construction costs in America to increase dramatically.

Meanwhile, Figure 10.2 makes it clear that on all three of these questions, the dominant force shaping the more welcoming attitudes is generational succession. The chart compares the answers given by the three cohorts when all three were aged twenty-five to thirty-five: More than two-thirds (67 percent) of the Anglo millennials, born after 1980, asserted that immigration mostly strengthens, rather than threatens, American culture. That view was held by just 52 percent of the Gen Xers and by 50 percent of the baby boomers when they were the same age.

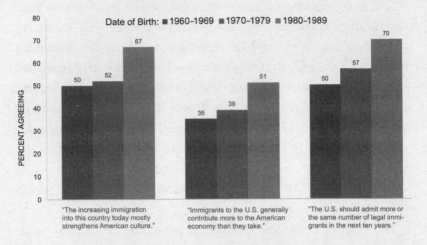

FIGURE 10.2: *Attitudes toward immigration among three cohorts of Harris County Anglos, all aged twenty-five to thirty-five*

Similarly, more than half of the millennials but only a third of the boomers believed that immigrants contribute more to the economy than they take. Fully 70 percent of the youngest group of Anglo adults called on the United States to admit more or the same number of legal immigrants in the next ten years as were admitted in the last ten years, a view expressed by just half of the respondents who were born in the 1960s.

This is what it means to be living in a time of dramatic social change. Today's older Anglos grew up in the America of the 1960s and 1970s; that was a profoundly different era from the 1990s and 2000s, when the younger generations were coming of age. Biography intersects with history to shape the way people experience the world: One of the most powerful predictors of comfort with new realities during a time of profound transition is in the nature of the particular historical period in which the respondents came of age.

Figure 10.3 provides further confirmation of this underlying dynamic. Harris County residents are falling in love across ethnic lines at a rate that accelerates with each generation. Younger Americans of all ethnicities across most of the country have been growing up in a world where ethnic diversity is part of their lived experience and close intergroup relationships are increasingly common. In most of America's major metro regions, the world of the 2000s and 2010s was a place of thriving interethnic friendships and increasing rates of intermarriage.

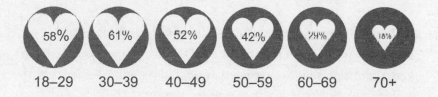

"Have you ever been in a romantic relationship
with someone who was not Anglo?"
(Percent saying, "Yes, I have":)

58%   61%   52%   42%   29%   18%

18–29   30–39   40–49   50–59   60–69   70+

FIGURE 10.3: *Interethnic romantic relationships by age
among Anglos (2007, 2011, 2014, 2016, and 2018)*

There is a well-known law of human nature that states, in essence: "What I am familiar with feels right and natural. What I'm unfamiliar with feels unnatural and somehow not quite right." The more recent generations of non-Hispanic whites take for granted what earlier generations still find difficult to accept. The ongoing processes of generational succession will surely help to smooth the unstoppable transition as this city and nation move inexorably into the multiethnic world of the twenty-first century.

★

The generational shifts are just as evident in Houston's African American community as they are among non-Hispanic whites: The data suggest that younger African Americans are also growing more comfortable with Houston's burgeoning diversity and they are less convinced that racism is a definitive barrier to their ability to succeed in America.

One of Dave's roommates is a performer in musical theater. A fourth-generation Houstonian, Dawn is a young African American woman, the great-granddaughter of a prominent lawyer who had been active in the civil rights movement. "I see being black as an advantage," she says when I ask her about her experience with racism. "Sometimes it makes people get out of my way. And that's okay with me."

"Not so fast," says her uncle Joe, a middle-school science teacher. We were gathered in the living room of the patriarchal home, all four generations present for a conversation about their experience with racism and discrimination across the decades. "The kids are in the arts and they don't experience it as much. But they also don't always recognize it when it happens."

"Yeah, you made my drama teacher cry when I was in a school play," says Dawn, rolling her eyes.

"Well from where I sat, he had the white kids with all the lines and the best songs, the Latino and black kids in supporting roles and doing the dance interludes, and here's Dawn with the best voice of everyone and she's got one line. One line! Not even a song! How could you not see the typecasting? The kids of her generation just don't see this kind of racism, even when it's in their face like this was."

Rachel, Dawn's sister, gathers snacks for her three-year-old in the kitchen. George, the tattooed Anglo artist husband and father of the child, takes over so she can join the conversation. She's headed out to rehearsal for a play to be presented in an EaDo theater. "I don't see discrimination as getting in the way of what I want to do. Sure, prejudice is out there, especially from those who haven't been around a lot of black people, but it doesn't stop me. I like being able to show them that we are not what they think we are. The arts are more open and that's why I stay in the field.

"My friends," Rachel continues, "talk about how things are getting worse for black people. But when you look at what my grandparents went through, how they lived, we are not talking about the same thing. In the arts you don't hear so many complaints about feeling oppressed."

"The harder thing," interjects Dawn, "is black people thinking we aren't black enough or that we are too bougie. But there are different ways to be black. Just because I'm interested in nerdy things doesn't negate my blackness. Just because Disney made me want to sing and I loved *The Great Mouse Detective* and *The Little Mermaid . . .*"

"Oh Lord, you played that video over and over again," Joe laughs, and the whole room erupts at the memory of how sick of it the adults became.

"And just because I'm educated and speak well," Dawn continues, "doesn't mean I'm not black."

*

Figure 10.4 asks the same question of African Americans as we asked of Anglos, inquiring if they had ever been in a romantic relationship with someone who was not of their ethnicity. Just 18 percent of the African American respondents who were aged seventy or older said that they had indeed been in a relationship of that sort. This was the case for 26 percent of those in their sixties, 35 percent among those aged fifty to fifty-nine, and slightly more than half of the respondents aged thirty to forty-nine. More than two-thirds (67 percent) of the youngest respondents, those aged eighteen to twenty-nine, said that they had indeed been in a romantic relationship with someone who was not African American.

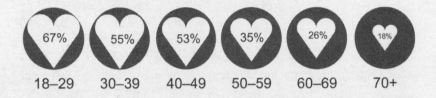

"Have you ever been in a romantic relationship with someone who was not African-American?"
(Percent saying, "Yes I have":)

67% 18–29 55% 30–39 53% 40–49 35% 50–59 26% 60–69 18% 70+

FIGURE 10.4: *Interethnic romantic relationships by age among blacks (2007, 2011, 2014, 2016, and 2018)*

Figure 10.5 digs deeper into these generational shifts by comparing four different age groups of African American respondents on questions about their perceptions of discrimination and the extent of equal opportunity in America today. Clear majorities at all ages continue to reject the suggestion that blacks and whites now have equal chances to succeed in America, but the relationship with age is also clear and consistent. The proportion who believed, for example, that blacks and other minorities have the same opportunities as whites increased from just 25 percent for the African Americans who were sixty and older to 43 percent among those under the age of thirty.

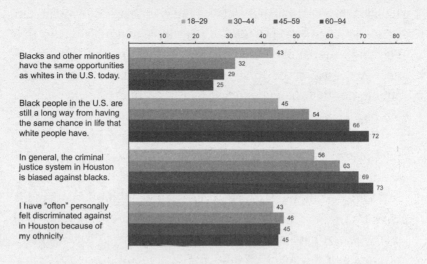

FIGURE 10.5: *Perceived discrimination by age among blacks (1999-2019, combined)*

Similarly, in alternating years, the survey participants were asked whether they agreed or disagreed that blacks are still a long way from having the same chance in life that white people have. Agreement with this assertion dropped from 72 percent among the oldest respondents to 45 percent among those aged eighteen to twenty-nine, the generation that came of age during Barack Obama's eight years in office. The same pattern was found when the respondents were asked if they thought the criminal justice system in Houston is biased in favor of blacks, biased against blacks, or generally gives blacks fair treatment. The proportions believing the system is biased against blacks dropped from 73 and 69 percent for those aged forty-five and older, to 63 and 56 percent for the younger respondents.

Younger blacks may be more optimistic about their life chances than older African Americans, but they are still much more sensitive than non-blacks to the continuing racial discrimination in America.

The black/white pay gap is as large today as it was during the Jim Crow era; African Americans in 2017 were making seventy-five cents on the dollar compared to whites.[85] In 2000, they were making eighty cents on the dollar. In this growing economy, the gap is widening, and it's happening faster in Texas than elsewhere in the country:

"The wealth gap among African Americans is even more serious," John Guess of HMAAC reminds me. "We don't have intergenerational wealth. Until we have more opportunities to build that kind of long-term success in families, the gap will keep widening." Many of his generation believe the attitudes of the millennials are naive and will change as they age. I think about Sandra Bland and Carl Hampton, and wonder if the police brutality in Houston during the 1970s and '80s is really a thing of the past.

Younger African Americans may believe that racial barriers are less impenetrable today, but that does not mean that they are also more likely than their elders to assert that discrimination has actually ended or that racist assumptions and stereotypes have disappeared. Blacks of all ages continue to run into explicit racism in their random encounters on streets, shops, and workplaces, or in interactions with the police. Both Denise Hamilton and the police sergeant's son feared for their lives during traffic stops.

The last item in Figure 10.5 indicates that the youngest African American adults in the Houston surveys are just as likely as those aged sixty and older (at 45 and 43 percent) to report that they have very often or fairly often felt discriminated against in Houston, even as younger blacks have also come to believe that the structural barriers of racism and discrimination are becoming less determinative in shaping the opportunities for success in America today. Moreover, wealthy blacks report experiencing just as much discrimination as do the least-affluent African Americans.

★

In each successive survey since 1992, we have asked respondents for their overall evaluation of the state of race and ethnic relations in the Houston area. There were plenty of ups and downs in these evaluations, but their overall direction is unmistakable. Across the last twenty-five years of surveys, and among all three U.S.-born ethnic communities, the overall evaluations have consistently grown more positive, and we are seeing friendships cross ethnic lines at an increasing rate. As usual, age is a key factor.

The main generational divide among African Americans has to do with whether or not they see racism as an obstacle that prevents success. For Anglos it is comfort with diversity and attitudes toward immigration. For Latinos the main divide is between U.S.-born and foreign-born in their friendships across the ethnic communities; and the same is true for Asians: the U.S.-born are far more likely than the immigrants to have close interethnic friendships. And it's in light of these shifts that the hope for a less polarized Houston and America emerges.

Beneath the gridlock of American politics and obscured by the overheated rhetoric in mainstream culture, individuals of all ages have been working quietly and effectively to develop more just and inclusive communities. Houston-area residents, at the forefront of these transformations, are called on to build something that has never existed before in human history—a truly successful, equitable, inclusive, and united multiethnic society, positioned for prosperity in the global, knowledge-based economy of the twenty-first century. The overall improvements in intergroup attitudes and the generational shifts the surveys reveal provide reasons to hope that those efforts might yet succeed.

"Yes, Steve, I know you really believe this," says Jenifer Bratter, my colleague in Rice's sociology department. "But I'm just not sure that the multiethnic inclusiveness you envision is going to hold true." Jenifer is a millennial. She has one black and one Anglo parent, and she argues that those of her generation, and even more so the members of the next generation (Gen Z), aren't identifying anymore with one particular race. "There is a whole new multiethnic category that's emerging." And though America's most diverse generation may not see the same ethnic categories that baby boomer sociologists and demographers use every day, it doesn't, according to Jenifer, mean that the millennials will be the architects of a less polarized and more inclusive America.

"Baby boomers were the big protestors and they were supposed to be solving the problems of racism and segregation, remember?" Jenifer prods during one of our Kinder Institute breakfast discussions at Rice. "They were busy integrating neighborhoods and schools. But when it came time for them to have kids and for those kids to start school, they all moved out to Katy and Sugar Land where the schools are whiter and better. When it comes time for millennials to make those decisions and for Gen Z as well, where will diversity be on their list of priorities? Will they choose education and homogeneity instead of multiethnic diversity? We don't know the answer to that yet."

Americans still generally live in relatively homogeneous silos, and even more so in Houston, one of the most economically segregated cities in America. In addition, as Nobel Prize–winning economist Joseph Stiglitz has shown,[86] as have so many others,[87] the younger generation will have a harder time succeeding economically compared to the baby boomers, who came of age during the broad-based affluence of the postwar era. The economy today is setting young people up not for the American Dream of intergenerational mobility, but for an American Plateau at best, or even a downhill slide, depending on whether or not they have successful and well-educated parents who can support them in school, or are living in a society that is prepared to invest significantly in their skills.

The greatest challenge facing our cities lies not in overcoming the fairly modest ethnic differences in attitudes and beliefs showing up in the surveys; it has to do instead with the educational and class divides that so profoundly constrict the life chances of the less-fortunate members of all ethnic communities. The only way to build a successful and equitable multiethnic society is to ensure that all the members of the rising generation in all of our communities have a reasonable chance to acquire the educational credentials and technical skills that today's economy requires.

CHAPTER 11

The New Importance of Quality of Place

The ideological thrust in Houston in the twentieth century has been anti-government, anti-regulation, anti-planning, anti-taxes, anti-anything that seemed to represent, in fact or fantasy, an expansion of the public sector or a limitation on the economic prerogatives and activities of the city's business community.

—Robert Fisher[88]

The Houston 2012 Foundation went to the U.S. Olympic Committee in 2002 with the perfect bid to host the 2012 games. They had state-of-the-art venues, new hotels, internationally recognized restaurants, and world-class museums. There were pristine sports facilities, along with plans to turn the Astrodome into the largest fully enclosed, fully air-conditioned track-and-field venue on the planet, and plenty of money to back the effort. The city's carefully developed plans called for magnificent new hotels and restaurants, and the first light-rail line linking downtown Houston to a four-hundred-million-dollar brand-new sports complex (at what is now Reliant Park). They had, according to the U.S. Olympic Committee, the most attractive bid of any of the other American cities still in the running—better offerings than New York, Los Angeles, San Francisco, or Washington, DC. They had the best collection of physical assets. The best plans. The tightest logistics.

The Foundation spent five years getting the plans together, and by the 2002 deadline for submission, their proposal was tight as a drum.

Though San Francisco was a logistical and political mess and New York would be a traffic-and-infrastructure nightmare, those two cities made the Committee's final cut. Houston received not a single vote. "Houston is big, admittedly super-sized in a Texas-Astrodome-LBJ kind of way. And according to those involved in the Olympic hosting competition, it had the most technically and financially sound bid among the municipal hopefuls. It only had one problem. It's Houston," read an article in the *San Francisco Chronicle*.

Houston Chronicle columnist Fran Blinebury quoted a member of the Olympic Committee's task force who said, "If it was just a matter of who we thought could organize the best-run games, Houston would probably win it easy . . . But you've got to consider that Paris is coming at you with the Eiffel freaking Tower and London with Big bleeping Ben. What is the symbol of Houston that we sell to the world? Is it a cowboy town? Is it the space city?

"They can crunch the numbers, spin the truth, and do more recounting of the votes than the state of Florida, and it always comes back to one point," Blinebury continued. "Image is everything. In the end, the ten deciding members of the USOC task force voted with their hearts and their digital cameras instead of their heads." And who wouldn't? The reality Houstonians didn't want to face in 2002 is that the city was clogged by freeways, peppered with ugly billboards, and had never put much thought into building beautiful public spaces. Nobody in their right mind would pick a city like Houston over Paris, San Francisco, or New York. Since that experience, Houstonians have spent a lot of time and money to improve the product, and they have tried to identify an iconic image they could sell at least to themselves, if not yet to the rest of the world.

Space City. Bayou City. Houston Proud. Houston Is Hot. Houston: So Much More to Explore. Enron City (when that was a good thing). The Energy Capital. Houston: The Real Texas. Expect the Unexpected. Nobody has really figured out how to describe what Houston is, not even the people who live here. Outside of Houston, the image has to do with the big, big hair and the big diamonds (that's Dallas, by the way), oil wells in backyards, the Houston Livestock Show and Rodeo (Houston has the biggest monthlong event in the nation, but has no actual cowboy history), and barbecue. But nobody's been able to capture the city in a marketing campaign or slogan.

In 2004, local communications firm ttweak went with the truth: HoustonItsWorthIt.com. The site opens with rapid-fire reminders of Houston's less-endearing features—the heat; the humidity; the flying cockroaches; the hurricanes and flooding; the traffic; the nonstop construction; the potholes; the billboards; the sprawl; the refineries; the pollen; the air pollution; the no hills or mountains—before arriving at the confident claim: "Houston. It's Worth It."

Area residents were invited to post their comments. Thousands responded, often with infectious tongue-in-cheek humor and descriptions of the unexpected silver linings they insisted might yet be found amid all the unattractive features. They wrote about Houston's numerous restaurants, with their panoply of cuisines in a city of burgeoning diversity. They pointed to the friendliness and welcoming spirit of the people, the low cost of housing, the extraordinary theater and museum districts, the impressive skyline, the birding and recreational areas surrounding the city, and the nearby beaches for sailing and fishing—though as one inner-loop resident interviewed by CultureMap.com asserted, "Galveston is great as long as you don't go in the water."

Another one of the comments read: "If Houston were a dog, she'd be a mutt with three legs, one bad eye, fleas the size of Corn Nuts, and buck teeth. Despite all that, she'd be the best dog you'd ever know." You often hear residents saying things like, "It's a nice place to live, but I wouldn't want to visit." And indeed, the surveys find that despite all the problems, people overwhelmingly do seem to like living in Houston. "I never expected to stay," Mandy Kao reminds me. "My whole family moved back to Hong Kong, even some of them that moved to

Vancouver before the handover to China in 1997. It would be easy for me to join them. But it's been such a good place to raise my kids."

John Mendelsohn, MD, left his post as chair of the department of medicine at Sloan Kettering in 1996 to take over as president of MD Anderson Cancer Center. He had a plum position at one of the world's best cancer centers in one of the world's greatest cities. But he loved the idea of building something new, in a place that encouraged thinking outside the box. "You don't get pigeonholed so easily here," he said. "You can come to Houston and reinvent yourself."

Denise Hamilton, who had been a backup singer in Los Angeles for Stevie Wonder and came to Houston to publish a magazine, said the same thing in talking about her move to the tech industry and the creation of her own company, WatchHerWork. "You're not trapped by your résumé. You are not defined by your past," she says. Being able to reinvent her career in Houston has helped her develop a national platform.

★

Houston may not be able to sell itself easily to the outside world, but the surveys continue to show that Houstonians themselves are clear in saying they wouldn't want to live anywhere else; they consistently give high ratings to life in the Houston area. This has been true across race, class, and generations for all the years of the surveys. It was even true during and after the oil bust. In the midst of the oil-boom collapse (1982–1987), Houston's population not only didn't shrink, it continued to grow, albeit at a slower pace, until things picked back up again in the early 1990s.

The survey participants readily complain (in part because we invite them to) about traffic, crime, pollution, and other inadequate city services (not to mention the hot summers, the no mountains, and the flying cockroaches!). But when asked how they would rate the Houston area in general as a place to live, decisively and increasingly (up from 71 percent in 2006 to 77 percent in 2018), area residents give ratings of *excellent* or *good*. Similarly, when the respondents were asked to compare Houston to most other metropolitan areas in the country, 78 percent in 2005 thought this region was a slightly better or a much better place in which to live; that favorable assessment grew to 90 percent in the 2013 survey, the last time the question was asked.

It's all well and good for Houstonians to love their city, and generations of families have tended to stay close to home. "Even if they go away to school," says Mike Treviño, "you see them coming back to give back. That's a Houston thing." But it's not so clearly the case anymore with today's global corporations. Jesse Jones and the Suite 8F Crowd operated from the premise that they could only succeed if Houston succeeded. Though 40 percent of the U.S. petrochemical industry is in Houston, most of Houston's oil and gas companies don't invest in the city in the same way previous generations did. "I still have them at the table," insists Bob Harvey, president of the Greater Houston Partnership. "And when I talk to people from other Chambers of Commerce around the country, they are surprised that we've kept senior corporate officers engaged."

Though Houston calls itself America's energy capital, "The city doesn't actually produce the oil anymore," economist Bill Gilmer reminds me. "Refining happens here." But it's a big enough chunk to be a major force in the overall U.S. economy. If all goes well with petrochem in Houston, it's a boon to the rest of America. Should what happens around the Ship Channel suddenly collapse, that would bring the whole country down with it.

"It's an employment cluster, like Silicon Valley is for digital, and Detroit was for cars. If you want to do oil and gas, you need to be in Houston." But Gilmer made the point that you can go anywhere else for just about everything else. "There are national companies that originated in Houston, like Continental Airlines [now merged with

United], AIG, Sysco, Waste Management, Men's Wearhouse, that are all trying to pull talent in from outside the state. And they are having a hard time attracting the best."

"When Houston had a strong economy while the rest of the country was struggling," says Greater Houston Partnership's vice president for research Patrick Jankowski, "then it was easy to draw talent from other states. But Houston's economy hasn't been countercyclical since the early 1980s." If people outside Houston continue to think the city is not only flat and hot for much of the year, but also ugly and dangerously polluted, few will choose to move here. That realization has dogged Houston from its beginnings, pushing it to make significant improvements in its public spaces and quality-of-life attributes.

★

The rejection of the Olympic bid ("Houston Is Ugly!" ran the headlines) made the national news on that day in 2002. That experience sparked a renewed determination among local business leaders, city officials, and philanthropists to make the additional investments that would be needed to beautify and modernize the city.

When Houston once again sought the national spotlight just two years later, this time as host to the 2004 Super Bowl, Hermann Park (Houston's Central Park) was undergoing a thirty-million-dollar renovation and the city's first light-rail line was up and running. That same year, construction began on "Discovery Green," a celebrated twelve-acre park in the heart of downtown Houston. By 2017, when the city once again hosted the Super Bowl, it was widely praised for its many fine restaurants, its vibrant art scene, its welcoming and diverse population, its abundant parks and green spaces, its public art exhibits, and its historical-preservation projects. Houston's effort to enhance its attractiveness had roots in a proposal made more than one hundred years earlier.

It was a disciple of the great landscape architect, Frederick Law Olmsted, the architect of New York's Central Park and San Francisco's Golden Gate Park, who would try in 1913 to awaken Houston to its need for public parks and to show the nascent parks commission that there was a ready-made natural network that could be put to use. Arthur Comey, Harvard professor and city planner, had been commissioned to draw up a plan for Houston. But instead of acting on his vision, the Parks Board filed it away, and then cemented over the arteries of bayous that could have turned Houston into a much more beautiful and greener city. Nearly a hundred years later, Comey's plan was unearthed and put into practice by a newly energized generation of architects and planners.

"This is the map of Houston we are used to seeing" (Figure 11.1), says award-winning architect Tom Bacon, in a Lionstone Investments conference room downtown. Dressed in jeans, a crisp white shirt, and black sport coat, Bacon turns on his computer to show a map of the concentric highways that ring the city. He's tall and slim, and he exudes an almost childlike enthusiasm. The Georgia native has a Southern lilt but not a full-on drawl, and speaks as fast as a New Yorker.

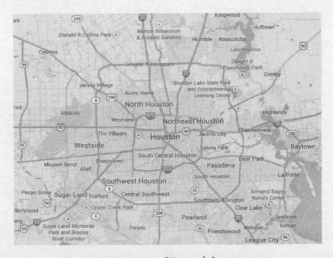

FIGURE 11.1: *A map of Houston's freeway system*
Source: Google.com, *"Map of Houston's Freeways"*

"Here's the map I've been using [Figure 11.2]. We have been so stuck on how the highways have made the city, that we have trouble seeing the way nature actually defines the terrain. We ignored it for a hundred years." What Tom showed me instead looked like a bulging artery in the east of the city, emanating out to the west in a fan of veins. To the southeast was Galveston Bay, wide and deep. Due east is the narrow Ship Channel, the dredged bayou that established Houston as the nation's second-busiest port, pouring out of Buffalo Bayou and its tributaries, spreading west as tentacles of water embrace all parts of the city, darting beyond the circular infrastructure of freeways that, try as they might, would never be able to contain it.

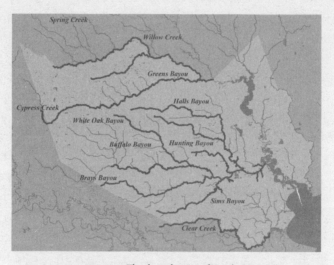

FIGURE 11.2: *The eleven bayous of Harris County*
Source: Google.com, "Map of Houston's Bayous"

The bayous, or "BI-yohs" as some locals call them, had always been treated as an afterthought or an inconvenience. They rise during storms and overflow their banks, flooding homes, streets, cars, and hospitals. They are both a source of fresh water and a conduit for sewage. The Army Corps of Engineers lined them with cement in the 1960s and 1970s and tried to straighten them out as much as possible; they became a smelly waste-drainage system, and remained that way until the sewage moratorium in the 1970s halted all new construction. When Bacon was tapped in 2004 by Mayor White to head the Parks Board, it was in the bayous and in Comey's vision as outlined in his 1913 report that Tom found the answer to building Houston's green space.

Here's what Comey wrote in 1913:

"[T]he backbone of a park system for Houston will naturally be its bayou or creek valleys, which readily lend themselves to parking and cannot so advantageously be used for any other purpose. These valleys intersect the city and surrounding country in such a way as to furnish opportunity for parks of unusual value within a comparatively short distance of most of the residential areas, including those of the future as well as the present. The normal type of bayou park will include a roadway as a boundary and parkway drive on the crest of the valley slope on either side, walks on the slope, and occasional lawns and playfields among the wooded areas. All the bayous should be parked except where utilized for commerce. . . . The bayous are natural parks already. Tree-growth and grass are good even in populous sections; the valleys include the only scenery with slopes, while occasional narrow bends furnish level playfields. . . . The long, narrow strips along the bayous will serve many communities; continuous walks can be laid out in naturalistic landscape; parkway drives along the banks of the bayou are capable of unusually park-like treatment. . . . The effect on land values and tax returns is equally beneficial, as bayous have little value under private control, and depreciate surrounding property through their poor development, but as parks they greatly enhance the value of their frontage and the neighborhood in general."[89]

★

On November 6, 2012, Houston voters overwhelmingly approved a bond referendum proposed by the Houston Parks Board that would provide one hundred million dollars in public money, to be matched by $130 million in private donations, to transform three thousand acres along Houston's bayous into more miles of linear parks than can be found in any other city in America. The Bayou Greenways 2020 Initiative is in the process of building 150 miles of hike and bike trails along the city's nine major bayous, creating additional green space and recreational venues in almost every neighborhood in the city. When the project is completed, 60 percent of all City of Houston residents will live within a mile and a half of a bayou trail, and Houston will be one of the greenest cities in America. A project of this sort, focused on the beautification of Houston's public spaces, would never have been pursued in the Houston of twenty years ago.

"You don't understand what we've done until you see it from the air," Bacon continues. "You get up in a helicopter—we take planners from other cities up there all the time—and it's a sea of green everywhere. It's not until you see it from above that you really understand how vast it is."

"Yes," I add, as I often do, "the greater Houston metro area covers almost the same geographical space as the entire state of Massachusetts. But," I hesitate to dampen Tom's excitement, "the Bayou Greenways 2020 Initiative isn't really going to be finished by 2020, is it?" We'd been hearing about this plan for many years and it didn't seem to be making that much progress. But Houston is nothing if not surprising.

"We might be a year late," he replied, "but that's it. The Greenways Initiative is just about done. We will have those 150 miles of linear parks along the major bayous, and six in ten city residents, in every neighborhood, across all levels of socioeconomic status, will be within walking distance of a bayou trail. We have been connecting the neighborhoods and parks by bridges; we've created gathering spots, and we've launched campaigns to encourage people to meet each other over food, outdoor concerts, kayaking, biking, hiking, and public gardens. Now we're looking at a new, more expansive project, called Beyond the Bayous. But that's for another conversation."

Some of Houston's earlier attempts at beautifying the city smack a bit of the Allen brothers' bait and switch. As you leave Bush Intercontinental, for example, you will see a lushly planted boulevard that stretches all the way east to the north/south artery, US 59. If you decide to pass up Hardy Toll Road to take the locals' route toward downtown, the aesthetics change. You will be greeted by ugly billboards, chain restaurants and stores, and by some of the least-attractive images to be found along any of America's highways.

While many Houstonians are pushing for walkable urbanism, pedestrians are still unexpected phenomena in Houston. Montrose, a cozy and chic neighborhood just north of the museum district, is advertised as well suited for walking. But sidewalks are upended by tree roots, and pedestrians too often need to cross the street when a sidewalk ends on one side and picks up on the other.

Though new developments in the River Oaks area are touted for their proximity to restaurants and shops, a friend described the challenge of walking four blocks to nearby Arnaldo's: "Brand-new sidewalks were already broken, and it took forever to cross Westheimer. Though there is a pedestrian crossing with a light, but it was new, and most cars didn't respect it even when it was red. We had to just wait for a break in the traffic." The effort to build safe "complete" streets, to slow the cars and trucks and invite walking and biking, will not be easy to accomplish in a city that through most of its history has been so totally dependent on the automobile. And for the time being, Houston is still the country's deadliest big city for pedestrians and cyclists.

During the 1980s and '90s, cities around the country and around the world tripped over each other offering incentives for relocation as many of Houston's most skilled individuals left for more robust and more attractive regions, where better school systems turned out more of the well-educated workforce that was going to be needed in the new economy. "It's hard to recruit people in robotics and digital technology to the oil industry in Houston," Patrick Jankowski reminds me when I ask the Greater Houston Partnership's senior vice president why recruitment has been so difficult. "Remember," he continues, "if digital specialists come to work in oil production in Texas, they will be sent out to the desert to live in a trailer. Silicon Valley in California, or Silicon Alley in New York or Austin or DC, where they can work in a comfortable office and live in what's considered to be a cool city, are going to be more attractive."

The answer to the question of how much longer oil and gas can sustain the Houston economy depends on your point of view. Some believe it will be forty to fifty years before the world will have moved decisively beyond fossil fuels. "I think there are about twenty to thirty years left," says Jim Hackett, former CEO of the exploration giant Anadarko. "And then the alternatives will kick in." Mike Treviño tends to agree. "And when that happens, Houston will be left in the dust. As companies try to rebrand as carbon-free and energy-focused instead of oil-and-gas focused, they'll leave this city. They'll consolidate wherever they are headquartered, and that isn't likely to be Houston."

★

The flooding the early settlers complained about has been made worse by the lax regulations in Houston. The Memorial Day (2015) and Tax Day (2016) floods were major five-hundred-year rain events. Meyerland, an affluent neighborhood along Braes Bayou, has been flooded out twice.

In August 2017, the biggest and wettest storm ever to hit the United

States hovered over Houston. Cars and homes were submerged. The Addicks and Barker dams were released, flooding the upper-middle-class neighborhood of Nottingham Forest, and destroying the homes that developers had known they were building inside a federal flood-control reservoir. In Houston, of course, it was all perfectly legal; and perfectly legal until a new law was enacted in 2019 for a seller not to disclose the flood history of a home to a prospective buyer, unless specifically asked.

Harvey hit in August 2017; it was unlike anything in American history. During the five days when the rains hovered, circling at a sluggish three miles per hour over the region, the storm dumped more than fifty-five inches of rain, reaching a total of some thirty-three trillion gallons of water, flooding more than 150,000 homes, destroying more than five hundred thousand vehicles, and causing damage estimated at more than one hundred billion dollars.

"Mattress Mack," as the famous owner of Gallery Furniture Jim McIngvale is known, sent his trucks out to pick up people who had been rescued from flooded homes and were helicoptered to highway overpasses where they were stranded in the rain for hours while awaiting transportation to shelters. He didn't wait for the city to tell him that these folks needed help. He brought them to his stores and gave them his ten-thousand-dollar mattresses to sleep on. He fed and housed evacuees for weeks, even donating furniture to some who were starting over.

Meanwhile, Lakewood Church, the headquarters of Joel Osteen's ministry, and one of the wealthiest churches in America, was roundly criticized for its failure to respond. The church, headquartered near Greenway Plaza just off US 59, claimed it could not open its doors to serve as a shelter because of the danger of additional flooding. "That's a load of crap," says a local attorney. "My office is right next door. I was in and out of it during the entire storm. There was no flooding in our area." The building is the former Compaq Stadium, where the Houston Rockets used to play, and it hosts some seventeen thousand worshippers in its Sunday services. Representatives of the church claimed they were waiting to hear from the city about what they could do to be helpful. The incident remains a blight on the prosperity-gospel preacher's reputation.

Local TV stations stayed on air twenty-four hours a day during the Harvey crisis, and some, like KHOU-TV, the CBS affiliate, decamped to the studios of competitors when theirs were flooded. To spell the exhausted local reporters, journalists were brought in from other parts of the country to help cover the story. In the aftermath, many wrote moving letters to Houston. They were deeply impressed by the generosity and compassion shown by so many ordinary citizens—like the Houston resident who had lost everything but his tractor, and then spent days pulling people to safety from their flooded neighborhoods. When asked why he was doing it, he responded that he was just glad he could lend a hand. At least his tractor could be put to use.

Harvey was a wake-up call for Houston residents. The 2018 survey, six months after Harvey hit, asked area residents about various initiatives that have been proposed to mitigate the impact of future storms and about their personal experiences with the hurricane. Almost one-third (32 percent) of the survey participants that year reported that their homes or vehicles were severely damaged during the storm.

Figure 11.3 depicts area residents' reactions to proposals that were calling for more stringent government regulations to reduce the impact of future flooding. The responses are shown by the extent to which the survey participants reported that their homes were actually damaged by the hurricane. As indicated in the chart, there were only very slight and inconsistent differences in the degree of support for these initiatives among those experiencing the three different levels of impact.

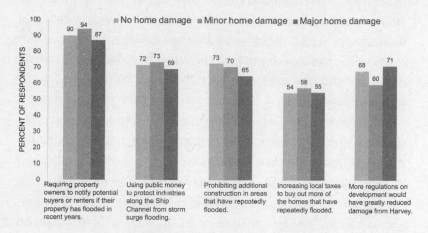

FIGURE 11.3: *Support for government initiatives to mitigate flooding, by the degree of home damage (2018)*

Whether they suffered any direct harm from the storm or came through the experience personally unscathed, the survey participants were equally insistent, by 91 percent overall, on the need to enforce more vigorously the requirement that property owners must notify potential buyers or renters if the property they are considering has flooded in recent years. By 72 percent, they favored using public money to protect the industries along the Ship Channel from hurricane surge flooding, and by the same percentage they supported prohibiting any additional construction in flood-prone areas. By 56 percent, they were in favor of increasing local taxes to enable government to buy out homes that have repeatedly flooded. And 66 percent agreed that if Houston had imposed more stringent regulations on development, that would have significantly reduced the damage caused by the hurricane.

An early sign that attitudes were shifting after the Harvey experience came when the Houston City Council voted in April 2018 to require all new developments in the area's floodplains to be built two feet above the projected water level in a five-hundred-year storm. Even more compelling was the bond referendum in August 2018 calling for $2.5 billion in flood infrastructure spending designed to help protect the area in future storms. It was by far the largest bond Harris County voters have ever been asked to approve, to be paid for by an increase in property taxes, yet it passed with more than 85 percent approval.

Effective flood mitigation will require moving, not just rebuilding, entire neighborhoods; declaring certain places to be off-limits to development; and calling for massive dikes and new reservoirs. Protecting homes from flooding will increase the cost of housing overall, result in less profit for builders and developers, and impose higher taxes on all area residents, whether or not they are living in flood-prone areas.

The overwhelming approval of the $2.5 billion bond referendum to fund improvements in the area's flooding infrastructure suggests that area residents may be more prepared than ever before to seriously reconsider the city's traditional philosophy of urban growth (its insistence on low taxes and minimal regulations), to push the city's business leadership into supporting more stringent controls on development, and to acknowledge the reality of climate change. But we didn't know if the new attitude would hold.

The opening question in each year's survey asks the respondents to name what they consider to be the biggest problem facing people in the Houston area today. Before Harvey, in the February 2017 survey, only 1 percent of the respondents thought of flooding and storms as the most salient problem in the Houston region. Shortly after that unprecedented rainfall event, in the 2018 survey, 15 percent spontaneously named the floods as the biggest problem. The number faded to just 7 percent in 2019, while mentions of traffic woes jumped from 25 to 36 percent.

As indicated in Figure 11.4, there was no change at all from 2018 to 2019 in the decisive majorities, at 76 and 75 percent, who agreed that the Houston region is almost certain to experience even more severe storms during the next ten years. But the public's support for more stringent government regulations declined. In 2018, 71 percent were in favor of prohibiting any additional construction in areas of Houston that have repeatedly flooded; that view was expressed by just 56 percent of the respondents in the 2019 survey. Similarly, though less dramatically, 50 percent in 2019, compared to 55 percent in 2018, were in favor of increasing local taxes to enable government agencies to buy out more of the homes that have repeatedly flooded. The instinctive resistance to an increase in government controls over the initiatives of the private sector is still embedded, it would seem, in Houston's basic DNA. As for floods, like so many other long-term threats: out of sight, out of mind.

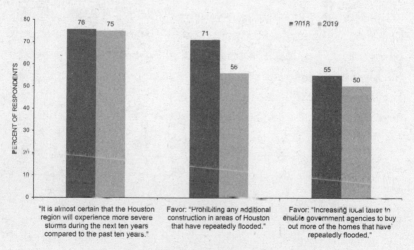

FIGURE 11.4: *The likelihood of future storms and support for flood-mitigation controls (2018-2019)*

Two other questions, depicted in Figure 11.5, show that continuing changes are indeed underway with regard to the broader understandings that area residents are bringing to these issues. Back in

2010, only 39 percent thought that the threat of climate change was a very serious problem. That concern grew to 46 percent in 2016, and then jumped to 52 percent in 2018, six months after Harvey. Instead of any lessening of concern in the following year as the salience of the storm receded, the perceived seriousness of climate issues was unchanged, at 53 percent, in the 2019 survey. When asked what they believed to be the primary cause of the changing climate, 64 percent in the 2018 survey (when the question was last asked) thought it was mainly caused by human activities. Only 58 percent took that position in 2015; just 48 percent in 2011.

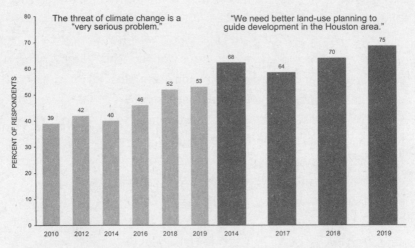

FIGURE 11.5: *Concerns about climate change and calls for better land-use planning*

The respondents in 2019 were also asked if they believed that we need better land-use planning to guide development in the Houston area, or if they thought instead that people and businesses should be free to build wherever they want. The proportion calling for more effective land-use planning grew from 64 percent in 2017 to 70 percent in 2018, and it increased even further to 75 percent in 2019. It really does look as if a broader shift of consciousness has been taking place among the residents of this famously free-enterprise oil-and-gas capital of America.

At the same time, the surveys underline the profound ambivalence that so many feel about how to respond to the growing dangers of flooding: Area residents continue to resist additional government interference in developer decisions, even as they also recognize more clearly than ever the region's deepening vulnerability to severe storms and the need for new dimensions of public action to strengthen resiliency.

★

The year 2017 marked the biggest one-time bump in tourism that Houston had ever seen. The Super Bowl was hosted in the city in February, and later that year the Astros won the World Series: Nearly twenty million people came to Houston during that year for reasons other than business. But compare these numbers to the more than sixty-five million who visited New York during 2017, fifty-eight million for Chicago, fifty million for Los Angeles, and twenty-five million for San Francisco. America's fourth largest metropolitan area clearly comes up short on the list of preferred tourist destinations.

Houstonians celebrate how much cleaner the air is now, and how the bayous support not only aquatic life but water sports. The city has landed on every list of the best foodie places to visit in America. Yet with all the improvements, Houston still rarely appears on lists of the top cities that you would want to live in or move to. And that has left a lot of loyal Houstonians scratching their heads.

To most outsiders it's not a mystery.

The impressive flyover of Houston, so celebrated by the Parks Board, generally looks to the west and north, where the seemingly endless expanse of green is indeed an impressive view. But turn to the south and east, and the view is impressive in another way: You will see vast fields of white, cylindrical tanks lining the Ship Channel all the way to Galveston Bay and out to the Golden Triangle along the Gulf. Houstonians who don't live in what is known as Cancer Alley get concerned about the air only when the wind shifts to the west, bringing the stench that Deer Park, Seaview, Harrisburg, and Manchester residents are accustomed to experiencing on a daily basis (the "smell of money," it used to be called).

Driving by the refineries at night is an eerie experience for the uninitiated. The vast structures seem to glow in the dark, clogged with access rigging lit up by ghostly lights. Vents stream fire into the night sky, making them look more like alien spacecraft than industrial plants. But the larger threat of their concentration in Houston, combined with lax regulations by the state, have put some Houstonians on high alert.

While Harvey poured down on Houston, the Arkema chemical plant in the city of Crosby, just outside the eastern portion of Houston's Beltway 8, lost power to its refrigeration when the building's electrical systems were disabled by rising water on the floodplain where the plant was built. As a result, the pressurized tanks could no longer contain the organic peroxides, and on August 31, 2017, the explosions began and residents within a 1.5-mile radius had to be evacuated. More than twenty-three thousand pounds of contaminants were released into the environment. The company was not required by Texas state law to report what the tanks were holding. Criminal charges have been filed; OSHA fines totaled some $91,000—not likely to have much effect on the company's standard operating procedures.

Aside from the Arkema incident and the Deep Water Horizon rig explosion in the Gulf of Mexico in April 2010, it's rare that environmental disasters in Houston make more than the local news. The early months of 2019 were rife with underreported incidents. March 17 brought a major conflagration that started across Galveston Bay in Deer Park at the ITC Chemical Refinery (the Intercontinental Terminals Company), which lasted more than a week. The entire Ship

Channel was forced to close when dangerous chemicals were released both from the burning tanks and the fire-retardant foam. The black cloud from the fire spread over the inner loop and drifted all the way to San Antonio, a three-hour drive to the west. It was so large that it masked the deadly emissions from a fire at Exxon Baytown that burned on March 16. Tanks at the KMCO refinery near the Arkema plant caught fire in early April, and in May 2019, the Ship Channel had to close for the second time when benzene and other deadly chemicals poured into Galveston Bay after a barge collision, and then washed on shore twelve to twenty-four hours before residents were notified.

Back in 2008, Hurricane Ike, a category 2 storm, landed in Galveston and sent a fourteen-foot storm surge up the Houston Ship Channel. It was by sheer luck that the surge brought substantial wind and water damage but no release of toxic chemicals. My colleague and friend, environmental lawyer Jim Blackburn, has shown that you would need just six more feet of storm surge, "and a back-side wind blowing south to north, and you would have had a twenty-million-gallon release of chemicals; 2,200 out of the 4,400 tanks would have flooded, and many would have failed. The tanks are not designed for flotation; they will pop up off their foundations; there will be more Arkema situations." The resulting fires and explosions would create an environmental disaster that would take down not only the region, but the entire U.S. economy. If anyone wanted purposefully to cripple the United States, the Houston Ship Channel is one of the most promising targets.

★

No other region in the country matches Houston's concentration of oil refining, petrochemical production, oil and natural gas transportation, and ocean-going tankers—not to mention its sprawling low-density car-dependent expansion facilitated by miles of freeways. One of the city's biggest environmental challenges continues to come from ground-level ozone, which is formed by a complex chemical reaction that combines the nitrogen oxides with the volatile organic compounds generated by the area's vehicles, power plants, and petrochemicals, whenever that dangerous soup is warmed in the presence of sunlight and heat. And Houston has an abundance of every ingredient.

For most of the twentieth century, Houston's business leaders were calling for unrestrained oil and gas production and the continued expansion of its petrochemical industries, while minimizing the pollution problems those developments were generating. They were enthusiastic participants in the national pro-business backlash that developed in opposition to the environmental regulations of the 1970s and '80s.

In the mid-1970s, the Chamber of Commerce funded an ambitious report (the Houston Area Oxidant Study), which sought to show that the federal air-pollution standards were based on questionable science and that any serious efforts to come into compliance with the new regulations were certain to cause severe harm to the entire economy. The study claimed there was no proven link between Houston's ozone levels and any harmful health effects, and the pollution was largely caused at any rate by activities outside the city's control. The standards promulgated by the EPA were unattainable, it asserted, short of actions that would completely disrupt the economy of the region.

Then came the wake-up call. During the 1990s, Bill Dawson, the environmental reporter for the *Houston Chronicle*, had been writing about the business elite's resistance to addressing air pollution issues, and in 1999, he wrote an article showing that Houston was gaining on Los Angeles in competition for the dubious title as the smog capital of America. L.A. had been making significant progress throughout the decade in reducing its high ozone levels, while Houston's pollution remained largely unchanged. On October 7, 1999, the lines converged. The headline in the *USA Today* newspaper read, "Houston, cough,

cough . . . We've got a problem, cough, cough!" And the *Los Angeles Times* proclaimed, "New Smog Capital of America Declared!"

Houston was on track to surpass Los Angeles that year in the total number of days that exceeded the federal ozone standards. On that particularly hot and humid October day, a cloud of ozone formed over southeast Houston. Students playing soccer at Deer Park High School were choking on the smog, complaining of aching chests and sore throats. An epidemic of new asthma cases was pouring into the area's hospitals. It was no longer possible to deny that Houston's pollution was having serious health effects, or that the city's carefully cultivated image as an attractive place to live and work was now profoundly at risk.

The national media cheerfully highlighted Houston's new status as the most severely polluted metro area in America. The city became a target for Al Gore's presidential campaign against Houstonian George W. Bush. Houston's civic and business leaders were jolted into acknowledging that the city did indeed have an air-pollution problem that would require serious public and private-sector attention. They were reluctantly beginning to acknowledge that more stringent regulations on emissions, rather than being anti-growth and antibusiness, were essential elements in the city's efforts to attract the talent that would grow its economy in the new era. For a while at least, Houston would no longer be at the forefront of the national opposition to all federal air-pollution regulations.

Early in the following year, the GHP created the Business Coalition for Clean Air and soon announced a variety of initiatives designed to strengthen industrial regulations and to reduce the city's ozone pollution. The BCCA went on to fund additional and more reliable scientific research, and it called for a series of actions that were carefully crafted to reduce Houston's ozone and particulate emissions without causing unacceptable damage to the region's critical refining and petrochemical industries.

In the ensuing years, Houston's leading companies, responding to both local and national pressures, were induced to make the investments that have gradually lowered their toxic emissions. Yet they continue to resist any strengthening of the regulations, and they still insist that Houston's petrochemical industry will decline precipitously if the costs of doing business increase any further. Twenty years after that October 1999 wake-up call, progress has clearly been made, but the region is still out of compliance with the EPA requirements for ozone and it remains close to noncompliance with regard to particulate pollution. At the same time, as my friend Angela Blanchard points out, if you want a seat or tires on that bicycle you're riding in order to cut emissions, you can't have it without Houston's petrochemicals.

★

Houston's freeways are a big part of the reason ozone is such a major problem, and those living alongside them face some of the most serious health challenges, particularly if they are children with asthma. Every year since 2013, the survey participants have spontaneously named traffic as the biggest problem in Houston. At least until recently, the approach the city has taken in its efforts to address mobility problems has been almost exclusively to build wider and longer highways. Critics claim that this time-honored strategy will never solve the real problem. "Trying to reduce traffic congestion by building more roads," it has been said, "is like trying to deal with your weight problem by buying a bigger pair of pants."

"I-10 might be the widest highway in America," says Tom Bacon, when I ask him about dealing with congestion. "Harris County welcomed TxDOT's plan to run it through Houston, because area leaders thought it would relieve our traffic problems. And it did for about the first five minutes. The problem is that Houston keeps spreading, and it doesn't take long for traffic on a new highway to exceed its capacity. We never think about building for density, and because of that blindness, we will continue to suffer." Visibly frustrated, he continues, "I-10 destroyed neighborhoods and cut off communities. Now we are doing the same thing with the I-45 expansion downtown."

The city of Houston itself extends across more than six hundred square miles and is home to slightly more than 2.2 million people. The 610 Loop, which defines the inner core of the city, spreads across more than fifty-five square miles; no other city has a core as expansive as that. You could place inside the overall city limits of Houston the cities of Chicago, Baltimore, Detroit, and Philadelphia. Those four urban centers contain among them a total population of more than 5.5 million, compared to the 2.2 million who live within Houston's city limits.

Spreading farther out, the nine-county Greater Houston Metropolitan area encompasses 10,072 square miles and contains some 6.5 million people. Figure 11.6 depicts the nine counties, highlighting the three largest. The overall geographical expanse of the area's nine counties is just slightly smaller than the entire state of Massachusetts (at 10,550 square miles) and considerably larger than the state of New Jersey (8,729 square miles).

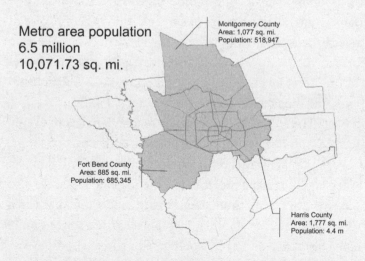

Metro area population
6.5 million
10,071.73 sq. mi.

Montgomery County
Area: 1,077 sq. mi.
Population: 518,947

Fort Bend County
Area: 885 sq. mi.
Population: 685,345

Harris County
Area: 1,777 sq. mi.
Population: 4.4 m

FIGURE 11.6: *The three largest counties in the Greater Houston Metropolitan region*

During the years after World War II, when Americans constructed the forty thousand miles of the Interstate Highway System and fled en masse to the newly developed suburbs, they were the parents of the baby boom. More than two-thirds of all U.S. households in 1970 had children living at home, and suburbia, with all its new homes and highways, was where they wanted to be. Thirty years later, in 2010, less than one-third of all American households had children at home; by 2020 the census projects that this will be the case for about one-fourth of all U.S. households; another one-fourth will consist of persons living alone; and the fastest growing segment of the overall population will consist of men and women over the age of eighty.

As the number of families with three or more children continues to decline, replaced by empty nesters wanting shorter commutes, young creatives postponing marriage and having fewer children, and growing numbers of single-person and elderly households—it is not surprising that many residents across the Houston region today (as in most metropolitan areas) are calling for more transit-oriented, high-density, walkable urbanism, and for "complete streets," reconfigured to accommodate not only motor vehicles, but also bikers and pedestrians. "With all these years of surveys," adds Bacon, "it's not like we need a focus group to figure out what residents want. We have that information already. We will never have a great city until we get it right at the street level, with shops and restaurants and cultural institutions, and then build upward from there; not outward."

As indicated in Figure 11.7, the survey respondents were evenly divided in their preference for living in areas with a mix of shops, workplaces, and restaurants or in single-family residential areas. When asked about housing preferences, the respondents were also split 50-50 between wanting a smaller home in a more urbanized area within walking distance of shops and workplaces or "a single-family home with a big yard, where you would need to drive almost everywhere you want to go."

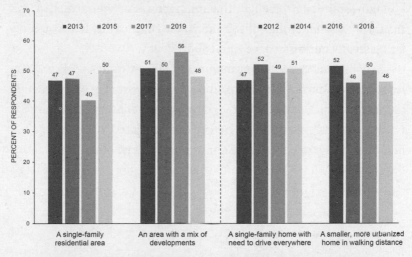

FIGURE 11.7: *The preference for "walkable urbanism" among Harris County residents*

The changing preferences are also the result of area residents' growing comfort with Houston's diversity. Just as the move out to the suburbs in the 1960s and 1970s was based on more than a desire for bigger spaces to accommodate larger families but was also motivated by fear of urban crime and discomfort with life in the inner core, so the new interest in returning to the city today is motivated by more than traffic woes and smaller households.

Living in denser urban areas means sharing public amenities, interacting in common spaces with people from different socioeconomic backgrounds and different ethnicities. Its attraction for area residents is therefore likely to depend in part on their comfort with the burgeoning diversity of urban places. After controlling for differences in age, gender, and education, the U.S.-born Anglos who said they would prefer to live in smaller, more urbanized homes within walking distance of shops and workplaces were also significantly more likely than those stating a preference for single-family homes in automobile-dependent suburbs to assert that Houston's diversity will be a source of great strength for the city, to believe that immigrants contribute more to the American economy than they take, and to approve of homosexuals being legally permitted to adopt children.[90]

As cohort succession continues and newer attitudes take root, cities will respond with policies that mirror the preferences and demands of their citizens. Social change, as always, happens first at the individual level, years, even decades, before it is translated into public policy and eventually transforms the community as a whole.

CHAPTER 12

Pathways to Success or Failure

It is not a question of alternatives to growth, but of alternative ways of growing.

—John McHale[91]

The official parade of cowboys and cowgirls, covered wagons and other horse-drawn vehicles takes place on the Sabine Street Bridge, where most of the money shots of downtown are taken, at the foot of Buffalo Bayou Park. The festival begins in the heart of downtown, at Bagby and Walker, the intersection where city hall and the Hobby Center for the Performing Arts stand kitty-corner to each other. The parade is an all-day event that launches the biggest celebration of the American West in the entire world.

For more than two weeks, Houston will be clogged with traffic, and nearly thirty-five thousand people vie—and pay—for the opportunity to volunteer at the rodeo. There's status among them, gold badges for longevity, and a hefty fee for a lifetime spot. Houstonians line up to wait for someone to drop out or die so that they can join the ranks, getting prime spots for the concerts—Tejano, blues, country, hip-hop, Elvis Presley, Santana, Los Tigres del Norte, Willie Nelson, Kacey Musgraves, Keith Urban, Blake Shelton, Cardi B—and a front-row seat to the prime attraction at the livestock show: Everyone wants to watch tiny tots trying to stay on sheep desperate to get rid of their riders in the Mutton Bustin' contest.

The Livestock Show and Rodeo has been part of the Houston experience in February and March of every year since 1931. Some things don't change, including the fact that Houston never actually had a history featuring cowboys, rodeos, or livestock. The spirit of the Allen brothers lives on, and so does the spirit of Jesse Jones. Nowhere else will you find this combination of inventive boosterism, public enthusiasm, and meaningful civic engagement.

Volunteering and giving back are two of Houston's most consistent qualities. If you compare cities by the health of their nonprofits, Houston ranks as either the most or the second most (after Pittsburgh) generous city in America in its support of charities of all kinds. In addition, it's not at all uncommon for Houstonians, like forty-three-year-old Lisa Helfman, to find ways to turn their personal struggles into charitable benefits for area residents.

"I was a successful lawyer at Vinson and Elkins," begins the quiet and centered petite director of public affairs at H-E-B grocery stores. "But I was eating really unhealthy food, I was addicted to Dr Pepper, I was working like crazy, and I was training for marathons. I finally hit a wall of exhaustion." Lisa changed her diet and her lifestyle, and found that by taking better care of herself, her life markedly improved, in the quality time she could now spend with her children, even in her success at work. "And I was on a mission to bring the message to anyone who would listen. I wanted to get healthy meals into areas that were known as food deserts, where pretty much nothing but processed food was available."

When she began to work on real-estate transactions for the medical center, she and Dr. Shreela Sharma, a public health and nutrition specialist, teamed up to address the problem. "Every day," says Lisa, "grocery stores throw out so much fresh produce that could be donated and could make a difference in the lives of children and families all over Houston. The problem wasn't just figuring out how to get the food to them, it was also helping people learn to incorporate healthy eating into their everyday lives. I didn't want to give up junk food or soda. I needed someone to teach me how to eat wisely. And then, when I felt the difference in my mood and energy, that's when I got hooked."

Sharma and Helfman connected with Texas grocery store chain H-E-B for donations of excess produce, to begin a nonprofit they call Brighter Bites. The program not only delivers bags of fresh food to kids in underserved areas; the groceries also contain recipes and instructions for preparing the meals. During the day at school, the children get to sample the food, inspiring their parents to make it for them at home. Brighter Bites has now spread beyond Houston and has some fifty thousand families in its network, partnering with Target, Walmart, Sysco, and other grocers for additional donations. In recognition of this work, Helfman was the 2019 winner of the Schweitzer Foundation Humanitarian of the Year Award.

Every day, it seems, Houston's hotels and clubs hold luncheons and galas honoring people like Lisa for the work they do in Houston in addressing needs that are too often short-changed in a city with such inadequately funded government programs. And in that, many find hope for Houston's future. "At the end of every presentation I do on Houston," Patrick Jankowski says, "I talk about how engaged Houstonians are in their community. We threw a party for the volunteers who picked up trash during the Super Bowl in 2017. There were ten thousand people there. All they got was a T-shirt and a plate of barbecue, but it was important to them to make sure Houston looked good during the week of national attention. So they came to help.

"And you remember," he continues, "the *New Yorker* cover on September 11, 2017, right after Harvey, don't you? It was an illustration of cars floating down Memorial Parkway adjacent to Buffalo Bayou. There's a red-and-white pickup truck with evacuees in the bed dressed in blue. All of the evacuees, black, white and brown, are hauling people out of a small motorboat that has pulled up beside the truck." This was the new multiethnic America in action.

The city has been reinvented, according to a 2018 article in *GQ*, as "The New Capital of Southern Cool." From kids dropping acid and making art on the lawn of the Menil Collection to some of the country's most unusual nightclubs, one Austin transplant claimed in the article that Houston was now cooler than Austin, mostly because it doesn't care about being cool. "Now that I'm leaving for the summer," a colleague told me, "my friends' kids are clamoring for my couch and guest bedroom, in the heat of July. The word is out among Generation Z." The food scene, some argue, is the main driver. There are many award winners, and restaurateurs from places like New York, such as B&B Butchers, are building their empires in Houston.

Disaffected Houston native Brett Martin wrote in that article about what he found upon his return after Hurricane Harvey had receded:

"I firmly believe that there's no such thing as a city that has more 'grit' or 'resilience' than any other; some are just unlucky enough to get the chance to show it. Still, the cracked-open metropolis that the rest of the country gazed upon in the immediate aftermath of Harvey was clearly one of deep communal ties, fierce civic pride, and wells of creative energy. There were the four employees of El Bolillo Bakery who, trapped by rising water, spent two days of the storm baking forty-four hundred pounds of flour's worth of bread and *pan dulce* to distribute to flood victims. There was the Houston Ballet, whose home theater was inundated but who pressed on with its season in makeshift digs all over the city. Something special, it became clear to those who might not have been paying attention, was going on here. In its youthfulness, its diversity (by some measures, the most diverse large city in America), and its explosive growth (an astonishing two decades of 25 percent in the greater metro area), Houston was looking more and more like the American city of the future. . .

"As for Houston's place in the Texas firmament, one businessman with shops in all three of the state's most famous cities broke them down for me thusly: Austin is like your young, hip millennial brother who always knows the latest cool thing. Dallas is the metrosexual middle brother that nobody really wants to spend time with. But Houston is the older, cooler sibling—he's got some miles on him, he's been through some stuff, but he totally knows what's cool and what's not.

"You love all your siblings, but you know which one you want to hang out with."[92]

★

"But none of all those good things will matter," says environmental lawyer Jim Blackburn, "if we don't stop pretending that Houston doesn't flood." Slim, salt-and-pepper hair, plaid shirt, jeans and cowboy boots, Blackburn has seen his fair share of environmental battles since he arrived in Houston as a newly minted lawyer to study environmental engineering at Rice in 1972. "My wife and I made a pact that we'd stay for a year," he says, echoing the familiar sentiment of so many accidental Houstonians.

"I was an environmental consultant on The Woodlands project, as it was being developed, and I worked with some of the best urban planners," Blackburn remembers. "At Rice I got to study the Texas coast using computers to measure the environmental impacts. Then Reagan got elected and the money for the program dried up, so I started teaching in the engineering department and began my environmental law practice. And that's when I hit my first wall. I had never failed at anything. But I quickly discovered that the state of Texas did not really want to protect the environment; they were only interested in issuing more permits. I drank too much and blamed the state institutions. But I haven't been drunk since 1986. That was the best decision I ever made."

Blackburn kept fighting with Texas companies, having his first real success when he got the Fort Bend County Landfill closed after the methane leakage was so bad that a man blew himself up when he lit a cigarette in a building adjacent to the site. "I learned how to fight in this part of the world. The big companies weren't used to being challenged. I learned that you have to convince them you can inflict financial or reputational pain in order to get them to the table. I learned to be an environmentalist *and* to talk about how companies can make money in less destructive ways. You have to talk about money, about jobs, about the economy. And I learned to compromise and to recognize that there is a graceful way to win or lose."

"Houston is much cleaner than it used to be," I offered, having seen the progress myself.

"Yes," he answered, "because it had to be. Houston's buddy, George H. W. Bush, supported the Clean Air Act, and the business community had to do something."

Many of Blackburn's victories turned into bigger environmental wins than even he had expected. By stopping the building of the Texas Copper Plant, the site is now a three-thousand-acre nature preserve adjacent to the causeway that crosses to Galveston Island. The defeat of the Wallisville Reservoir project left a twenty-thousand-acre wetland preserve intact. What would have been the function of the reservoir is instead performed by a benign saltwater barrier, a resolution Blackburn helped to develop. It solved the problem for the Army Corps of Engineers without the disruption that would have been caused by the building of an additional reservoir.

"But the problem is that, way back during the Suite 8F time, and into the 1950s and sixties, Houston made a silent pact, that the east side would be petrochem, the west side would be left to the developers, and neither would interfere in each other's territory. It was a kind of deal with the devil. The corporations are silent about the pollution here, about how many are getting sick around the Ship Channel on the east, and about the huge problem on the west side with particulates and ozone along the freeways. As a result, Houston has some of the worst pollution in the country."

If you are unfamiliar with navigating the east side, as most Houstonians who don't live near the Ship Channel are, you are unlikely to know how to avoid getting stuck at a train signal in that part of town for fifteen or more minutes as half-mile-long trains pass through. It takes a local's experience to know where to turn off when you see the signal in the distance, to find the underpasses and alternate routes. Google Maps, Waze, Apple Maps—none of them takes account of the train traffic when they suggest a route. Most westsiders don't even realize how much cargo—much of it petrochemicals—moves through Houston on any given day.

These are the same kinds of trains that have exploded into infernos across the world, destroying towns in the UK, North Dakota, Mississippi, Oregon, Ontario, Illinois, West Virginia, Virginia, and more. Called "train bombs" by environmentalists, so far, none have exploded in Houston.

Bill Gilmer, economist at the University of Houston, reminds me that the worldwide demand for oil grew from thirty million barrels per day in 1965 to nearly one hundred million in 2018. This in the face of increasing demand for alternative forms of energy, all of which, of course, require fossil fuels to develop. If you ride a bike instead of driving a car, you won't have a seat or tires without the products Houston's petrochemical plants turn out. The same goes for manufacturing wind turbines—Texas is now America's top state for wind energy production—and solar panels and batteries for electric cars. Weaning the world off fossil fuels will take a great deal of time and commitment. This is why Blackburn talks about finding ways for corporations to make money while protecting the environment. "You can do both at the same time," he says.

One of Blackburn's biggest concerns for the future of the environmental movement in Houston is the lack of any compelling vision of what an environmentally sensitive economy might actually look like. "Everybody in the movement is busy fighting against what they don't want, but nobody is saying what could work." He formed Bayou City Initiative, a group now reaching about two hundred thousand area residents, who are passionate about the environment. Among the initiatives they are fighting for are raising homes above the floodplain, buying out those that have repeatedly flooded, and restoring the Houston-area prairies to improve water absorption.

"I listen to oil executives and economists tell me all the time that you simply cannot reduce the world's dependence on fossil fuels, at least not anytime soon," I challenged Blackburn. We are old friends and I was sure he'd take the bait.

"Of course you can," he insisted, as I knew he would. "We have to start thinking about how to build circular systems instead of consumer economies. We are so in love with the idea of getting rich just by making more stuff for more people to buy. But that isn't sustainable. There are plenty of green solutions for the economy. I started the Texas Coastal Exchange to help petrochemical companies become carbon-neutral by recapturing the carbon they produce. They are invited to make a donation that will pay farmers to turn their land back into prairies in order to sequester carbon emissions. If you get a big enough piece of land, oil companies could sell carbon-neutral gasoline through the process of carbon-banking.

"The farmers would continue to make money—the donations from the Exchange would pay them for the use of their land. They aren't growing much right now besides corn for cattle, and that corn is what's making cattle produce methane. If you let them eat what they normally eat, which is prairie grass, their systems work better and you help solve the methane problem. Once you let the prairies restore themselves, they will not only absorb carbon, they will also absorb more water, and that will help with flooding."

It seemed like such an obvious solution, you had to wonder why the oil and gas industry wasn't endorsing it. Jim smiled at my question. "Houston makes every bad, toxic thing in the world. We have to have a plan other than letting it run till it can't run anymore. Industry knows that green solutions are the only future for fossil fuels. But the first question they ask is how can they build it with their own technology, like a vacuum to suck the carbon out of the air or a pipeline to get it into the ground." Blackburn couldn't suppress a belly laugh that bubbles up, and neither could I. It was astonishing to both of us that such successful, educated business leaders wouldn't want to take full advantage of how nature itself offers some of the best cleansing alternatives.

"We have so many different forms of energy here," insists Blackburn. "We have wind—more than any other state—we have solar, and in Houston we have the biggest industrial complex in the United States. We can maintain that manufacturing base while we are finding ways to make its products less damaging," Blackburn says. "The mix of products will change as consumers make different demands. If we voted with our money to insist on carbon-neutral gas, all the oil and gas companies would sequester their carbon. But they aren't even offering consumers the choice."

★

As a developer of commercial real estate and chair of the Houston Parks Board, Tom Bacon has spent years working on the answer to what makes a great city. Like Blackburn, he's on board with the celebration of the environment. When I ask him what he thinks it would take to build a better city, he draws a triangle. He labels the base as health. On each of the two sides he writes *transportation*. The three points are an affordable home, a good job, and recreation facilities. And at the center is education.

Bacon, like many other business leaders in Houston, is especially worried about the degree to which Houston ISD is failing in its responsibility to prepare students for jobs in today's knowledge-based economy. "Those numbers you give every year, Steve, are scary,"

Bacon says. He's referring to the data showing that, while 60 percent of all the jobs in America now require postsecondary education, more than 70 percent of all the graduating seniors in Houston-area high schools are, by some key measures, unprepared for a college education and without the skills today's jobs require.

"Those numbers have to scare everyone," says Scott McClelland. It's a recipe for mass poverty, and "education is the only pathway out of poverty." The 2019 chairman of the board of the Greater Houston Partnership has also put education at the center of his agenda. As president of H-E-B Houston, McClelland has overseen, during the course of twenty-nine years, the growth of a local Texas chain into the sixth largest grocer in America. "But stop and look at this," says the lanky, bespectacled, and energetic Southern California native as we cross an open hallway to the offices at Central Market, the chain's flagship high-end store.

"I just love this view," he says, barely able to suppress his pleasure at the sight. On one side of Central Market is an explosion of locally grown produce, like the biggest indoor farmers' market you've ever seen. There is an oversized gourmet market; a cheese aisle as big as most New York City specialty stores; fish and meat, all locally sourced; and selections of specialty items curated by Houston's dedicated foodies.

"Forty-five percent of all Harris County schools are rated C, D, or F, and that number goes up to 55 percent for the schools you attend if you are a person of color," McClelland says. "Since education is *the* pathway out of poverty, that number has to bother everyone. All kids are our kids. You can't just talk about 'my kids,' especially if you're in the business world. This is our future workforce. If you improve the quality of schools by just a 20 percent increase in graduates, that will help fifty- to sixty-thousand kids to be ready for the Houston work-force. It's not everyone, but we can make a difference."

McClelland is a cofounder of GHP's new education initiative, Good Reason Houston, which grew out of Early Matters, a previous effort to provide universal pre-K education to all children in Houston. I served for five years on the executive board of Early Matters; I attended a lot of meetings, saw a lot of concern being expressed by wonderful nonprofits and other dedicated Houstonians, but after all that time, it seemed clear to me that not a single additional child had been helped as a direct result of our years of meeting together. So I challenged McClelland to make the case that Good Reason, which had expanded into an even larger mandate, taking on the entire spectrum of education, from cradle to career, was different from Early Matters and would really be able to move the needle. He sent me to the new superintendent of one of the worst-performing districts in the metropolitan area.

Superintendent LaTonya Goffney is the first outside hire in recent years to run Aldine ISD, where 90 percent of the students are living in poverty. "I have run small and medium school systems before," says Goffney, who turned around the Lufkin schools in East Texas. "And I've partnered with private-sector organizations as well. How effective they are depends on who's running them. It depends on whether that person has just fallen in love with working with children, or if they've fallen in love with results.

"If you're not in love with results, then not much happens. Good Reason," she insists, "has made it possible for me to make a difference. Their CEO, Alex Hales Elizondo, brings knowledge of resources and systems that I might not have found out about on my own. She's become a partner in helping me think through problem-solving in the district. When things seemed overwhelming, she was there with ideas and solutions."

Goffney tells the story of how education was her own pathway out of poverty. "The only reason I am here talking to you," she says, "is because of the education I received. My mother had me when she was fifteen. She made some bad choices about drugs and she lived with a drug dealer. I witnessed abuse, depression, addiction. My grandmother took me to live with her when I was in the fifth grade.

Some teachers noticed I was smart and started encouraging me. My grandmother cleaned house for a local Anglo family. We called her employer 'boss lady,' because she seemed to have magical powers to make everything possible. She helped me personally a lot." Goffney took the job as superintendent at Aldine because, as she says, "I believe in making a difference for those not born in the ballpark of success."

Not quite a year into her job, Goffney has already had an impact. The schools in Aldine have increased their pre-K enrollment by 5 percent just by providing an opportunity for parents to enroll their children in school at the district's new pre-K awareness festival. And with financial help from Good Reason, they've implemented a bonus system to attract the best principals and teachers into the schools that need the most help, similar to the program that demonstrably helped improve the Dallas school system. Good Reason also helped Goffney change a failing curriculum by insisting on systematic classroom assessments and on the need to challenge the kids more powerfully in order to bring them up to grade-level reading.

"We found out that teachers were going too easy on the kids, giving them lower than grade-level textbooks. If my teachers and counselors had felt sorry for me and didn't push me, I wouldn't be where I am today. We have a moral obligation not to lower our expectations for these kids. If they aren't reading at grade level, they won't pass the state-level tests, they can't graduate, and then what options are available to them? We have to learn to see possibility and not just circumstances. Yes, we are starting from a tough place, but we have good families and good kids here. I'm excited about what happens when you raise expectations, and I wouldn't be so excited about the future without Good Reason Houston."

The surveys have found that Houston-area residents themselves are changing in their understanding of the critical importance of education. They are clearly more ready than in earlier years to get behind improvements in the public schools. In the 2018 survey, for the first time in all the years since the question was initially asked in 1995, a clear majority (by 56 to 42 percent) affirmed that the public schools will need significantly more money in order to provide a quality education.

McClelland claims that this new understanding has now finally bubbled up to the state legislature. "In this last session," he says of the one completed in the first quarter of 2019, "they released eleven billion dollars for education." Governor Abbott signed the bill in June. "Some of that money is bound to have an effect in Houston," McClelland says. "The question is whether or not we will spend it strategically. I think Alex and Good Reason will make a difference."

★

Anyone who conducts reliable survey research on the attitudes and beliefs of the general public will be struck as we have been by how often the generally progressive views recorded in surveys of this sort seem to be at odds with current public policies. The disconnect between public opinion and politically effective opinion seems particularly striking in the case of Houston and Texas.

The surveys find, for example, that while Texas statutes have made it increasingly difficult for women to obtain an abortion, Houston-area residents are firmly opposed to laws that would further restrict access to the procedure. As Stan Marck and many others continue to battle for reform against the anti-immigrant policies of the state and federal government, Houstonians themselves increasingly favor granting a path to citizenship for illegal immigrants. While the federal government refuses to act on gun reform, area residents, in this open-carry city and state, are calling (by 85 percent) for background checks on anyone who wants to buy a gun.

More than ever, Harris County residents support strengthening the safety net to reduce the inequalities, knowing, as LaTonya Goffney's story demonstrates, that none of us succeeds purely on our own and intervention is needed in almost all cases to counteract the effects of poverty. Despite the defeat of the Houston Equal Rights Ordinance in 2016 and Houston's moniker as the execution capital of America, Houstonians are growing more in favor of gay rights and more opposed to the death penalty. The views expressed by Houston-area residents are almost always echoed in the national polls, but they are hardly reflected at all in the way public policy today generally gets shaped and sustained in state and federal legislatures.

An editorial in the *Houston Chronicle* in May 2015 took note of this discrepancy. The article described the "Texas myth" as a place that "relishes the death penalty, that's obsessed with guns, that's anti-education, anti-science, anti-immigrant, and anti-environment." This is often the image Texas presents to the world. It's not exactly one the state's elected leaders run away from, but as the newspaper noted, drawing on findings from the Houston surveys, it's far from the one that the majority of Texans would embrace when they are asked about these issues in the privacy of their homes.

A friend sent me an email after reading that editorial. If Texans are as progressive as they say they are in the surveys, he wondered, why don't they simply elect people to office who share their views? "What I don't understand is that those same ordinary Texans keep electing the very politicians who too frequently perpetuate the myths and the stereotypes," my friend wrote.

At the most general level, the surveys show clearly that the general public has been expressing more progressive views over the years, and as in the state's other major cities (Dallas, Austin, San Antonio, El Paso), area residents are now more firmly affiliated with the Democratic Party (48 percent in our 2019 survey, up from 35 percent in 2005), even as the Republicans (at just 29 percent in 2019) have gained a supermajority in Texas. The defeat of Ann Richards by George W. Bush after her one term as governor in 1995 marked the end of the

Democratic Party as a force of any consequence in Texas.[93] Not a single Texas-wide officeholder today is a Democrat.

That gap of 19 points in political party affiliation (48 percent Democrat, 29 percent Republican) in this, the largest city in one of the reddest states in America, underlines the degree to which, despite their growing strength, Democrats continue, at least so far, to be sidelined from meaningful political participation at the statewide level. The exception is Houston city government, which is supposedly nonpartisan but has been controlled by Democrats since 1974.

Once again, the views of the general public are at odds with the political agendas that have been shaping public policy in state and national legislatures. The disconnect between private opinion and public action is the result of many forces—older, more conservative voters more consistently showing up at the polls; highly motivated single-issue voters dominating local elections; voter suppression through tougher ID laws; the disproportionate power of the moneyed donor class; and blatant redistricting.

In the early 2000s, Texas Republicans dominated the legislature and were able to put into place a sweeping redistricting plan intended to create a permanent Republican majority in the U.S. House of Representatives. Today, the entire Texas delegation to the U.S. House has twenty-five Republicans and eleven Democrats. As a result of creative gerrymandering, the city of Austin, the center of liberal sentiment in the state of Texas, has a total of six congressional districts, but only one of its elected representatives is a Democrat.[94]

The redistricting has made winning in the primaries tantamount to getting elected. Primary voters are generally more intense and more committed in their political views than the electorate as a whole, and most registered voters feel little incentive to go to the polls in the general elections, since they consider most of the outcomes to be foregone conclusions. Not surprisingly, Texas cities like Houston and Dallas have lower voter turnout rates than most other major cities in America.

Citizens who are intensely pro-gun, pro-life, or anti-gay are more likely to vote on those issues alone than are those who support gun control or gay rights, but who hold a variety of other views with equal conviction. In 2013, for example, at the same time that the U.S. Congress was defeating every effort to strengthen controls over access to handguns and the state legislature was pushing for right-to-carry laws, 81 percent of the respondents in that year's survey said they were *strongly* in favor of requiring universal criminal background checks for all gun sales in America. That public demand is unlikely to get translated into legislation anytime soon, since those who are opposed to any such restrictions are more likely to advocate for that position and to vote on the basis of that one issue alone than those who are generally (but not so fervently) in favor of what they consider to be common-sense gun regulations.

In the 2016 survey, the pro-life respondents, by 31 to 12 percent, were more than twice as likely as those who were pro-choice to say they would vote on the basis of that one issue alone. Even as the state of Texas has sought in a variety of ways to enact legislation that severely limits a woman's access to abortion, the majority of area residents are firmly opposed to any law that would make it more difficult for a woman to obtain an abortion and fully in support of a woman's right to make that decision herself. But public policy is more likely to respond to the intensity with which such views are held.

★

In a democracy, even one as flawed and slow to respond as is the current American version, when the views of the general public have shifted decisively, they tend eventually to be heard in the shaping of public policy. We have seen the policy changes with regard to the legalization of gay marriage, and it may also be happening in response to the public's changing attitudes toward the death penalty.

Harris County residents have been rethinking their earlier, long-time support for capital punishment. As indicated in Figure 12.1, the percent of survey participants who said they were in favor of the death penalty for persons convicted of murder dropped decisively from 75 percent in 1993, to 61 percent in 2011, and to 56 percent in 2019. In alternating years, the respondents were asked to choose among three forms of punishment for persons convicted of first-degree murder —the death penalty, life imprisonment with no possibility for parole, or life imprisonment with a chance for parole after twenty-five years. The percentages who chose the death penalty as the most appropriate punishment dropped from 41 percent in 2000 to 26 percent in 2018.

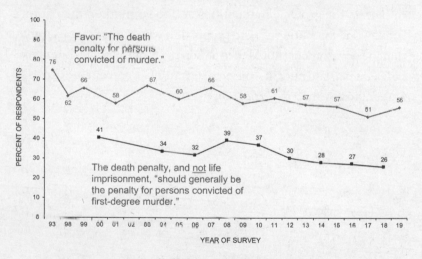

FIGURE 12.1: *Support for the death penalty in Harris County (1993–2019)*

The revelations of discriminatory sentencing, of innocent persons being freed from death row just before their scheduled executions, and of botched lethal injections have been steadily eroding support for capital punishment; at the same time, the monetary costs of seeking the death penalty rather than life imprisonment have increased dramatically. Texas executed thirteen prisoners in the year 2018, down from forty in 2000. No one from Harris County was executed in 2017, and no new prisoners have been sentenced to death since 2014. Executions resumed in 2018 and have continued, but only for the most extreme cases. The continuing decline in the use of the death penalty is at least in part a reflection of growing opposition on the part of the general public.

The most recent surveys also document an increasing acceptance of the need for stronger government action to expand economic opportunity and to moderate the impact of concentrated disadvantage. As shown in Figure 12.2, area residents expressed stronger support in 2018 and 2019 than in any previous years for effective public actions to redress the growing inequalities and to strengthen the nation's "equalizing institutions." The proportion who agreed, for example, that the government should take action to reduce income differences between rich and poor in America grew from 45 percent in 2010 to 59 percent in 2012 and to 66 percent in 2018.

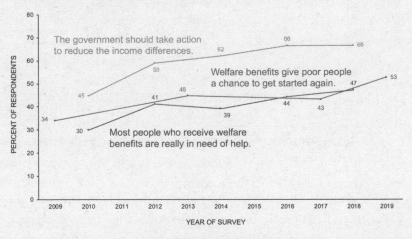

FIGURE 12.2: *Support for government programs to reduce the inequalities in America (2009–2019)*

The respondents were asked if they thought most people who receive welfare payments are really in need of help or are taking advantage of the system. When the question was first asked, in 1994 (not shown in Figure 12.2), only 24 percent agreed that the people receiving welfare benefits are really in need and are not cheating the system. The numbers grew further from 30 percent in 2010 to 47 percent in 2018. On a similar question, 53 percent in 2019, up from 34 percent ten years earlier, affirmed that welfare benefits generally give poor people a chance to get started again, rather than encouraging poor people to stay poor and dependent.

∗

When people are asked how they see the world, their responses usually reflect what psychologists call "motivated beliefs," the assumptions we make about social reality that enable us to feel more comfortable with our lot in life and our position in society. If you are wealthy and successful in America, you will generally be motivated to believe that anyone can succeed if they're willing to work hard and that government interventions only hurt the poor by slowing the growth generated by the free-enterprise system. If you are unsuccessful, you will be equally motivated to believe that people are poor because of circumstances they can't control, and that government has an affirmative role to play in strengthening the social safety net and enhancing economic opportunities.

These are precisely the differences by income and education that we find among Anglos and Hispanics in the surveys: The Anglo and Latino respondents who are earning more money in better jobs are generally more firmly opposed than their less affluent counterparts to government efforts to reduce poverty and inequality in America. Strikingly, we do not find those same differences by income among African Americans. Unlike Anglos and Hispanics, black Houstonians generally do not become more convinced that the game is fair, even as they have succeeded in playing it.

"That's because our emergence into the middle and upper economic classes is more recent, rare, and fragile," says Judson Robinson. "We see many of us falling backward. They may have made it, but they are likely supporting a bunch of family members who haven't. That kind of drag can and does break many."

The Anglo and Latino respondents in the surveys who were earning lower wages in the Houston workforce were consistently more likely than their wealthier counterparts to call for stronger public programs. Among Anglos with personal incomes of more than $75,000, only 24 percent believed that government should do more to solve our country's problems; but that was the position taken by 36 percent of those making $25,000 to $50,000.

Among the U.S.-born Latinos, the negative association between personal earnings and beliefs about the role of government was even clearer. Fully 61 percent of the least-affluent respondents called for more government action, compared to 50 percent of those reporting incomes of $50,000 to $75,000, and to just 33 percent of the Hispanics who had even better jobs and were earning higher incomes.

For the black respondents, in contrast, there was no meaningful relationship between the respondents' personal earnings and their attitudes toward government programs. Among the African Americans who reported personal incomes of at least $75,000, 64 percent agreed that the government should do more to solve the country's problems. This was also the position taken by 63 percent of those making $25,000 to $50,000.

Similarly, when asked about federal health insurance to cover the medical expenses of all Americans, 63 percent of the least well-paid Anglos were in favor of universal coverage, compared to just 28 percent of the most highly paid. The contrast among Latinos was equally clear and even more consistent: 80 percent of those making less than $25,000 were in favor of federal health insurance, but support drops to 47 percent among those reporting personal incomes of more than

$75,000. Once again, there was no relationship among African Americans: The most highly paid blacks (at 86 percent) were not much different from the least affluent (at 79 percent) in their almost unanimous support for universal health care.

The same empirical relationships were found when the survey participants were asked about their perceptions of discrimination. The less affluent Anglos and Latinos were more likely than their better-paid counterparts to believe that members of their ethnic community are very often or fairly often discriminated against in the Houston area, and they were more likely to report that they themselves have personally felt discriminated against because of their ethnicity.

The data show no relationship between personal incomes and perceived discrimination among African Americans. If anything, they point in the opposite direction. The most successful blacks, those who are earning at least $75,000 a year and who are presumably employed in predominantly Anglo workplaces, may actually be somewhat more likely to report that they have often personally felt discriminated against, at 56 percent, compared to 42 percent among those making $25,000 to $50,000, and they are no different in this regard from the least well-paid African Americans, those who are working full-time for very low wages in the Houston marketplace.

Indeed, wealthy blacks frequently report being followed by security when shopping in expensive retail outlets. They describe their fear when driving while black and being stopped and asked for proof that their BMW, or Mercedes, or Maserati is really theirs. Wealthy black women often have a hard time getting served in department stores and restaurants. "I have bought more Prada over the years than I should have," says forty-nine-year-old Rebecca, "just to prove to the staff that told me they didn't have anything for me, that I could afford their products."

These divergent internal patterns among these three ethnic communities offer important insights into the different realities people experience in their daily encounters with economic opportunities and with the structural barriers that constrain mobility in today's economy. Among African Americans, race still matters: Racial solidarity trumps class interests. Intragroup solidarity remains a powerful source of strength in African Americans' continuing struggles for freedom, justice, and equality.

The suggestion some are making, that class now supersedes race as the most politically salient factor in determining the fates and perspectives of black Americans, is not confirmed by the survey data. The data offer little support for the claim by journalist Eugene Robinson and others that a new class-based "dis-integration," a definitive splintering by socioeconomic status, is taking place within the African American community today.[95] While the U.S. Census may be documenting the growing class divisions among blacks in America, we are not seeing in the surveys, at least not yet, anything that looks like a decisive shattering of African American solidarity.

Beliefs about the role of government and concerns about discrimination are views that tend to be associated with political party affiliation. Despite a recent rise in Republican circles of working-class populism, Republicans and Democrats generally continue to differ on the need for public intervention to strengthen the social safety net. The survey participants were asked if they would call themselves a Republican, Democrat, Independent, or something else. If they did not indicate a preference, they were asked if they thought of themselves as closer to the Republican or Democratic Party. The respondents who chose Republican or Democrat on either of these questions were categorized as identifying with that party.

As indicated in Figure 12.3, among Anglos and Hispanics, those who are earning higher incomes are consistently more likely to be affiliated with the Republican Party. More than seven out of ten of the non-Hispanic whites who report earning more than $75,000 in the Houston workplace think of themselves as Republicans, compared to less than half (48 percent) of those with personal incomes below $25,000. The comparable figures for Latinos are 51 percent for those earning the highest incomes and 27 percent for the least affluent. Among African Americans, in contrast, 72 to 80 percent said they thought of themselves as Democrats regardless of their economic circumstances.

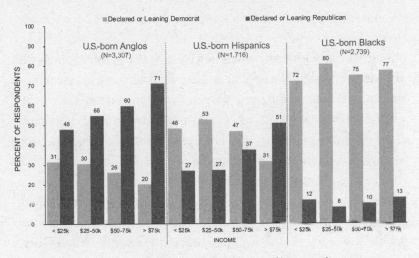

FIGURE 12.3: *The relation between personal income and political party affiliation in three communities*

The African American community is distinctive in the degree to which racial solidarity, an abiding sense of peoplehood, the recognition of a shared history and shared prospects continue to be more important than individualistic class interests in shaping perspectives on public-policy issues. That intragroup cohesion among African Americans is a major source of strength and promise in the continuing struggle for equal opportunity and racial justice in today's increasingly polarized society.

Despite the loud voices venting their anger and fear in response to the changes that are underway in this country, when ordinary Americans are asked systematically about these issues in the privacy of their homes, the findings from the surveys over the years make it clear that most Americans are quietly accepting and even embracing the new realities. Public opinion is changing, and the shifts in the views of the general public, if they continue in this direction, will surely be reflected eventually in public policies.

★

My old friend Blackburn has a vision for how to live intelligently with Houston's ecology. "We need to develop an image for what the city can be, and that means being smart about living with water. It is low, flat, and full of bayous; it rains a lot, and we will always flood. Solving for flooding is *the* window, because it will take us into the densification we need, building upward instead of out over the floodplains and in the flood zones. I think we are at a point where important new changes are both possible and imperative. Houston has to find another path.

"It was technology that defined Houston in the twentieth century. It will be adaptation that will define it in the twenty-first century. I think most companies want to find a better path if they can make it work financially. And we environmentalists need to be much more adept at thinking in economic terms, in thinking about livelihoods, in thinking about jobs. We will have to help the refining and chemical industries find their way to carbon neutrality. We need to make it easier for new leadership to emerge in the industry. I don't think Houston will fail, but we might have to hit a wall first. And this will be very hard for a proud city. The legal fights over the years have allowed me to see a path forward to build some better things, and to end the life of a few bad things. And all of it makes me smile."

CHAPTER 13

Where Will Houston Go from Here?

The occasion is piled high with difficulty, and we must rise with the occasion. As our case is new, so we must think anew, and act anew.

—Abraham Lincoln[96]

In almost every conversation for this book, we have asked civic and spiritual leaders as well as the general public to tell us about their hopes and dreams, their concerns and conclusions regarding Houston's future. Tom Bacon said, "Because of the surveys, we know what Houston thinks and what it wants. We know who Houstonians are. Nobody has to come in and do a focus group to find out. We know they want good schools, walkability, and public transportation. But the biggest risk to Houston's future is that we will just keep muddling along. Instead of being strategic, we will spend randomly on inadequate solutions, trying to solve a bigger problem with insufficient funds and leadership. The biggest threat to our future is that we will lower our aspirations, based on the false belief that our dreams for building a great city aren't possible. They *are* possible. We can have great education, strategic urbanization, and an inclusive city."

Bacon, with his company's powerful data visualizers, has tracked the accelerating growth of cities. "People are increasingly looking for access to better education, health care, jobs, opportunities, the amenities of a city and the opportunity not to spend all day in a car getting from home to work and back again." Though nobody has quite gotten it right, he argues that cities need to form partnerships with their "city accelerators," organizations with the cutting-edge knowledge and critical resources that come out of the nation's most prestigious universities, think tanks, and philanthropic organizations.

On his list are MIT, UC Berkeley, George Washington University, Bloomberg Associates, Brookings Institute, the Rockefeller Family, the Bass Family, Alphabet, and JPMorgan. All of these organizations have partnered with local governments and businesses to accelerate responsible urban densification. The same is happening in Houston with the committed philanthropy of Houston Endowment, the Kinder Foundation, and the Brown Foundation, among others.

The iconic 1939 Sears flagship department store in Houston's Midtown was closed in 2018. It is situated along the light-rail line that originates at NRG Stadium, heads north through Hermann Park, past Rice, the museum district, and into downtown. The building was acquired through a public/private partnership to become part of Houston's new Innovation Corridor, spearheaded by Rice University in partnership with other universities and foundations.

The impetus for building the new one-hundred-million-dollar start-up hub that will anchor the planned innovation district came from a 2017 study by Accenture indicating that while Houston has a strong economy overall, it still has too little in the way of an incubation ecosphere or a venture-capital culture prepared to invest in the engines of a post-petrochem-based economy—such as new energy systems, the life sciences, aerospace, big data, a Smart Cities Accelerator Program, and new digital technologies. Ion, the newly named headquarters for the sixteen-acre South Main Innovation Corridor, is expected to open in the first quarter of 2021.

The question is whether all these efforts are going to be a story of too little, too late.

The education gap is here now and its implications are disconcerting, to say the least. Every year, tens of thousands of young people leave Houston high schools unprepared for the available jobs. What happens to a city when a growing number of its citizens are unable to participate meaningfully in the economy, becoming increasingly impoverished and desperate? The social system will surely collapse at some point.

It is as yet not at all clear whether we Americans will be able to rise to the occasion, meeting the challenges and needs of our fellow citizens, committed to building a truly sustainable, inclusive economy. Will we come to understand that these are all *our* children? They will be the workers, citizens, taxpayers, and voters in Houston and America in the years ahead. If today's young people, who are disproportionately Hispanic and African American, are unprepared to succeed in the new economy, our city and yours will not have much of a future. And neither will America.

Rabbi Samuel Karff, for one, is optimistic, believing that this spiritually driven city has tremendous positive potential. "When the community is mobilized," he says, "and when we have been able to transcend our narrow economic or political interests and work together to achieve goals based on a moral stance, where we are not benefiting personally, that has had an impact—desegregation, getting a public defender for Harris County, fighting for civil rights, immigration reform, and the civil disobedience by the sheriff and city government in Houston, who have been unwilling to enforce punitive immigration laws. All this is very powerful." Karff was referring to the Harris County sheriff's refusal to cooperate with ICE in incarcerating undocumented immigrants who have committed no crime other than being in this country without the right papers.

So many good things are happening in this city that it's tempting to embrace Karff's optimism, and I often feel that way about Houston myself. It is easy to get discouraged if all we pay attention to are the loudest voices in the media. What the Houston surveys have shown, over and over again, is that Houstonians who care about education and celebrate the coming together of all the world's peoples are not only not alone, they are in the majority. And their numbers are growing. The systematic surveys that have been tracking responses over thirty-eight years are clear in this regard.

Still, I worry about the city's mounting problems, especially the burgeoning gap in access to quality education; the growing pockets of concentrated poverty, homelessness, and despair; the persistence of environmental racism; the region's increasing vulnerability to flooding; its position as a hub for human trafficking. And I wonder how it will all play out in an age when the norms of inclusion and social justice seem to be flaunted on a daily basis both in Austin and in Washington.

"I think we will muddle through," says my friend the rabbi. "Positive social change can most dramatically take place when you mobilize enlightened self-interest, when people realize it is ultimately going to help them. Moral idealism by itself is a much weaker motivation. But you need both. One of the affirmations of religion is that ultimately a society cannot survive unless it remains true to its basic moral principles.

"The new economy has left too many behind. We have to provide a support system for the victims of this changed economy, such as early childhood education and job training for adults. It's a crime that preschool isn't universal. It's the only way to get a level playing field. Every child needs at least one parent who is a combination of unconditional and tough love. And if you don't have that and your parents are overwhelmed by trying to put food on the table, then they can't address these issues, and society has to provide the needed support systems and mentoring opportunities."

Scott McClelland is convinced that Houston's business community is ready to pitch in. "At our 2019 GHP luncheon, do you know what got the biggest standing ovation? It was when we said that the city must provide opportunity for all. The crowd cheered like crazy. We are asking how to ensure that everyone can succeed. And this is why we are different from most other big cities. We do a better job at embracing diversity and welcoming new people. Texans are friendly, and Houstonians are friendlier. And now we are looking hard at how to address the city's socioeconomic inequalities. That's why I'm so focused on education."

We can build a truly successful universal city and nation, the first of its kind in human history. We can position Houston and America for continued prosperity as the twenty-first century unfolds, and we are doing many of the right things. Where we are failing most spectacularly is in making the critical sustained investments that will broaden access to quality education and lifelong learning so that all area residents are enabled to compete and thrive in today's high-tech, knowledge-based, global economy.

In *The New Localism*, Brookings Institution fellows Bruce Katz and Jeremy Nowak posit that the best opportunities for shaping the future of America will come from its major cities. The nation's metropolitan regions are the new centers of industry and innovation. They have the potential to draw on local power to finance the future through transformative investments in innovation, infrastructure, and inclusion.[97]

Today more than ever, cities need to become the real problem-solvers, the vehicles for helping people and places adapt to the profound changes wrought by globalization, technological innovation, and the epic transition in the nation's ethnic composition. Houston has turned out to be at the forefront of the ongoing economic, technological, and demographic transformations, so this city has a special responsibility to help point the way toward a thriving America, one that is prepared to meet the challenges of today and tomorrow.

Katz and Nowak are looking toward a worldwide urban revolution, through which cities become more inclusive and embracing of diversity as they rescue and reinvent themselves on the frontlines of a changing economy, as they become innovation hubs and dominant players on the world stage. Houston's economic future will depend on its ability to harness the new energy technologies, to become the third coast (along with Boston and San Francisco) for the life sciences, supported by the world's largest conglomeration of medical institutions, and to develop a full-fledged entrepreneurial ecosystem, stimulating new ideas and new wealth in the high-tech sectors of today's economy. The city needs to become an urban destination of choice, building communities that are more beautiful, healthier, greener, safer, and more walkable, even as it accommodates the one million additional people who are expected to be moving into Harris County during the next twenty years.

Ultimately, we will need to become a true learning society overall, in which everyone from birth through retirement has access to opportunities for new learning and personal growth. The old one-life/one-career imperative is rapidly giving way to the expectation that in this time of constant change and longer life spans, Americans will experience some five or six career changes during their working years. We are condemned, if that's the word, to lives of continual learning, and we need to build the educational infrastructure to ensure that those opportunities are available to all of us.

The impending revolution in robotics and artificial intelligence will exacerbate the inequalities, but it may also stimulate the growth of a more humane society, one that celebrates the kinds of empathetic and caring jobs that are best performed by human beings and are generally beyond the reach of digital algorithms. Perhaps cities will be full of people who are living richer human lives. If we have less physical work to do, perhaps we can be more open to becoming artisans again, becoming poets, potters, and philosophers, like those who, back in the days of the European city-states, helped move the West out of the Dark Ages and into a greater acceptance of reason and science.

A critical question has to do with how the wealthiest 20 percent of Americans (the privileged, well-educated "fortunate fifth") will ultimately respond to the new imperatives. Predominantly composed of aging non-Hispanic whites, they are the ones with the concentrated resources today who are in a position to fund the new initiatives through their taxes and philanthropy. Will they recognize a responsibility not only to ensure the success of their own children and grandchildren, but to invest significantly in all the children in the community?

One of the compelling negative scenarios for the future of America has been called "the secession of the fortunate fifth."[98] It asserts that the wealthiest Americans have essentially seceded from the rest of the country, and are saying to the city, state, and nation, "Don't raise my taxes, and build more prisons." If true, this would seriously undermine any realistic hopes for the years ahead, since it is ultimately on the values and commitments of the most privileged Americans that the country's future will depend.

The Houston surveys do not support that negative assessment of the most fortunate and powerful segment of the population, at least not in any obvious and straightforward way. When we separate out the Anglo respondents who report both household incomes greater than $150,000 and a postgraduate education (having an MA, JD, MD, PhD, etc.), and we compare their views with all the other non-Hispanic whites who participated in the surveys in the years from 2010 to 2019, we find no evidence for the secession argument.

The wealthiest and most highly educated non-Hispanic whites are, if anything, *more* inclined than the other Anglo respondents, by 46 to 39 percent, to *agree* that government has a responsibility to help reduce the inequalities between rich and poor in America. By 50 to 44 percent, they are more adamant in asserting that the public schools in Houston will need significantly more money to provide a quality education. By 46 to 36 percent, they are more likely to believe that welfare benefits generally give poor people a chance to get started again, rather than encouraging them to stay poor and dependent.

We sociologists have a tendency to overemphasize the differences in attitudes and beliefs that are found across the traditional divides by age, education, income, ethnicity, and gender. We sometimes forget that the overlap among the groups is usually far greater than the differences in overall tendencies. Across all the sociological divisions, we are much more alike in our attitudes and beliefs than we are different, and most of us have been changing in more progressive directions over the years in our views of the present and the future.

Almost four decades of systematic surveys have documented significant change in the attitudes and beliefs of Houston-area residents, and the national polls indicate that similar changes hold true for the American public as a whole. Across the traditional divides, respondents in the more recent surveys have been expressing significantly more support than in earlier years for policies to reduce the inequalities and address the needs of the poor; they have been calling for more spending on public education and for more stringent controls on development to reduce the region's vulnerability to future flooding and enhance its quality-of-life attributes. The surveys also show ever more clearly that area residents are embracing Houston's diversity and feeling more comfortable in a world of thriving friendships across the various ethnic communities, religious beliefs, and sexual orientations.

It remains to be seen whether the business and civic leaders of Houston can build on these attitude changes and undertake the critical investments that will be needed to position the region for sustained prosperity in this new era of economic, demographic, and technological transformation.

These are the challenges facing all of America. The jury is out, not only for Houston, but for the rest of the country as well.

Acknowledgments

For almost four decades, the survey research on which this work is based has been made possible by the collaboration of colleagues at Rice University and by many good friends and faithful supporters in the wider Houston community and beyond. I am indebted to far more people than I can possibly acknowledge.

I would like to thank first the succession of talented Rice undergraduates who participated each year in the spring semester course that developed, carried out, analyzed, and reported on the findings from the annual surveys. And I'm deeply grateful to Rosie Zamora and Dick Jaffe for launching their research firm, originally called Tele-surveys of Texas, at just the right moment, and for working with us from the beginning to make this research possible and to ensure its professional quality.

I'm thankful as well for the steadfast support I received in the early years of the surveys from my longtime colleagues in the Rice Sociology Department (Bill Martin, Chandler Davidson, Elizabeth Long, and Chad Gordon) and from Lyn Ragsdale when she served as Dean of the Social Sciences (2006–2016). I'm grateful to Rice president David Leebron and university representative Y. Ping Sun, who so quickly recognized the value of this research in reaching beyond the Rice hedges with survey findings that would inform and inspire the wider Houston community.

I am indebted to my current colleagues both in the Rice Sociology Department and at the Kinder Institute for Urban Research. I'm especially grateful for the leadership and support of the Institute's director, Bill Fulton, and for Jie Wu, the director of research management at the Institute, who for more than a decade has played a crucial role in helping to ensure the quality and accuracy of our analyses of the survey findings.

This thirty-eight-year project would not have been possible without the continued generous support and encouragement of individuals and organizations from well beyond Rice. I'm deeply indebted to the Kinder Foundation and to Nancy and Rich Kinder for their extraordinary endowment gift to fund the Institute and for their continued help and sage advice throughout the years. Generous support has also come from numerous corporations and organizations, among them: Amegy Bank, Bank of America, BP America, Bracewell LLP, CenterPoint Energy, Chevron, ExxonMobil, Fiesta Mart, Frost Bank, Gallery Furniture, Gensler, H-E-B Houston, Houston Endowment Inc., JPMorgan Chase, KHOU-TV Channel 11, Silver Eagle Distributors, Sterling Bank/Comerica, United Way of Greater Houston, and Wells Fargo.

A great many individual friends have made personal gifts to the Institute to help ensure the continuation of the annual studies. I'm thinking especially of Laura and Tom Bacon, Anne and Albert Chao, Kathryn and Hank Coleman, Molly and Jim Crownover, Patti and Richard Everett, Sis and Hasty Johnson, Melissa and Steve Kean, Stephanie Larsen, Reinnette and Stan Marek, Franci Neely, Becky and Ralph O'Connor, and Phoebe and Bobby Tudor.

I have been amazed and humbled every year by the extent to which members of the wider Houston community have embraced this research and have shown how much they value the objective snapshot of Houston that the surveys provide, tracking the way this city has been changing from one year to the next. At the Kinder Luncheon in

May 2019, more than 1,750 Houstonians came to the event to hear about the latest findings and to ensure with their support that the surveys will continue.

I am deeply grateful to Amy Hertz, distinguished editor and author, who teamed up with me to write this book and has a well-deserved place on the title page. Amy was indispensable in helping to turn my sometimes dry academic prose into rich illustrative stories about this city, and in giving voice to the people of Houston themselves— particularly those who sat down with us for lengthy interviews and whose perspectives in these pages have so greatly enriched and deepened our understanding of this remarkable city. In the process of completing the manuscript itself, we received expert guidance from Elizabeth Kaplan, Ben Loehnen, Carolyn Kelly, and the many other professionals associated with Simon & Schuster.

And to my family: I'm thankful for my siblings (Rosemary Coffey and John Klineberg), who continue to watch over their younger brother. And on so many levels and for so much more than I can say, I am grateful to my wife (Peggy), to our two children and their spouses (Geoffrey and Ursula, Kathy and Rick), and to our five grandchildren (Julia, Maggie, Anna, Coles, and Emily). This book is dedicated to them. I cannot imagine living my life without them in it.

Notes

Chapter 1: Getting to Houston

1 The survey we conducted in 1969 with a representative sample of parents and adolescents living in the inner city of Tunis captured the transitional nature of Tunisian society: More than 40 percent of the fathers and almost 90 percent of the mothers in the survey had obtained no formal education whatsoever. Every one of their children had been to school, and 70 percent of the adolescents in the sample were still in school at the time of the interviews. [See Stephen L. Klineberg, "Parents, Schools, and Modernity: An Exploratory Investigation of Sex Differences in the Attitudinal Development of Tunisian Adolescents," *International Journal of Comparative Sociology* 14 (1974): 221–244.]

2 Thomas J. Cottle and Stephen L. Klineberg, *The Present of Things Future: Explorations of Time in Human Experience* (New York: The Free Press, 1974).

3 Joel Garreau, *The Nine Nations of North America* (New York: Avon Books, 1981).

4 Pete A. Y. Gunter and Max Oelschlaeger, *Texas Land Ethics* (Austin: University of Texas Press, 1997), 25–26.

Chapter 2: The Quintessential American City: Houston, 1836–1982

5 David McComb, *Houston: A History* (Austin: University of Texas Press, 1981), 6.

6 Much of this historical account is drawn from the following works: Joe R. Feagin, *Free Enterprise City: Houston in Political and Economic Perspective* (New Brunswick: Rutgers University Press, 1988); David McComb, *Houston: A History* (Austin: University of Texas Press, 1981); Martin Melosi and

291

Joseph Pratt, eds., *Energy Metropolis: An Environmental History of Houston and the Gulf Coast* (Pittsburgh: University of Pittsburgh Press, 2007); Robert D. Thomas and Richard W. Murray, *Progrowth Politics: Change and Governance in Houston* (Berkeley: Institute of Governmental Studies, 1991); and Beth Anne Shelton et al., *Houston: Growth and Decline in a Sunbelt Boomtown* (Philadelphia: Temple University Press, 1989).

7 McComb, *Houston: A History*, 46.

8 From Craig Hlavaty, "See How Houston Was Marketed to the Rest of the World in 1836," *Houston Chronicle*, August 29, 2018.

9 McComb, *Houston: A History*, 14–15.

10 William C. Barnett, "A Tale of Two Texas Cities," in *Energy Metropolis: An Environmental History of Houston and the Gulf Coast*, eds. Martin V. Melosi and Joseph A. Pratt (Pittsburgh: University of Pittsburgh Press, 2007), 185–206.

11 St. Clair Griffin Reed, *A History of the Texas Railroads* (Ann Arbor: University of Michigan, 1941), 63.

12 From Betty T. Chapman, "Plow and Locomotive on City Seal Illustrate Origins of Houston" (http://www.houstontx.gov/abouthouston/city seal .pdf), *Houston Business Journal*, May 6-12, 2005.

13 McComb, *Houston: A History*, 96.

14 From John Melloy, "Energy Output from Shale Rock Could Match 20th Century Oil Boom," March 30, 2011.

15 Joseph Pratt, "A Mixed Blessing," in *Energy Metropolis: An Environmental History of Houston and the Gulf Coast*, eds. Martin Melosi and Joseph Pratt (Pittsburgh: University of Pittsburgh Press, 2007), 26.

16 Steven Fenberg, *Unprecedented Power: Jesse Jones, Capitalism, and the Common Good* (College Station: Texas A&M Press, 2011).

17 Feagin, *Free Enterprise City*, 120–143.

18 Chandler Davidson, "Houston: The City Where the Business of Government is Business," in *Public Policy in Texas*, W. M. Bedichek and N. Tannahill (Glenview: Scott, Foresman & Co, 1982), 275–288.

19 Paul A. Levengood, "For the Duration and Beyond: World War II and the Creation of Modern Houston" (PhD diss., Rice University, 1999).

20 Mark Gottdiener, Ray Hutchison, and Michael T. Ryan, *The New Urban Sociology*, 5th ed. (Boulder: Westview Press, 2015), 5.

21 Feagin, *Free Enterprise City*, 45–72.

22 Martin Melosi and Joseph Pratt, eds., "Introduction," in *Energy Metropolis: An Environmental History of Houston and the Gulf Coast* (Pittsburgh, University of Pittsburgh Press, 2007), 3–4.

23 Richard Louv, *America II* (New York: Penguin Books, 1983), 56–68.

24 Ada Louise Huxtable, "Houston Is the Future . . . ," *Houston Chronicle*, February 22, 1976, 4, 7.

Chapter 3: Launching the Systematic Study of a City in Transition

25 James Fallows, "Houston: A Permanent Boomtown," *The Atlantic*, July 1985, 16–28.

26 Paul Recer, "A Texas City That's Busting Out All Over," *U.S. News & World Report*, November 27, 1978, 47–48.

27 Term suggested by Tory Gattis, well-known Houston blogger (houston-strategies@googlegroups.com).

28 Note that "Anglo" is the term most often used in Texas to refer to the demographic the Census designates as "non-Hispanic white," so we will use these two terms interchangeably.

29 Stephen Fox, "Houston 2000: Looking Back," in *Good: Houston 2000*, ed. T. Beauchamp (Houston, 2000), 81–84.

30 Feagin, *Free Enterprise City*, 162.

31 Beth Anne Shelton et al., *Houston: Growth and Decline in a Sunbelt Boomtown* (Philadelphia: Temple University Press, 1989), 48.

31 Robert D. Bullard, *Dumping on Dixie: Race, Class, and Environmental Quality*, 2nd ed. (Boulder: Westview Press, 1994).

33 "Texas Inc.," *Houston Chronicle*, June 10, 2019.

34 "A City's Growing Pains," *Newsweek*, January 14, 1980, 45.

36 Paul Gapp, "The American City, Challenge of the 80s: Houston, Texas," *Chicago Tribune*, March 30, 1980.

37 William K. Stevens, "As Houston's Amenities Bloom, Its Services Decay," *New York Times*, May 28, 1981.

38 Earl Babbie, *Survey Research Methods*, 2nd ed. (Belmont: Wadsworth Publishing, 1990), 70–71.

39 Jim Asker, "Traditional Labels Don't Apply," *Houston Post*, August 22, 1982, 1A, 3A.

40 Stephen L. Klineberg, "The Houston Area Survey, 1982," *Action Briefs,* no. 2 (November 1982).

41 Increasingly in those early years, as invitations kept coming to present the findings to local corporations, nonprofits, and other organizations, I would gently ask my hosts if they would be willing in exchange to make a tax-deductible contribution to Rice University to help support the surveys. The community responded with remarkable appreciation and generosity.

It soon became apparent that we would have all the funding needed to underwrite a longer-term and more ambitious research program.

42 The American Sociological Association highlighted this research in their national newsletter in 1985, reminding the profession of how valuable such surveys can be for the wider community. [See Carla B. Howery, "Community Surveys Train Students, Provide Service," *ASA Footnotes*, vol. 13, no. 3 (March 1985): 1–2.]

43 Stephen L. Klineberg, "Environmental Concern through Boom and Bust: Seven Years of Surveys in Houston, Texas," presented at the American Sociological Association (Atlanta, Georgia, August 1988).

44 The responses from all thirty-eight years are "weighted" to correct for variations in the likelihood of selection and to align the samples more closely with known population characteristics. This helps to ensure that the data we report will accurately reflect the characteristics of Harris County's overall population with regard to such key dimensions as race or ethnicity, age, gender, education, and homeownership. When asking about changes over time, we examine the weighted responses given by successive representative samples of Harris County residents responding to identically worded questions that have been positioned similarly in the survey instrument.

45 In the 1980s, for example, we asked about support for the ERA, the nuclear freeze, U.S.-Soviet relations, and traditional family structures (e.g., "It is more important for a wife to help her husband's career than to have one herself"). In the 1990s, there were questions about zoning, recycling, and AIDS. The early 2000s brought to the fore issues of affirmative action, the Katrina evacuees, and the nature of mental illness. More recently, the surveys have asked about interracial dating, the challenge of riding a bicycle in Houston, and the experience of Hurricane Harvey in 2017.

46 When Jaffe and Zamora decided to retire from the survey business in 2004, after twenty-two years of fruitful collaboration, for the next seven years (2005–2011) we worked with the Survey Research Institute at the University of Houston. Since 2012, the intensive, thirty-minute interviews have been conducted by SSRS, one of the country's premier research organizations, operating out of Glen Mills, Pennsylvania.

Chapter 4: When All the Good Fortune Suddenly Ended

47 Thomas and Murray, *Progrowth Politics*, 62.

48 David Maraniss, "John Connally and the Auction of a Lifetime," *Washington Post*, January 18, 1988.

49 T. R. Fehrenbach, *Seven Keys to Texas* (El Paso: Texas Western Press, 1983).

50 Mike Snyder, "Long-Overlooked East Aldine on Cusp of Transformation," *Houston Chronicle*, May 2, 2016.

51 Bill Bishop, *The Big Sort: Why the Clustering of Like-Minded America Is Tearing Us Apart* (New York: Houghton Mifflin, 2008).

52 http://www.equality-of-opportunity.org/assets/documents/abs_mobility _summary.pdf.

Chapter 5: The Growing Opportunity Gap

52 Tony Wagner, *Making the Grade* (New York: RoutledgeFalmer, 2002), 19.

53 Roberto Suro, *Strangers Among Us: Latino Lives in a Changing America* (New York: Vintage, 1998), 17.

54 James J. Heckman, "Lifelines for Poor Children," *New York Times*, September 15, 2013.

Chapter 6: The Moral Core of a Paradoxical City

55 Mustafa Tameez, interview, February 26, 2019.

56 Thomas R. Cole, *No Color Is My Kind: The Life of Eldrewy Stearns and the Integration of Houston* (Austin: University of Texas Press, 1997).

57 William A. Lawson, "Harris County Makes History with Public Defender's Office," *Houston Chronicle*, November 11, 2010.

58 Stephen L. Klineberg and David A. Kravitz, "Ethnic Differences in Predictors of Support for Municipal Affirmative Action Contracting," *Social Science Quarterly* 84, no. 2 (May 19, 2003): 425–40.

59 Frans de Waal, *Age of Empathy* (New York: Harmony Books, 2009), 2.

Chapter 7. The Black/White Divide

60 Laurence J. Payne, interview, February 9, 2019.

61 Valerie A. Lewis, Michael O. Emerson, and Stephen L. Klineberg, "Who We'll Live With: Neighborhood Racial Composition Preferences of Whites, Blacks, and Latinos," *Social Forces* 89, no. 4 (June 2011): 1385–1407.

Chapter 8: The Demographic Transformations

62 *Anthony Bourdain: Parts Unknown*, "Houston," aired October 2016, CNN.

63 John F. Kennedy, *A Nation of Immigrants*, revised and enlarged (New York: Harper Perennial, 1964).

64 Ben J. Wattenberg, *The First Universal Nation* (New York: Macmillan, 1991), 9. We are indebted for much of this discussion of the new immigration to Alejandro Portes and Rubén G. Rumbaut, *Immigrant America: A Portrait*, 3rd ed. (Berkeley: University of California Press, 2006), to Dowell Myers, *Immigrants and Boomers* (New York: Russell Sage Foundation, 2007), and to William Frey, *Diversity Explosion: How New Racial Demographics Are Remaking America* (Washington: Brookings, 2015).

65 https://www.nytimes.com/2004/09/26/books/arts/dance-the-dancer -whodefected-twice.html.

66 Nestor Rodriguez, "Hispanic and Asian Immigration Waves in Houston," in *Religion and the New Immigrants*, eds. Helen Rose Ebaugh and Jane S. Chafetz (Walnut Creek: AltaMira Press, 2000), 29–42.

67 Frey, *Diversity Explosion*, 107–130.

68 Lisa Falkenberg, "For Muslim Americans, a Time of Angst and Sadness," *Houston Chronicle*, February 18, 2017.

69 Michael O. Emerson, Jenifer Bratter, Junia Howell, P. Wilner Jeanty, and Mike Cline, *Houston Region Grows More Racially/Ethnically Diverse, with Small Declines in Segregation* (Houston: Kinder Institute for Urban Research, 2012).

Chapter 9: The New Face of Houston

70 Laura Murillo, interview, March 22, 2019.

71 Rogene Gee Calvert, interview, September 7, 2017.

72 Mihir Zaveri, "Lina Hidalgo, a 27-Year-Old Latina, Will Lead Harris County, Texas' Biggest County," *New York Times*, November 8, 2018.

73 "This is Not Mexico," *Washington Post*, March 27, 2019.

74 William A. Vega, Michael Rodriguez, and Elisabeth Gruskin, "Health Disparities in the Latino Population," *Epidemiologic Reviews* 31 (August 27, 2009): 99–112.

75 https://www.houstonchronicle.com/opinion/outlook/article/I-was-homeless-Then-I-was-admitted-to-Harvard-13676129.php.

76 Ronald Reagan, "Ellis Island" (speech), September 1, 1980, Ronald Reagan Presidential Library & Museum.

77 The video depicting Syed's experience is here: https://www.youtube.com /watch?v=SjgXbQLVX4o.

78 Stephen L. Klineberg and Jie Wu, *Diversity and Transformation among*

Asians in Houston: Findings from the Kinder Institute's Houston Area Asian Survey (1995, 2002, 2011) (Houston: Rice University Kinder Institute for Urban Research, February 2013).

79 Elliot Aronson, *The Social Animal*, 7th ed (New York: W. H. Freeman, 1995), 223–25, 339–42.

Chapter 10: Generational Divides in a Time of Transition

80 Email message received on June 24, 2016.
81 Lawrence Wright, *God Save Texas* (New York: Knopf, 2018), 258.
82 https://www.nytimes.com/interactive/2014/07/15/us/questions-about-the-border-kids.html.
83 "Protesters in California Block Busloads of Immigrant Children and Families," *Washington Post*, July 2, 2014.
84 William G. Mayer, *The Changing American Mind: How and Why American Public Opinion Changed between 1960 and 1988* (Ann Arbor: University of Michigan Press, 1992).
85 https://www.houstonchronicle.com/business/article/The-black-white-wage-gap-is-growing-It-s-worse-13771318.php.
86 Joseph Stiglitz, *Globalization and Its Discontents* (New York: Norton, 2017).
87 We have been greatly aided in our understanding of the nature and implications of the new, knowledge-based economy, and of the increasing inequalities it has generated, by the work of many first-rate scholars over the years. Among them, we are particularly grateful for the following: Jacob S. Hacker and Paul Pierson, *Winner-Take-All Politics* (New York: Simon & Schuster, 2010); Richard Florida, *The New Urban Crisis* (New York: Basic Books, 2017); Frank Levy, *The New Dollars and Dreams* (New York: Russell Sage Foundation, 1998); Timothy Noah, *The Great Divergence* (New York: Bloomsbury Press, 2012); Robert D. Putnam, *Our Kids* (New York: Simon & Schuster, 2015); Richard V. Reeves, *Dream Hoarders* (Washington, DC: Brookings Institution Press, 2017); Robert B. Reich, *The Work of Nations* (New York: Knopf, 1991); and Robert B. Reich, *Aftershock* (New York: Knopf, 2010).

Chapter 11: The New Importance of Quality of Place

88 Robert Fisher, "The Urban Sunbelt in Comparative Perspective: Houston in Context," in *Essays on Sunbelt Cities and Recent Urban America*, eds. R. Fairbanks and K. Underwood (College Station: Texas A&M University Press, 1990), 33–58.

89 Arthur Comey, "City Beautiful" Report: *Save Buffalo Bayou* (1913), 10.

90 Stephen L. Klineberg and Emily Braswell, "Is Houston About to Experience an 'Urban Renaissance'? Findings from the Kinder Houston Area Survey (1995–2012)," *Cite: The Architecture + Design Review of Houston*, 2012, 34–39.

Chapter 12: Pathways to Success or Failure

91 John McHale wrote these insightful words in an article published in the *Futurist* magazine in 1979.

92 Brett Martin, "The New Capital of Southern Cool," *GQ*, September 2018.

93 Wright, *God Save Texas*, 200–01.

94 Wright, *God Save Texas*, 195–196.

95 Eugene Robinson, *Disintegration: The Splintering of Black America* (New York: Doubleday, 2010).

Chapter 13: Where Will Houston Go from Here?

96 From Lincoln's Second Annual Message to Congress, 1 December 1862.

97 Bruce Katz and Jeremy Nowak, *The New Localism* (Washington: Brookings Institution, 2017).

98 Robert B. Reich, *The Work of Nations* (New York: Vintage, 1992).

Bibliography

Aronson, Elliot. *The Social Animal*, 7th ed. New York: W. H. Freeman & Co., 1995.

Asker, Jim. "Traditional Labels Don't Apply: Survey Reveals Conservative, Liberal Mix Here." *Houston Post*, August 22, 1982, 1A-3A.

Babbie, Earl. *Survey Research Methods*, 2nd ed. Belmont: Wadsworth Publishing Company, 1990.

Barnett, William C. "A Tale of Two Texas Cities." In *Energy Metropolis: An Environmental History of Houston and the Gulf Coast*, edited by Martin V. Melosi and Joseph A. Pratt, 185-206. Pittsburgh: University of Pittsburgh Press, 2007.

Bishop, Bill. *The Big Sort: Why the Clustering of Like-Minded America Is Tearing Us Apart*. New York: Houghton Mifflin, 2008.

Bullard, Robert D. *Dumping on Dixie: Race, Class, and Environmental Quality*, 2nd ed. Boulder: Westview Press, 1994.

Bullard, Robert D. *Invisible Houston: The Black Experience in Boom and Bust*. College Station: Texas A&M University Press, 1987.

Carleton, Don E. *Red Scare! Right-Wing Hysteria, Fifties Fanaticism, and Their Legacy in Texas*. Austin: Texas Monthly Press, 1985.

Cottle, Thomas J., and Stephen L. Klineberg. *The Present of Things Future: Explorations of Time in Human Experience*. New York: Free Press, 1974.

Davidson, Chandler. "Houston: The City Where the Business of Government is Business." In *Public Policy in Texas*, by W. M. Bedichek and N. Tannahill, 275-88. Glenview: Scott, Foresman & Co, 1982.

De Leon, Arnoldo. *Ethnicity in the Sunbelt: A History of Mexican Americans in Houston*. College Station: Texas A&M University Press, 2001.

Ehrenhalt, Alan. *The Great Inversion and the Future of the American City*. New York: Alfred A. Knopf, 2012.

Emerson, Michael O., Jenifer Bratter, Junia Howell, P. Wilner Jeanty, and Mike Cline. *Houston Region Grows More Racially/Ethnically Diverse, with Small Declines in Segregation.* Houston: Kinder Institute for Urban Research, 2012.

Emerson, Michael Oluf, and Kevin T. Smiley. *Market Cities, People Cities: The Shape of Our Urban Future.* New York: New York University Press, 2018.

Fallows, James. "Houston: A Permanent Boomtown." *Atlantic*, July 1985, 16–28.

Feagin, Joe R. *Free Enterprise City: Houston in Political and Economic Perspective.* New Brunswick: Rutgers University Press, 1988.

Fehrenbach, T. R. *Seven Keys to Texas.* El Paso: Texas Western Press, 1983.

Fenberg, Steven. *Unprecedented Power: Jesse Jones, Capitalism, and the Common Good.* College Station: Texas A&M Press, 2011.

Fisher, Robert. "The Urban Sunbelt in Comparative Perspective: Houston in Context." In *Essays on Sunbelt Cities and Recent Urban America*, edited by R. Fairbanks and K. Underwood, 33–58. College Station: Texas A&M University Press, 1990.

Florida, Richard. *The New Urban Crisis: How Our Cities Are Increasing Inequality, Deepening Segregation, and Failing the Middle Class—And What We Can Do about It.* New York: Basic Books, 2017.

Fox, Stephen. "Houston 2000: Looking Back." In *Good: Houston 2000*, edited by T. Beauchamp, 81–84. Houston, Texas, 2000.

Friedman, Thomas J. "From Hands to Heads to Hearts." *New York Times*, January 4, 2017.

Frey, William H. *Diversity Explosion: How New Racial Demographics Are Remaking America.* Washington, DC: Brookings Institution Press, 2015.

Gapp, Paul. "The American City, Challenge of the 80s: Houston, Texas." *Chicago Tribune*, March 30, 1980.

Garreau, Joel. *The Nine Nations of North America.* New York: Avon Books, 1981.

Gunter, Pete A. Y., and Max Oelschlaeger. *Texas Land Ethics.* Austin: University of Texas Press, 1997.

Heckman, James J. "Lifelines for Poor Children." *New York Times*, September 15, 2013.

Houston Chronicle editorial. "American Mirror: New Rice Institute Could Make Houston a Key Influence on Urban Policy." *Houston Chronicle*, March 16, 2010.

Howery, Carla B. "Community Surveys Train Students, Provide Service." *ASA Footnotes* 13, no. 3 (March 1985): 1–2.

Huxtable, Ada Louise. "Houston Is the . . ." *Houston Chronicle*, February 22, 1976, 4, 7.

Institute for Urban Studies. *HouMAP: Houston Metropolitan Area Project: Survey of the Houston-Galveston Planning Region.* Houston: University of Houston, 1976.

Kaplan, Barry J. "Houston: The Golden Buckle of the Sunbelt." In *Sunbelt Cities: Politics and Growth since World War II*, edited by R. M. Berhard and B. R. Rice, 196–212. Austin: University of Texas Press, 1983.

Katz, Bruce, and Jeremy Nowak. *The New Localism: How Cities Can Thrive in the Age of Populism.* Washington, DC: Brookings Institution Press, 2017.

Kennedy, John Fitzgerald. *A Nation of Immigrants*, revised and enlarged edition. New York: Harper Perennial, 1964.

Klineberg, Stephen L. *The 2019 Kinder Houston Area Survey: Tracking Responses to the Economic and Demographic Transformations through 38 Years of Houston Surveys.* Rice University: Kinder Institute for Urban Research, May 2019.

Klineberg, Stephen L. "Parents, Schools, and Modernity: An Exploratory Investigation of Sex Differences in the Attitudinal Development of Tunisian Adolescents." *International Journal of Comparative Sociology* 14 (1974): 221–44.

Klineberg, Stephen L. "The Houston Area Survey, 1982." Rice Institute for Policy Analysis: *Action Briefs*, no. 2 (November 1982).

Klineberg, Stephen L. "Environmental Concern through Boom and Bust: Seven Years of Surveys in Houston, Texas." Presented at the annual meeting of the American Sociological Association, Atlanta, Georgia, August 1988.

Klineberg, Stephen L. *Houston's Ethnic Communities, 3rd ed: Updated and Expanded to Include the First-Ever Survey of Houston's Asian Communities.* Houston: Rice University Publication, 1996.

Klineberg, Stephen L. "Religious Diversity and Social Integration among Asian Americans in Houston." In *Asian American Religions: The Making and Remaking of Borders and Boundaries*, edited by Tony Carnes and Fenggang Yang, 247–62. New York: New York University Press, 2014.

Klineberg, Stephen L., and David A. Kravitz. "Ethnic Differences in Predictors of Support for Municipal Affirmative Action Contracting." *Social Science Quarterly* 84 (2003): 425–40.

Klineberg, Stephen L., and Emily Braswell. "Is Houston About to Experience an 'Urban Renaissance'? Findings from the Kinder Houston Area Survey (1995–2012)." *Cite: The Architecture + Design Review of Houston* 90 (2012): 34–39.

Klineberg, Stephen L., and Jie Wu. *Diversity and Transformation among Asians in Houston: Findings from the Kinder Institute's Houston Area Asian Survey (1995, 2002, 2011).* Rice University: Kinder Institute for Urban Research, February 2013.

Klineberg, Stephen L., Jie Wu, Kiara Douds, and Diane Ramirez. *Shared Prospects: Hispanics and the Future of Houston; Findings from the Houston Surveys (1994–2014)*. Rice University: Kinder Institute for Urban Research, 2014.

Levengood, Paul A. "For the Duration and Beyond: World War II and the Creation of Modern Houston, Texas." PhD diss., Department of History, Rice University, 1999.

Levy, Frank. *The New Dollars and Dreams: American Incomes and Economic Change*. New York: Russell Sage Foundation, 1998.

Lewis, Valerie A., Michael O. Emerson, and Stephen L. Klineberg. "Who We'll Live With: Racial Composition Preferences of Whites, Blacks, and Latinos." *Social Forces* 89 (2011): 1385-407.

Logan, John R., and Harvey L. Molotch. *Urban Fortunes: The Political Economy of Place*. Berkeley: University of California Press, 1987.

Lopate, Phillip. "Pursuing the Unicorn: Public Space in Houston." In *Ephemeral City: Cite Looks at Houston,* edited by Barrie Scardino, William F. Stern, and Bruce C. Webb, 9–23. Austin: University of Texas Press, 2003.

Louv, Richard. *America II*. New York: Penguin Books, 1983.

MacManus, Susan A. "Managing Urban Growth: Citizen Perceptions and Preferences." In *The Future of the Sunbelt: Managing Growth and Change,* edited by S. C. Ballard and T. E. James, 132–161. New York: Praeger, 1983.

Mayer, William G. *The Changing American Mind: How and Why American Public Opinion Changed between 1960 and 1988*. Ann Arbor: University of Michigan Press, 1992.

McComb, David G. *Houston: A History*, rev. ed. Austin: University of Texas Press, 1981.

Melosi, Martin V., and Joseph A. Pratt, eds. *Energy Metropolis: An Environmental History of Houston and the Gulf Coast*. Pittsburgh: University of Pittsburgh Press, 2007.

Murdock, Steve H., Michael E. Cline, Mary Zey, P. Wilner Jeanty, and Deborah Perez. *Changing Texas: Implications of Addressing or Ignoring the Texas Challenge*. College Station: Texas A&M University Press, 2014.

Murdock, Steve H., and Stephen L. Klineberg. "Demographic and Related Economic Transformations of Texas: Implications for Early Childhood Education and Development." In *Investing in Early Childhood Development: Evidence to Support a Movement for Educational Change*, edited by Alvin R. Tarlov and Michelle Precourt Debbink, 159–76. New York: Palgrave-Macmillan, 2008.

Myers, Dowell. *Immigrants and Boomers: Forging a New Social Contract for the Future of America*. New York: Russell Sage Foundation, 2007.

Newman, Katherine S., and Hella Winston. *Reskilling America: Learning to Labor in the Twenty-First Century.* New York: Metropolitan Books, 2016.

Newsweek, "A City's Growing Pains." *Newsweek,* January 14, 1980, 45.

Payne, Laurence J. *The Heart of HoUSton: Lessons in Servant Leadership.* Houston: Bright Sky Press, 2013.

Portes, Alejandro, and Rubén G. Rumbaut. *Immigrant America: A Portrait,* 3rd ed. Berkeley: University of California Press, 2006.

Pratt, Joseph A. "A Mixed Blessing: Energy, Economic Growth, and Houston's Environment." In *Energy Metropolis: An Environmental History of Houston and the Gulf Coast,* edited by Martin V. Melosi and Joseph A. Pratt, 21–51. Pittsburgh: University of Pittsburgh Press, 2007.

Putnam, Robert D. *Our Kids: The American Dream in Crisis.* New York: Simon & Schuster, 2015.

Recer, Paul. "A Texas City That's Busting Out All Over." *U.S. News & World Report,* November 27, 1978, 47–48.

Reich, Robert B. *The Work of Nations: Preparing Ourselves for 21st-Century Capitalism.* New York: Vintage Books, 1992.

Reich, Robert B. *Aftershock: The Next Economy and America's Future.* New York: Knopf, 2010.

Robinson, Eugene. *Disintegration: The Splintering of Black America.* New York: Doubleday, 2010.

Shelton, Beth Anne, Nestor P. Rodriguez, Joe R. Feagin, Robert D. Bullard, and Robert D. Thomas. *Houston: Growth and Decline in a Sunbelt Boomtown.* Philadelphia: Temple University Press, 1989.

Shelton, Kyle. *Power Moves: Transportation, Politics, and Development in Houston.* Austin: University of Texas Press, 2017.

Smith, Barton A. *Handbook on the Houston Economy, 1989 Edition.* Houston: University of Houston Center for Public Policy, 1989.

Stevens, William K. "As Houston's Amenities Bloom, Its Services Decay." *New York Times,* May 28, 1981.

Stiglitz, Joseph. "Equal Opportunity, Our National Myth." *New York Times,* February 17, 2013.

Suro, Roberto. *Strangers Among Us: Latino Lives in a Changing America.* New York: Vintage Books, 1998.

Taylor, Paul. *The Next America: Boomers, Millennials, and the Looming Generational Showdown.* New York: PublicAffairs, 2014.

Thomas, Robert D., and Richard W. Murray. *Progrowth Politics: Change and Governance in Houston.* Berkeley: Institute of Governmental Studies Press, 1991.

Thurow, Lester. "Companies Merge; Families Break Up." *New York Times*, September 3, 1995, 11.

Vega, William A., Michael Rodriguez, and Elisabeth Gruskin. "Health Disparities in the Latino Population." *Epidemiologic Reviews* 31 (2009): 99–112.

Waldinger, Roger. *Strangers at the Gates: New Immigrants in Urban America.* Berkeley: University of California Press, 2001.

Wattenberg, Ben J. *The First Universal Nation: Leading Indicators and Ideas About the Surge of America in the 1990s.* New York: Macmillan, 1991.

Wright, Lawrence. *God Save Texas: A Journey into the Soul of the Lone Star State.* New York: Knopf, 2018.

Index

About the Author

Stephen L. Klineberg is a graduate of Haverford College and holds an MA from the University of Paris and a PhD from Harvard. He is the founding director of the Kinder Institute for Urban Research, a multidisciplinary "think-and-do tank" at Rice University working to advance understanding of the most important issues facing Houston and other leading urban centers. Klineberg joined Rice's sociology department in 1972, and in 1982 he and his students initiated an annual study, now called the "Kinder Houston Area Survey," which for thirty-eight years has been tracking systematically the remarkable changes in the demographic patterns, economic outlooks, experiences, attitudes, and beliefs of Houston residents.